T0143599

RECONNOITERING THE LANDSCAPE OF EDGE INTELLIGENCE IN HEALTHCARE

RECONNOITERING THE LANDSCAPE OF EDGE INTELLIGENCE IN HEALTHCARE

Edited by
Suneeta Satpathy, PhD
Sachi Nandan Mohanty, PhD
Sirisha Potluri, PhD

First edition published 2024

Apple Academic Press Inc.
1265 Goldenrod Circle, NE,
Palm Bay, FL 32905 USA
760 Laurentian Drive, Unit 19,
Burlington, ON L7N 0A4, CANADA

CRC Press
2385 NW Executive Center Drive,
Suite 320, Boca Raton FL 33431
4 Park Square, Milton Park,
Abingdon, Oxon, OX14 4RN UK

© 2024 by Apple Academic Press, Inc.

Apple Academic Press exclusively co-publishes with CRC Press, an imprint of Taylor & Francis Group, LLC

Library and Archives Canada Cataloguing in Publication

....

CIP data on file with Canada Library and Archives

....

Library of Congress Cataloging-in-Publication Data

....

CIP data on file with US Library of Congress

....

ISBN: 978-1-77491-436-6 (hbk)
ISBN: 978-1-77491-437-3 (pbk)
ISBN: 978-1-00340-184-1 (ebk)

About the Editors

Suneeta Satpathy, PhD
SOA University, Bhubaneswar, Odisha, India.

Suneeta Satpathy, PhD, is currently working in the Center for AI & ML, SOA University, Bhubaneswar, Odisha, India. Her research interests include computer forensics, cybersecurity, data fusion, data mining, big data analysis, and decision mining. In addition to her own research, she has guided many postgraduate and graduate students. She has published papers in many international journals and conferences in repute. She holds two Indian patents. Her professional activities include roles as editorial board member and/or reviewer of the Journal of Engineering Science, Advancement of Computer Technology and Applications, Robotics and Autonomous Systems, and *Computational and Structural Biotechnology Journal.* She is a member of the Computer Society of India, International Society for Technology in Education, Orissa Information Technology Society, and Association for Computing Machinery. She received her PhD from Utkal University, Bhubaneswar, Odisha, in 2015, with a Directorate of Forensic Sciences, MHA scholarship from Govt of India.

Sachi Nandan Mohanty, PhD
School of Computer Science & Engineering (SCOPE), VIT-AP University, Amaravati, Andhra Pradesh, India

Sachi Nandan Mohanty, PhD, is affiliated with the School of Computer Science & Engineering (SCOPE), VIT-AP University, Amaravati, Andhra Pradesh, India. He has edited 24 books in association with Springer and Wiley as well as over 120 papers in international journals. His research areas include data mining, big data analysis, cognitive science, fuzzy decision-making, brain-computer interface, cognition, and computational intelligence. Professor Mohanty has received several best paper awards during his PhD at IIT Kharagpur at an international conference at Beijing,

China, and at the International Conference on Soft Computing Applications organized by IIT Rookee (2013). He was awarded a best thesis award (first prize) by the Computer Society of India in 2015. He has guided 10 PhD scholars. Dr. Mohanty is a Fellow of the Institute of Engineers and a senior member of IEEE Computer Society, Hyderabad chapter. He also a reviewer for the *Journal of Robotics and Autonomous Systems* and *Computational and Structural Biotechnology Journal* (both published by Elsevier) and *Artificial Intelligence Review and Spatial Information Research* (published by Springer). Dr. Mohanty received his PostDoc from IIT Kanpur in the year 2019 and PhD from IIT Kharagpur, India, in the year 2015, with an MHRD scholarship from Govt of India.

Sirisha Potluri, PhD
Department of Computer Science and Engineering, Faculty of Science and Technology, ICFAI Tech, ICFAI Foundation for Higher Education, Telangana, India

Sirisha Potluri, PhD, is affiliated in the Department of Computer Science and Engineering in the Faculty of Science and Technology at ICFAI Tech, ICFAI Foundation for Higher Education, Telangana, India. Her research areas include cloud computing, edge computing, artificial intelligence, and data analytics. She has more than eight years of teaching experience. She taught various subjects, including Computer Programming using C, Python Programming, Data Structures, Core JAVA, Advanced JAVA, OOP using C++, Operating Systems, Distributed Operating System, Human Computer Interaction, C# and .NET Programming, Computer Graphics, Web Technology, UNIX Programming, Distributed and Cloud Computing, Data Mining and Warehousing, Scripting Languages, Database Management Systems, Software Engineering, and Software Process Management. She has presented research papers at national and international conferences and published 24 research articles in international peer-reviewed journals. She has edited three books from global publishing houses and published several book chapters. She is a member of IEEE and a reviewer for various journals. She received the TN Global Research award as a Young Scientist on 5th March 2022.

Contents

Contributors

Nidhi Agarwal
Department of Information Technology, KIET Group of Institutions, Delhi-NCR, Uttar Pradesh, Ghaziabad, India

Kavitha Athota
Department of Computer Science and Engineering, Jawaharlal Nehru Technological University, Hyderabad, Telangana, India

Vaishali B. Bhagat
Research Scholar, Computer Science and Engineering, Sant Gadge Baba Amravati University, Amravati, Maharashtra, India; Assistant Professor, P. R. Pote College of Engineering and Management, Amravati, Maharashtra, India

R. Kiruba Buri
Department of Computer Science and Engineering, University College of Engineering, Anna University, Rajamadam, Pattukottai, Tamil Nadu, India

Saswati Chatterjee
Sunstone Eduversity, Kolkata Campus, Kolkata, West Bengal, India

Prakhar Deep
Project Manager, Tech Mahindra, NSEZ Noida, Uttar Pradesh, India

Nisrutha Dulla
School of Humanities, KIIT Deemed to be University, Bhubaneswar, Odisha, India

Fatima Fariah
Department of Computer Science and Information Technology, Amity Institute of Information Technology, Amity University, Jharkhand, India

A. B. Gadicha
Head CSE Department, P. R. Pote College of Engineering and Management, Amravati, Maharashtra, India

Jossy P. George
Department of Data Science, Christ University, Lavasa, Pune, Maharashtra, India

W. Jaisingh
School of Computing Science and Engineering, VIT Bhopal University, Bhopal, Madhya Pradesh, India

T. Jayasankar
University College of Engineering, BIT Campus Anna University, Tiruchirappalli, Tamil Nadu, India

Parmeshwara Joga
Researcher, Department of Computer Science and Engineering, Faculty of Science and Technology – IcfaiTech, ICFAI Foundation for Higher Education, Hyderabad, Telangana, India

C. Karpagam
Department of Computer Science with Data Analytics, Dr. N.G.P. Arts and Science College, Tamil Nadu, India

Puranam Revanth Kumar
Department of Electronics and Communication Engineering, IcfaiTech (Faculty of Science and Technology), IFHE, Hyderabad, Telangana, India

Shalini Mahato
Department of Computer Science and Engineering, Indian Institute of Information Technology, Ranchi, Jharkhand, India

P. Maheswaravenkatesh
University College of Engineering, BIT Campus Anna University, Tiruchirappalli, Tamil Nadu, India

Shirin Sharon Masih
Sunstone Eduversity, Kolkata Campus, Kolkata, West Bengal, India

Bibhu Kalyan Mishra
Sri Sri University, Cuttack, Odisha, India

Shruti Mishra
Vellore Institute of Technology, Chennai, Tamil Nadu, India

Sachi Nandan Mohanty
School of Computer Engineering, VIT-AP University, Andhra Pradesh, India

Preethi Nanjundan
Assistant Professor, Department of Data Science, Christ University, Lavasa, Pune, Maharashtra, India

Deepika Nasika
Department of Computer Science and Engineering, Jawaharlal Nehru Technological University, Hyderabad, Telangana, India

Chinmaya Ranjan Pattanaik
Department of Computer Science and Engineering, Ajay Binay Institute of Technology, Cuttack, Odisha, India

Sirisha Potluri
Assistant Professor, Department of Computer Science and Engineering, Faculty of Science and Technology – IcfaiTech, ICFAI Foundation for Higher Education, Hyderabad, Telangana, India

Sugyanta Priyadarshini
School of Humanities, KIIT Deemed to be University, Bhubaneswar, Odisha, India

Deepthi Rapaka
Researcher, Department of Computer Science and Engineering, Faculty of Science and Technology – IcfaiTech, ICFAI Foundation for Higher Education, Hyderabad, Telangana, India

Soumya Samarpita
FOS, Sri Sri University, Cuttack, Odisha, India

Sandeep Kumar Satapathy
Vellore Institute of Technology, Chennai, Tamil Nadu, India

Suneeta Satpathy
Center for AI & ML, SOA University, Bhubaneswar, Odisha

R. Pandi Selvam
PG Department of Computer Science, Ananda College, Devakottai, Tamil Nadu, India

B. Shilpa
Department of Electronics and Communication Engineering, IcfaiTech (Faculty of Science and Technology), IFHE, Hyderabad, Telangana, India

G. Sucharitha
Associate Professor, Department of Computer Science and Engineering, Institute of Aeronautical Engineering, Hyderabad, Telangana, India

Sukanta Chandra Swain
School of Humanities, KIIT Deemed to be University, Bhubaneswar, Odisha, India

V. M. Thakare
Professor and Head, PG Department of Computer Science and Engineering, Sant Gadge Baba Amravati University, Amravati, Maharashtra, India

S. K. Yadav
Shri JJT University, Vidya Nagari, Jhunjhunu, Rajasthan, India

Anagha Zachariah
Vellore Institute of Technology, Chennai, Tamil Nadu, India

Abbreviations

AC	access categories
AC-GAN	auxiliary classifier generative adversarial network
ADM	anomaly detection module
ADNI	Alzheimer's disease neuroimaging initiative
AF	atrial fibrillation
AI	artificial intelligence
AIDS	acquired immune deficiency syndrome
AIFS	arbitration IFS
AKA	authenticated key agreement
AODV	ad hoc on-demand distance vector
AP	access point
AR	augmented reality
ART	anti-retroviral therapy
BAN	body area network
BBN	body-to-body network
BCG	Ballistocardiogram
BLE	Bluetooth low energy
BMI	body mass index
BOLD	blood-oxygen-level-dependent
BP	blood pressure
CAD	computer-aided diagnosis
CC	cloud computing
CDNs	content distribution networks
CHD	coronary heart disease
CI	cloud intelligence
CNN	convolution neural network
COVID-19	coronavirus disease 2019
CP-ABE	ciphertext policy attribute-based encryption
CRL	certificate revocation list
CS	compressed sensing
CV	computer vision
DBNs	deep belief networks
DCGAN	deep convolutional generative adversarial network
DDoS	distributed denial of service
DH	Diffie-Hellman
DL	deep learning
DNNs	deep neural networks

DoS	denial of service
DRL	deep reinforcement learning
DSR	dynamic source routing
D-VAE	dual-variational autoencoder
EAs	evolution algorithms
EBGAN	energy-based conditional GAN
EC	edge computing
ECC	elliptic-curve cryptography
ECG	electrocardiogram
ECRP	energy-aware cross-layer routing protocol
EDCA	enhanced distributed channel access
EECC	European edge computing consortium
EEG	electroencephalogram
EHIDF	edge-based hybrid intrusion detection framework
EHR	electronic health records
EI	edge intelligence
EoT	edge-of-things
ETSI	European Telecommunication Standards Institute
EVS	enhanced value substitution
EWS	early warning scores
FC	fog computing
FDA	Food and Drug Administration
FHE	fully homomorphic encryption
fMRI	functional magnetic resonance imaging
GAN	generative adversarial network
GAN-BVRM	GAN-based Bayesian visual reconstruction model
GATs	graph attention networks
GCN	graph convolutional neural networks
GET	graphene electronic tattoo
GLM	general linear regression model
GPU	graphics processing unit
Gr/PMMA	graphene/polymethylmethacrylate
GUI	graphical user interface
HCI	human-computer-interaction
h-d	helper-device
HDM	hybrid detection module
HEMA	hydroxyethyl methacrylate
H-IoT	healthcare-internet of things
HIV	human immunodeficiency virus
HMMs	hidden Markov models
HRP	horseradish peroxide
ICT	information and communication technology
IDS	intrusion detection system

ILIs   influenza-like illnesses
IoE   Internet of Everything
IoHT   Internet of Health Things
IoMT   Internet of Medical Things
IoST   Internet of Smart Things
IoT   Internet of Things
IPG   implanted pulse generator
IT   information technology
KPIs   key performance indicators
M2M   machine-to-machine
MANET   mobile ad hoc network
MCC   mobile cloud computing
MEC   multi-access edge computing
MEMS   microelectromechanical systems
MFS   medical features selection
MI   mutual information
ML   machine learning
MLP   multilayer perceptron
mMIMO   massive MIMO
mmWave   millimeter wave
MPR   multi-point relay
MR   mixed reality
MSE   mean squared error
MyTMed   my/treatment/medication
NFV   network function virtualization
NLP   natural language processing
OBL   oppositional-based learning
OCSP   online certificate status protocol
OMKELM-IDS   optimal mixed kernel extreme learning machine-based intrusion
                detection system
OT   operational technology
PBA   phenylboronic acid
PCC   Pearson correlation coefficient
PCR   polymerase chain reaction
PCs   personal computers
PDA   personal digital assistant
PPG   photoplethysmography
PSM   perceptual similarity metric
PTT   pulse-transit-times
QOCSA   quasi-oppositional cuckoo search algorithm
QoS   quality of service
RANs   radio access networks
RE   residual energy

RELM	regularized extreme learning machine
RL	reinforcement learning
RNN	recurrent neural network
RRC	radio resource control
RSSI	received signal strength indicator
SAEs	stacking auto-encoders
SC-GAN	similarity conditions generative adversarial network
SDM	signature detection module
SDNs	software-defined networks
SLAM	simultaneous localization and mapping
SSIM	structural similarity index measure
TC	topology control
TCId	traffic category identifications
TIA	transient ischemic attack
TT	training time
TTI	transmission time intervals
UAVs	unmanned aerial vehicles
UMass	University of Massachusetts
URLLC	ultra-reliable and low-latency communication
UWB	ultra-wideband
VAE	variational autoencoder
VMs	virtual machines
VPD	vaccine-preventable disease
VR	virtual reality
WBAN	wireless body area network
WCE	wireless capsule endoscope
WHO	World Health Organization

Preface

Revolution in healthcare, as well as demand for efficient real-time healthcare services, corresponds with the progression in edge computing (EC), artificial intelligence (AI)-mediated techniques, deep learning (DL), IoT applications for healthcare industries, and cloud computing (CC).

People today demand newer and more sophisticated healthcare systems, ones that are more personalized and matches the speed of modern life. With the exponential and rapid growth in the healthcare industry there are also growing challenges in solving complex real-life cases.

With the application of edge computing and automated intelligence, intuitions are incorporated into the existing healthcare analysis tools for identifying, forecasting, and preventing high-risk diseases. This book provides a comprehensive research idea on edge intelligence (EI) technology providing an insight to researchers about the healthcare industry trends, and future perspectives, as well as to healthcare professionals and the public health sector in making better data-driven decisions.

The scope of the book covers major areas of edge intelligence in healthcare data analysis with all emerging technologies like AI-based techniques, machine learning (ML), IoT, cloud computing, and deep learning with an illustration of its design, implementation, and management of smart and intelligent healthcare systems. The book has been constructed with the aim of assimilating and publishing research works and ideas that can be a valuable addition to the existing healthcare industries and help healthcare professionals and researchers explore future trends and simplify decision-making.

The book encompasses 14 chapters. Chapter 1 lays out the foundation of edge intelligence with its possible applications in healthcare industries. The chapter also marks a detailed study of all researches that have een conducted with edge computing for healthcare applications so that it can be an assisting technology in the battle against high-risk diseases. Chapter 2 extends the narration of Chapter 1 about edge intelligence as a cutting-edge technology to showcase the advantages and highlights of the adoption of intelligent edge models toward smart healthcare infrastructure. The chapter also outlines the perspective challenges and forthcoming research directions being applied within diversified technologies. Chapter 3 introduces smart healthcare model d to increase the use of AI and edge technologies and then addresses the possible problems and future research directions that could arise when these different technologies are combined. Chapter 4 recommends the emergence of a high level of security while transferring real-time data to cloud-based architecture, as medical data security is a matter of prime concern for both patient and doctor. The chapter advocates the implementation of Net-Medi (internet-based medical system) in healthcare industries so as to maintain security and make it flawless. Chapter 5 focuses on the latest advancements in different types of wearable sensor technologies and their application for monitoring health status to justify the economical and easy-to-use component for real-time monitoring.

Chapter 6 discusses a variety of edge computing techniques for disease prediction. Chapter 7 concentrates on e-health services and e-security solutions through IoT devices which have redesigned the healthcare systems to improve the quality of care for transgender patients who are generally ignored and get stuck in a perilous situation. Chapter 8 discusses ubiquitous health monitoring and addresses the collision problem with energy-aware cross-layer routing protocol (ECRP) for prioritizing service differentiation. Chapter 9 introduces the eLifeCare platform as a smart Healthcare Scenario in Ambient Assisted Living.

Chapter 10 stresses the fact that Edge Computing allows computation-intensive AI applications to run on edge hardware and further debates that edge intelligence can limit the virus spread during pandemics. Chapter 11 outlines the research gaps and challenges in the field of neuroscience in decoding and analysis of visual perception from neural patterns. Further, the chapter addressed the use of fMRI Analysis for visual image reconstruction. Chapter 12 highlights that edge computer technology is developed for healthcare progress in order to provide individuals with more quality and balance in their lives. The chapter also gives an idea of how the (IoST) method of solving edge problems with the help of medical healthcare therapy has recently been applied. Chapter 13 presents an experimental application of an effective OMKELM-IDS technique for the detection and classification of intrusions in the edge computing environment. Chapter 14 proposes a framework intended to generate the graphical user interface (GUI) by integrating big data concepts along with machine learning methodologies and Edge computing Concepts. The chapter further justified the pipelining of the existing structure with a complete GUI framework, which can be done to avoid repeated training of the ML methodologies in the addition of new data for the desired predictions.

PART I

Introduction to Edge-Intelligence in Healthcare

CHAPTER 1

Edge Intelligence and Its Healthcare Application

SOUMYA SAMARPITA

¹FOS, Sri Sri University, Cuttack, Odisha, India

ABSTRACT

Edge artificial intelligence (Edge AI), sometimes known as edge intelligence (EI), is the junction of edge computing (EC) and artificial intelligence (AI). The purpose of this technology is to escort AI abilities to edge of the network. The term "intelligent edge" refers to data analysis and solution development at the source of the data. In a variety of healthcare contexts, EI is a vital enabler technology. By analyzing data from medical equipment such as glucose monitors, blood pressure (BP) monitors, stress detection and alerting clinicians to potentially harmful results, edge could improve remote patient monitoring. EI is awaited to pave the way for the latest framework that incorporates EC and AI. Smart sensory objects, AI, machine learning (ML), edge analytics, deep learning (DL), and cloud computing (CC) concatenation are causing a revolution in healthcare, and linked healthcare is attracting a lot of attention from the industry, government, and healthcare organizations. There is an advancement of latest technologies for maintaining a happy and prospers life in this globe. Therefore, advanced smart healthcare framework is designed for human beings to meet their health needs. It is therefore imperative to investigate the various approaches to be applied in developing EI designs. Therefore, the study is intended to understand this fact with regards to smart healthcare and the challenges of various applications of the design.

Reconnoitering the Landscape of Edge Intelligence in Healthcare.
Suneeta Satpathy, Sachi Nandan Mohanty, and Sirisha Potluri (Eds.)
© 2024 Apple Academic Press, Inc. Co-published with CRC Press (Taylor & Francis)

1.1 INTRODUCTION

Edge intelligence (EI) is a new concept which intends to include edge computing (EC), artificial intelligence (AI), and other related applications. AI at the edge is a concept for developing AI operations that span centralized data centers and devices that are closer to humans and physical things outside the cloud. Around the world the deployment of AI applications is known as Edge AI. Using network's edge, the user does AI calculation keeping in view the stored data rather than the use of cloud computing (CC) facility. Therefore, it is named as "edge AI." Any location can be referred by network's edge because of the worldwide internet facilities which includes a store, a factory, a hospital, or everyday equipment like traffic lights, self-driving cars, and cell phones [6]. Applications of AI are always supported by developed models, computing power as well as massive datasets. Human users use different equipment for developing communications skills which are created as a major attribute [28].

Since the early 2000s, surveys on healthcare technology have appeared in publications. IT is now being used in healthcare to create smart technologies which elevate health diagnosis and deliver useful treatment. EI aims to create a single manifesto for AI on edge technologies. This technology is to be discovered by utilizing various resources in close proximity [18]. Therefore, EI aims at incorporation of AI and cognitive intelligence which is very relevant for human behavior in the field of EI. Many new platforms like industry, healthcare, and territorial control can be utilized with EC of AI techniques. This could be set with IoT healthcare platforms which will be more relevant as well as understandable. Such modern technologies enable real-time health controlling on smart technology which enhances some powers in controlling their health. It is stated that wearable and embedded smart IoT sensors can take real-time data collection. This data is analyzed by with the help of "machine learning (ML)" and "deep learning (DL)" techniques in order to detect hidden patterns and it is also helpful to warn about crucial situations [1]. EC can be used with several edge devices and local servers for the interactive and effective processing of healthcare sensor data. There is more advancement in the field of EI which leads towards smart healthcare platforms.

EI have reference to a network of connected mechanisms and appliance that gather, cache, process, and analyze data in close proximity to where it is acquired, with the goal of improving data processing quality and speed while also protecting data privacy and security. The appearance of EC has had a significant impact on the growth of the healthcare application. When considering the vast amount of data created by things on the healthcare system, it provides a lot of advantages. Things in healthcare can employ EC to do more complex data processing methods, allowing them to provide more services to users. People can also capture outlines of facilities using the EC paradigm in the field of healthcare. Hospital equipment also deals with patient data at the network's edge to satisfy privacy concerns.

Over the last few decades, the advent of sensor technology into our regular lifestyle has provided economy, relaxation, and enhanced health. Medical sensors have become more widely used as technological breakthroughs have reduced their cost and size [9]. In clinical application, sensor integration has been considerably enhanced for the quality and safety of healthcare applications. It also develops remote health monitoring, diagnostic imaging and birthing care since the last few years. Different types of sensors like electrocardiogram (ECG), humidity, oximeter as well as glucose sensors can be used for the patient with healthcare applications when it is needed.

1.1.1 EMERGENCE OF EDGE INTELLIGENCE (EI)

The merging of AI and EC techniques is known as "edge intelligence." The combination is natural because it offers significant benefits to traditional EC applications. The term "intelligent edge" refers to a procedure in which data is evaluated and aggregated near to where it is captured in a network. As demonstrated in Ref. [29], the significance of the data obtained by edge nodes can also be unlocked by AI approaches. High-quality judgments could be made at the edge by mining a vast amount of multi-modal data, resulting in improved service quality. Edge has drawn great attention as a new research area in recent years. EC and AI approaches, when combined; provide convenient intelligent applications for people in their daily lives that are less reliant on centralized storage [25]. EI has been driven to the perspective by EC approaches and drawn by AI applications. Data, model, and computation are known to be the three most crucial aspects for an intelligent application.

EI research has gotten a lot of attention lately, due to the growth popularity of implementing AI applications in the healthcare system using the framework of EC [29]. Numerous healthcare systems have turned to CC to provide cost-effective and sustainable solutions for processing and storing enormous amounts of data collected by a variety of biosensors. EC, which acts as a layer between end-user devices and remote cloud data centers, is a new way to overcome the limits of cloud-based healthcare [7]. EI focuses on the following six operations in accordance with the current status of EI technology [30]:

    i.   Collection;
    ii. Communication;
    iii. Computing;
    iv. Caching;
    v.   Control; and
    vi. Collaboration.

There are various classification systems for smart healthcare. They can be divided into categories based on data type, device type, or specialized use cases [6]. The following are the primary healthcare classifications based on use cases:

    i.   Health-aware mobile devices;
    ii. Real-time health tracking;
    iii. Healthcare data distribution;
    iv. Emergency management platforms.

1.1.2 ADVANTAGES OF EDGE INTELLIGENCE (EI)

Edge AI's main benefit is that it extends high-performance processing capabilities to the edge, where the location of IoT devices and sensors are found. AI EC allows AI applications to run on field devices, processing data and running ML and DL algorithms. DL calculations are intended to be pushed as far as feasible from the cloud to the edge by EI. This permits the implementation of several extended, minimal, dependable, and intelligent services. EC is being used in a growing number of real-world applications because of its considerable advantages.

The introduction of EC has had a huge impact on healthcare's expansion. When it comes to the large volume of data generated by items on healthcare, it offers numerous benefits. The following are a few benefits of EC:

    i.   It allows data created by things to be processed close to the source, relieving the network of the significant strain of data transmission.

ii. It reduces data communication and transmission time, resulting in a significant reduction in data processing delay, which is crucial for real-time applications.

iii. Processing data at the network's edge can also assist protect confidential details from being released, as certain data may be private and contain vital messages from users.

1.2 SCOPE OF EDGE INTELLIGENCE (EI)

Edge AI is a new and developed concept of AI. Now-a-days researchers are actively in studying this area in healthcare applications. In healthcare applications, where real-time processing and huge data consumption are critical, EC is particularly effective. As previously stated [32], in 2009, there was a study on "edge-based prototype" to support mobile voice command recognition which is constructed by Microsoft. There is no clear concept for EI in the field of research in its early stages. It is rapidly evolving and serving as a key facilitator for a variety of applications, ranging from medical diagnostics to alien inquiry.

On the cloud, ML systems have been effectively deployed. For many purposes, the cloud is the best place to run ML algorithms. ML computations closer to the edge, on the other hand, may be appropriate for applications that link to the physical world. Many authors use the terms "information technology" (IT) and "operational technology" interchangeably (OT) [24].

AI is also generating a lot of buzz in the healthcare industry. Many technologies and cutting-edge AI-powered computing have, of course, been successfully deployed to assist medical professionals [21]. A creative hierarchy should be built for effective EI systems. Furthermore, current EI ideas mostly emphasize on the inference phase, presuming that the AI model is trained in the power cloud datacenters, because the training phase consumes substantially more resources than the inference stage. To enhance the overall performance of the training and inference system, EI should be the framework to enhance the overall performance of the training system. That framework should be fully used through the hierarchy of edge nodes, end devices and cloud datacenters. As indicated in Figure 1.1, EI is classified into six stages which are shown below based on the amount of data. The range of EI scores is from one to six.

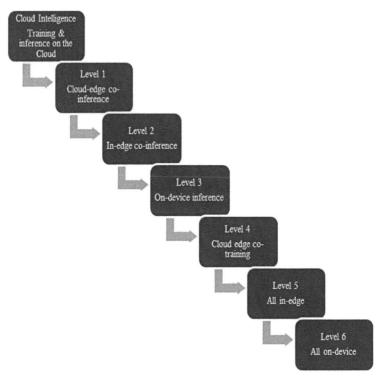

FIGURE 1.1   Stages of edge intelligence.

Source: Adapted from Ref.[4]

1.3 APPLICATION SCENARIOS

When we look at EC in the context of today's life, we can see how it has steadily crept into increasing corners of our world. The following are examples of application layout:

- i. Smart healthcare;
- ii. Smart city;
- iii. Smart manufacturing;
- iv. Smart home;
- v. Self-determining vehicle;
- vi. Self-directed robot.

In the EI context, there will be customization of advanced AI frameworks through ML algorithms. Running on the edge is required for AI applications such as smart healthcare, autonomous vehicles, smart manufacturing, smart home, smart city, and autonomous robots. Figure 1.2 shows various AI applications for successful execution of AI algorithms on the edge.

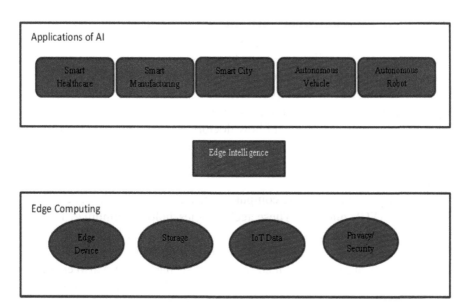

FIGURE 1.2 Edge intelligence's motive.

1.3.1 HEALTHCARE SCENARIO

EC has been used in a variety of contexts due to its benefits and technological advancements. The performance of healthcare system can be improved by using EC concept in healthcare system. Personal and confidential information is a critical issue which is used in medical services as well as data security system. The fast rise of the population has put a huge pressure on current health services. Emerging innovations are required to deal with medical crises, diagnosis, and procedures in a timely, accurate, and cost-effective manner. Smart healthcare informs people about their health issues and empowers them to manage a few of them independently. This section summarizes EC application scenarios in the healthcare world.

Healthcare has been rapidly utilizing information technologies to deliver smart solutions intended to speed up health tests and treatment in recent years [5]. These systems deliver intelligent monitoring systems and medical automation services in a variety of environments and situations, allowing for a significant reduction in physician visit expenses and an overall improvement in patient care quality. "Big data," "internet of things (IoT)," and "cloud" have all helped to promote the modernization healthcare systems and hence the quality of medical treatments. Smart healthcare services allow people and doctors to intelligently handle and respond to medical demands remotely, reducing hospitalization and helping patients and doctors in intelligently predicting, detecting, diagnosing, and treating diseases [7]. Some people are apprehensive about the treatment process to have trust in a digital system in order to diagnose or anticipate their illnesses. As a result, they typically oppose the use of smart technologies because they lack sufficient knowledge of how the system operates and how doctors engage with it and, indirectly, with patients. It is currently used in computer methods and communication technologies including wireless sensor networks, radio frequency identification and cell phones [2].

Examples of cutting-edge computer science technology include CC, fog computing (FC), and EC. These technologies help to minimize low-cost storage capacity and satisfy the needs of a cost-effective healthcare system. There are some new technologies like 6G, ultra-wide band (UWB), and Wi-Fi 6 which are very significant in present scenario. These also enable for modernizing the healthcare system including healthcare monitoring, assessment, and treatment programs [9].

Patients nowadays want a more complex and personalized healthcare system capable of keeping the pace of contemporary life. The field of health and biomedicine is entering a data-driven era. The advancement in medical equipment provides data about a person's health state. Citizens are using smart edge technologies to track their physical state as health awareness has grown. Pre-hospital medical technology is offered in the form of basic life support where the emergent patient is treated before arriving at the hospital [28]. EI improves the current system with the help of training the sharing system which recognizes medical images and improves treatment efficiency. EC is a cost-effective platform for collecting sensor data by supplying compute resources. Now-a-days for efficient resource development, AI has become the focus of interest in the field of healthcare system.

The EC approach also enhances the efficiency of real-time monitoring. It automatically tracks the status of a patient and rigorously monitors their real-time health status [29]. Real-time monitoring is critical for detecting clinical worsening early on. Patients' signs are recorded in a variety of ways, including audio and video. Different algorithms can be used to examine a patient's health and provide clinicians with the appropriate guidance. This type of research can be used to help those with chronic conditions. For example, in order to avoid cardiovascular illness, such as heart's beating frequency and blood pressure (BP), wearable devices can be used to analyze the health condition of the patient.

1.3.2 BACKGROUND INFORMATION AND RELATED WORK

Several research have investigated collaborative learning systems based on EI in recent years. The glorification of some terms like "smart sensory things," "artificial intelligence" (AI), "machine learning" (ML), "deep learning" (DL), "internet of medical things" (IoMT), and "edge analytics" with the combination of CC is causing a revolution in healthcare. Many applications, such as healthcare, will benefit from the use of AI and ML algorithms in tandem with EC. Latest studies that look at these new themes in healthcare tend to emphasize on the forms of monitoring that EC can give, such as EEG, heart rate monitoring, fall detection, and so on.

Information fusion, according to chapter [30], is a key strategy for boosting EI's capabilities in terms of collecting, communication, processing, caching, control, and collaboration. In terms of agile connection, real-time services, data optimization, application intelligence, and security and privacy protection, EI can address the key needs of healthcare system. "Artificial intelligence" and "human intelligence" are firmly interwoven at the edge of networks in social EI to study the collective capability of both humans and technology [22]. In several tasks, including as relational inference, cognitive, and emotion detection, and non-structured problem-solving, human intelligence has been found to be superior to AI. Researchers have ascertained the importance of EI in the "cyber-human evolution" in chapter [19], as well as the obstacles that edge AI systems will face in the coming years. They've demonstrated that how EC becomes more complicated which is inherent in AI applications and ML workflows, and how new methodologies are required to use hierarchical edge architectures for the AI lifecycle. They identified three types of EI use cases in terms of stake: personal health aides, smart public spaces, predictive maintenance, and overlapping.

Recent improvements in EC, such as new hardware and software that have arisen in recent years to describe the difficulties of CC in the current situation, have been explained in Ref. [14]. Hardware advancements are in keeping with the trend of introducing additional layers that enable parallelization of processes. Meanwhile, the software research lines are focused on increasing data processing speed as well as system security. For decision making, anomaly detection, predictive risk evaluation, therapy counseling, and so on, a variety of AI and ML-based technologies can be used efficiently [5]. To meet the requirements of real-time operation, reduce latency, and limit energy usage, multimodal activity prediction, fall detection and prevention, medical automation, and emergency healthcare require inference to be conducted as close to the sensor nodes as possible.

In terms of how the integration of EC, service computing, and AI can help to provide highly dispersed heterogeneous smart devices represented as services that can be used in a variety of smart application scenarios. As a result, facilitating AI implementation on these devices can enable smart and efficient systems like connected healthcare. In another work [8], a unique, dynamic, and trustworthy framework for AI subtask composition in the environment of EC for smart healthcare applications is presented. The main goal of this chapter is to make AI jobs easier to deploy on "resource-constrained" edge devices.

The IoMT is a combination of devices and software used in healthcare. These can be connected through cutting-edge communication technology. Hospital visits and massive pressure on medical system of a patient can be reduced which will enable him to give more health information through communication network. In Ref. [10], it has been discovered that edge-IoT applications can provide clinicians, caretakers, and physicians with an advanced experience without interruption, from any location and at any time. Edge AI's solution has also been found to be superior to cloud-based solutions. It has been discovered that using social platforms for healthcare communication is hampered by concerns about confidentiality, data flooding, poor reliability, confidentiality, and integrity.

In recent years, EI-based collaborative learning methodologies have been used to DL models, demonstrating higher classification performance as a result of expanded coverage on massive volumes of training data gathered at the edge of devices. According to the findings, partitioned model training has been recognized in Ref. [23] as the best strategy to use in the setting of resource restricted IoT edge devices. Because different researchers have varied perceptions of collaborative learning strategies, the existing methodologies in their work have been divided into three categories: distributed ML, partitioned model training, and data encryption. The distributed nature of IoT systems poses various technological obstacles for ML in IoT [24].

The researchers in study [4] focus on setting for Assisted Living scenario in which a smart home environment is used to help elderly people at home by making reliable automated difficult decisions using IoT sensors, smart healthcare equipment, and edge nodes. The study presented a revolutionary EC architecture and the "eLifeCare" platform, which is specifically built for healthcare, to demonstrate how all AI techniques encourage and strengthen one other [17]. Proposes utilizing the concept of FC in healthcare IoT systems by establishing a specified intelligence layer between sensor nodes and the cloud. Researchers must cope with an EC architecture that allows processing to take place at devices or gateways. This cuts down on needless data transmission and processing complexity, which is vital for applications like critical patient monitoring and analysis.

Through healthcare-internet of things (H-IoT), IoT plays a role in healthcare. Numerous projects providing IoT architectures for smart health monitoring have been developed in less than 10 years. It's a complicated system that includes medicine, microelectronics, health systems, AI, and more [11]. This enables remote patient monitoring in hospitals and at home, with the goal of improving healthcare quality, detecting, and controlling emergencies, and lowering healthcare costs. Big data analysis is required, according to researchers, before using the data for monitoring, diagnosis, or prediction. The analysis and management of data is still a study topic. Instead of focusing on cloud compute, edge, fog, and cloud infrastructure must be integrated to spread data processing responsibility.

The massive amount of data generated poses new storage, transport, and processing issues. Processing big medical data on the cloud backend presented issues such as "digital security" and "communication propagation delay." FC addresses these issues by applying processing, storing, filtering, and AI of local data. This FC is a new concept which is merged to employ these attributes in cloud and wearable devices. The work [15] has been processed in the function of ML based EI in the fog layer. The adaptive properties of "smart e-health internet of things" applications in the field of "ambient assisted living" are discussed in the chapter [13]. An adaptive sensing mechanism based on the analysis of contemporary and non-contemporary sensor data, features extracted from the gathered data, and AI optimization is presented to efficiently implement the integrated batteries of smart sensors and communication resources.

In clinical practice, U-Fall can attain extremely high sensitivity and specificity. Investigators used a real-world widespread health monitoring application to illustrate the efficacy and effectiveness of the "fog computing paradigm" in health monitoring in their paper [3]. According to them, "fall" is a primary cause of mortality and morbidity in stroke patients. The classification of basic data acquired by health sensors is usually done using basic or complicated algorithms, depending on the device's computer capabilities, and is a popular research topic in healthcare-related computing [6]. Because robust algorithms are required for devices with limited storage and computational resources, activity-based recognition is the most prominent classification study in healthcare EC. A huge-scale healthcare system paired with real-time data capture necessitates the analysis and security of a vast amount of data.

In variety of fields, "cross-domain use case study" is described in detail in a number of applications [18]. Researchers merged smart cities, health, agriculture, and food computing to highlight how multimodal sensors may be used in a variety of ways. Edge-based remote monitoring systems that use various types of smart sensors for the installation of healthcare systems are common in IoT healthcare frameworks. Researchers in chapter [1] focused particularly on the issues that health surveillance systems face. These issues are divided into two groups such as static patient monitoring and dynamic patient monitoring. At home, office or hospital, there is a need of static patient monitoring whereas dynamic patient monitoring follows the patient outside of these settings.

All throughout the world, the fifth generation (5G) wireless network is being used. The entire 5G network is capable of delivering high maximal data transfer rates, exceptionally low communication response times, and pervasive connectivity. The 6G network has been proposed as the next generation of the 5G network to satisfy requirements that are beyond the capabilities of 5G [26]. An adaptive operations-framework is developed by EC which is a potential method. It enables scalability of IoMT applications by reducing service latency. In the research [27], "latency-energy efficient sensor nodes task" offloaded for job implementation in "edge-enabled sensor networks" is also investigated with end-to-end latency and battery capacity.

Future smart health systems could use applications on edge devices with AI capabilities to revolutionize disease detection and monitoring. Researchers evaluated a minimalist strategy for "obstructive sleep apnea" severity assessment, severity estimation, and progression tracking in a home scenario employing wearable in the study [16]. They selected the optimal feature set derived from the "polysomnogram" using the recursive feature elimination technique. They investigated the effectiveness of obstructive sleep apnea severity classification with all ranked features to a subset of features available from either electroencephalography or heart rate variability and the duration of SpO2 level using a multi-layer perceptron model. The chapter [21] describes an "EI-based Smart Health Systems" that can determine whether or not a person gets stressed out a lot. Their smart health system, which is based on EI, measures heart-rate variability and informs users to their stress levels. This work uses IoT devices to continually monitor a person's heart rate because it is difficult for a medical practitioner to determine a person's age from pulse because both are nonlinear.

For management efficiency, high durability, flexibility, and deployment automation, the AI apps will be deployed on a lightweight container "orchestration platform." A container-based EC system has been presented by the researchers in the study [12]. To monitor and care for patients in the recovery stage in real-time, a web-based applications and smart care mobiles are designed to help doctor and nurse in medical services. To deal with the patient's facial emotion detection and treatment of heart disease, the researchers have proposed to use EC services through AI application scenario. Also, CC environment can be organized to secure the patient's data in a scalable and secure way. Researchers in Ref. [31] developed an ECG-based heartbeat detection technology and a lightweight framework called CareEdge to provide an innovative and effective model for EI. The "CareEdge" framework connects IoT and edge devices through multi-user EI architecture. To connect the integrated IoT-Edge-Cloud ecosystem, "CareEdge" makes extensive use of edge network resources.

Adopting human-computer-interaction (HCI) technology in a smart health system can improve it by accurately detecting people's emotions and acting effectively to assist them in changing their lifestyle. Research [20] on recognizing emotions from audio is developing day by day for healthcare in a wisely regulated environment, with other data sources. Their proposed system is being used to contribute to audio-based emotional healthcare in any intelligently controlled setting. With a restricted audio-based emotion dataset acquired from sound sensors in edges, the system can also be tested on edge devices. A health policy-related method called "distributed medical database access control 11" was examined in the publication [2]. The credentials, such as users and medical data, cannot be hidden via public networks since it is linked to a digital certificate. Their research aims to maintain security and privacy between framework technologies like "Gaggle and GaggleBridge."

1.4 CONCLUSION

The use of the AI paradigm in EC scenarios is referred to as EI. The capacity to construct EI applications and services will open up a completely new set of applications and services. AI has outperformed expectations in terms of identifying new opportunities for technologies from various fields. The use of EI-based tactics is changing people's lives, particularly in healthcare. Edge technology enhances smart healthcare services by decreasing latency, network stress and power consumption by processing locally. AI basically introduces the smartness to the system and improves the smart healthcare systems. The integration of AI and EI technologies improves the intelligence of smart healthcare system components and provides numerous benefits. As wearable technology and smartphone applications are consigned with real-time monitoring and diagnosis of patients, the results of EC in healthcare becomes more significant. Healthcare practitioners can benefit from EI's predictive risk analysis and increased health awareness. Embracing a mix of EC and AI, in particular, can pave the path for addressing a variety of difficulties in the domain of smart healthcare.

KEYWORDS

- **artificial intelligence**
- **edge computing**
- **edge intelligence**
- **healthcare**
- **real-time monitoring**
- **smartphone applications**
- **wearable technology**

REFERENCES

1. Amin, S. U., & Hossain, M. S., (2020). Edge intelligence and internet of things in healthcare: A survey. *IEEE Access, 9*, 45–59.
2. Bakkiam, D. D., & Al-Turjman, F., (2021). Lightweight privacy-aware secure authentication scheme for cyber-physical systems in the edge intelligence era. *Concurrency and Computation: Practice and Experience*, e6510.
3. Cao, Y., Hou, P., Brown, D., Wang, J., & Chen, S., (2015). Distributed analytics and edge intelligence: Pervasive health monitoring at the era of fog computing. In: *Proceedings of the 2015 Workshop on Mobile Big Data* (pp. 43–48).

4. Fasciano, C., & Vitulano, F., (2020). Artificial intelligence on edge computing: A healthcare scenario in ambient assisted living. *Proceedings of the Artificial Intelligence for Ambient Assisted Living (AI* AAL. it 2019).*

5. Greco, L., Percannella, G., Ritrovato, P., Tortorella, F., & Vento, M., (2020). Trends in IoT based solutions for health care: Moving AI to the edge. *Pattern Recognition Letters, 135*, 346–353.

6. Hartmann, M., Hashmi, U. S., & Imran, A., (2019). Edge computing in smart health care systems: Review, challenges, and research directions. *Transactions on Emerging Telecommunications Technologies*, e3710.

7. Hayyolalam, V., Aloqaily, M., Özkasap, Ö., & Guizani, M., (2021). Edge intelligence for empowering IoT-based healthcare systems. *IEEE Wireless Communications, 28*(3), 6–14.

8. Hayyolalam, V., Otoum, S., & Özkasap, Ö., (2022). Dynamic QoS/QoE-aware reliable service composition framework for edge intelligence. *Cluster Computing*, 1–19.

9. Javaid, S., Zeadally, S., Fahim, H., & He, B., (2022). Medical sensors and their integration in wireless body area networks for pervasive healthcare delivery: A review. *IEEE Sensors Journal.*

10. Kamruzzaman, M. M., Alrashdi, I., & Alqazzaz, A., (2022). New opportunities, challenges, and applications of edge-AI for connected healthcare in internet of medical things for smart cities. *Journal of Healthcare Engineering, 2022.*

11. Khan, S., Arslan, T., & Ratnarajah, T., (2022). Digital twin perspective of fourth industrial and healthcare revolution. *IEEE Access, 10*, 25732–25754.

12. Le-Anh, T., Ngo-Van, Q., Vo-Huy, P., Huynh-Van, D., & Le-Trung, Q., (2021). A container-based edge computing system for smart healthcare applications. In: *International Conference on Industrial Networks and Intelligent Systems* (pp. 324–336). Springer, Cham.

13. Lin, Y., Wang, J., & Sahama, T., (2022). An adaptive framework for smart e-health IoT applications using asynchronous data under edge computing services. In: *Australasian Computer Science Week 2022* (pp. 257–260).

14. Mendez, J., Bierzynski, K., Cuéllar, M. P., & Morales, D. P., (2022). Edge intelligence: Concepts, architectures, applications and future directions. *ACM Transactions on Embedded Computing Systems (TECS).*

15. Priyadarshini, R., Barik, R. K., Dubey, H. C., & Mishra, B. K., (2021). A survey of fog computing-based healthcare big data analytics and its security. *International Journal of Ambient Computing and Intelligence (IJACI), 12*(2), 53–72.

16. Rahman, M. J., & Morshed, B. I., (2021). A minimalist method toward severity assessment and progression monitoring of obstructive sleep apnea on the edge. *ACM Transactions on Computing for Healthcare (Health), 3*(2), 1–16.

17. Rahmani, A. M., Gia, T. N., Negash, B., Anzanpour, A., Azimi, I., Jiang, M., & Liljeberg, P., (2018). Exploiting smart e-health gateways at the edge of healthcare internet-of-things: A fog computing approach. *Future Generation Computer Systems, 78*, 641–658.

18. Raith, P., & Dustdar, S., (2021). Edge intelligence as a service. In: *2021 IEEE International Conference on Services Computing (SCC)* (pp. 252–262). IEEE.

19. Rausch, T., & Dustdar, S., (2019). Edge intelligence: The convergence of humans, things, and ai. In: *2019 IEEE International Conference on Cloud Engineering (IC2E)* (pp. 86–96). IEEE.

20. Uddin, M. Z., & Nilsson, E. G., (2020). Emotion recognition using speech and neural structured learning to facilitate edge intelligence. *Engineering Applications of Artificial Intelligence, 94*, 103775.

21. Vatti, R. A., Vinoth, K., & Sneha, Y., (2020). Edge intelligence for predicting and detecting cardiac pathologies by analyzing stress and anxiety. *Journal of Critical Reviews, 7*(18), 2816–2822.

22. Wang, D., Zhang, D., Zhang, Y., Rashid, M. T., Shang, L., & Wei, N., (2019). Social edge intelligence: Integrating human and artificial intelligence at the edge. In: *2019 IEEE First International Conference on Cognitive Machine Intelligence (CogMI)* (pp. 194–201). IEEE.

23. Welagedara, L., Harischandra, J., & Jayawardene, N., (2021). A review on edge intelligence based collaborative learning approaches. In: *2021 IEEE 11th Annual Computing and Communication Workshop and Conference (CCWC)* (pp. 572–577). IEEE.

24. Wolf, M., (2019). Machine learning+ distributed IoT= edge intelligence. In: *2019 IEEE 39th International Conference on Distributed Computing Systems (ICDCS)* (pp. 1715–1719). IEEE.

25. Xu, D., Li, T., Li, Y., Su, X., Tarkoma, S., Jiang, T., & Hui, P., (2020). *Edge Intelligence: Architectures, Challenges, and Applications.* arXiv preprint arXiv:2003.12172.

26. Xu, D., Li, T., Li, Y., Su, X., Tarkoma, S., Jiang, T., & Hui, P., (2021). Edge intelligence: Empowering intelligence to the edge of network. *Proceedings of the IEEE, 109*(11), 1778–1837.

27. Yadav, R., Zhang, W., Elgendy, I. A., Dong, G., Shafiq, M., Laghari, A. A., & Prakash, S., (2021). Smart healthcare: RL-based task offloading scheme for edge-enable sensor networks. *IEEE Sensors Journal, 21*(22), 24910–24918.

28. Zhang, X., Wang, Y., Lu, S., Liu, L., & Shi, W., (2019). OpenEI: An open framework for edge intelligence. In: *2019 IEEE 39th International Conference on Distributed Computing Systems (ICDCS)* (pp. 1840–1851). IEEE.

29. Zhang, T., Li, Y., & Chen, C. P., (2021). Edge computing and its role in industrial internet: Methodologies, applications, and future directions. *Information Sciences, 557*, 34–65.

30. Zhang, Y., Jiang, C., Yue, B., Wan, J., & Guizani, M., (2022). Information fusion for edge intelligence: A survey. *Information Fusion, 81*, 171–186.

31. Zhen, P., Han, Y., Dong, A., & Yu, J., (2021). CareEdge: A lightweight edge intelligence framework for ECG-based heartbeat detection. *Procedia Computer Science, 187*, 329–334.

32. Zhou, Z., Chen, X., Li, E., Zeng, L., Luo, K., & Zhang, J., (2019). Edge intelligence: Paving the last mile of artificial intelligence with edge computing. *Proceedings of the IEEE, 107*(8), 1738–1762.

CHAPTER 2

Edge Intelligence – The Cutting Edge of the Healthcare Industry

SIRISHA POTLURI,[1] PARMESHWARA JOGA,[2] DEEPTHI RAPAKA,[2] and
G. SUCHARITHA[3]

[1]*Assistant Professor, Department of Computer Science and Engineering, Faculty of Science and Technology – IcfaiTech, ICFAI Foundation for Higher Education, Hyderabad, Telangana, India*

[2]*Researcher, Department of Computer Science and Engineering, Faculty of Science and Technology – IcfaiTech, ICFAI Foundation for Higher Education, Hyderabad, Telangana, India*

[3]*Associate Professor, Department of Computer Science and Engineering, Institute of Aeronautical Engineering, Hyderabad, Telangana, India*

ABSTRACT

The demand for economical and efficient real-time services is increasing due to the technological swift and revolution. To meet our growing demands and handle real-life complex challenges there is a significant need for intelligent computing methods. We have several computing models to address these challenges. Particularly, the edge computing (EC) model can decrease network latency and resource energy consumption by shifting processes nearer to the data sources in contrast to the conventional cloud and IoT-enabled healthcare methods. Moreover, by getting automated intuitions into intelligent and smart healthcare methods, artificial intelligence (AI) offers the opportunity of identifying and forecasting high-risk diseases and sicknesses in advance, reducing medical expenses for patients, and proposing efficient medical treatments and solutions. Our objective of this research is to showcase the advantages and highlights of the adoption of intelligent edge

Reconnoitering the Landscape of Edge Intelligence in Healthcare.
Suneeta Satpathy, Sachi Nandan Mohanty, and Sirisha Potluri (Eds.)
© 2024 Apple Academic Press, Inc. Co-published with CRC Press (Taylor & Francis)

models toward smart healthcare infrastructure. Furthermore, we discourse perspective challenges and forthcoming research directions ascending when assimilating these diverse technologies.

2.1   INTRODUCTION

Edge computing (EC) contains decentralized and distributed computing architecture and infrastructure. It provides local data processing and quicker access to the edge network. Several characteristics: improved bandwidth optimization, faster response, scalability, and reliability of the EC technology allow it extremely to appropriate for several applications [1]:

1. **Efficient Bandwidth Optimization:** Due to local data processing on the edge nodes the quantity of data to be moved to the cloud for data processing is decreased. This in turn decreases the network traffic and increases the reliability and efficiency of the system.

2. **Spontaneous Response:** Data processing on the edge nodes allows and produces an instantaneous and spontaneous response to services. Due to this advantage of EC, it is treated as the best solution for real-life problems.

3. **Scalability:** Distributed EC provides a simple path to scalability that supports the expansion of the edge nodes. Scalability can be accomplished by merely increasing the computing nodes and their capacity through an arrangement of IoT and edge infrastructure. Moreover, different end-users will not enforce considerable bandwidth requirements on the existing network due to the utilization of processing capabilities of the EC devices. Due to this advantage of EC, it is incredibly flexible for real-life applications.

4. **Reliability:** Data processing is more reliable as it is safe from security issues and network problems.

2.2   THE ARCHITECTURE OF EDGE COMPUTING (EC)

Key components [2] of the EC are:

1. **Cloud Layer:** This is a public/private cloud computing (CC) model and is a repository for various applications and models that are container-based workloads. These cloud models also host and run several applications that are required to orchestrate and accomplish

the operations on edge nodes. Edge workloads will interact with cloud workloads to accomplish tasks. The cloud layer is also a source and target to the other nodes to provide required data.

2. **Edge Device:** In the edge framework, an edge device is a special infrastructure that has integrated local compute capacity. Interesting and significant work is performed on powerful edge devices.

3. **Edge Node:** In the edge framework, an edge node is a Broadway of mentioning to any edge device/server/gateway using which EC operations can be performed.

4. **Edge Cluster/Server Infrastructure:** An edge cluster/server infrastructure is a broad-purpose computer setup that is positioned in a remote processes ability such as a manufacturing factory, retail industry, hotel administration, distribution environment, or banking model. An edge cluster/server infrastructure is usually constructed with an engineering framework and is commonly used to execute enterprise-level workloads with shared services.

5. **Edge Gateway:** In an edge framework, an edge gateway can host enterprise-level application workloads with shared services. It also accomplishes network tasks such as protocol transformation, network dissolution, network tunneling, firewall security, and wireless network connection. While some edge devices in the edge framework can serve as a partial gateway, other edge gateways are further frequently isolated from edge devices.

IoT sensors in the edge framework are used to collect and transmit the data and allow onboard computation, memory, and loading. Edge devices attach to the different nodes and the infrastructure is shown in Figure 2.1.

2.3   EDGE INTELLIGENCE (EI)

Edge intelligence (EI) is observed when machine learning (ML) and EC are merged. As the name recommends, it is an area that handles providing intelligent insights attained through data processing at a local level in an edge network. The significant objective and purpose of EI are to advance the data processing with great quality, speed, and privacy of data [3, 4]. With all its advantages of EC, it came into existence with ML and artificial intelligence (AI) applications. The significance of EI is represented in Figure 2.2.

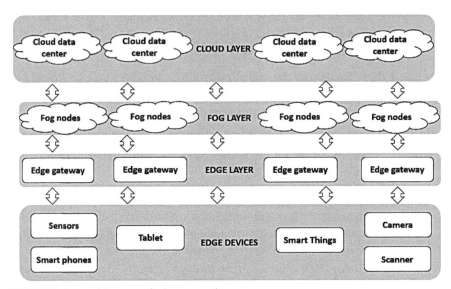

FIGURE 2.1   Architecture of edge computing.

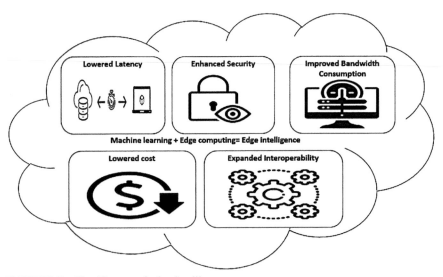

FIGURE 2.2   Significance of edge intelligence.

2.4   APPLICATIONS OF EDGE INTELLIGENCE (EI)

In several applications, it would be extremely advantageous to process and handle data on the local device where it's produced. In this crucial need EC plays a vital role. EC supports decentralized and local data processing and decreases data dependence on the cloud environment [5, 6]. Prime applications, which utilize the full benefit of EC technology are represented in Figure 2.3.

1. **Autonomous or Self-Driven Vehicles:** Autonomous vehicles are intelligent and smart vehicles. The instant decision to sojourn for a pedestrian walking in front of an autonomous or self-driven vehicle must be done immediately. Trusting a remote server to take this decision is not sensible. Moreover, vehicles that apply EC technology can relate more competently because they can interconnect with each other nodes first as contrasting to giving data on road accidents, climate or weather conditions, traffic environments, or diversions to a remote cloud server first.

2. **Healthcare Infrastructure:** Health monitors or devices can have a close watch and maintenance on chronic health conditions for several patients. It can protect lives by directly notifying caregivers when assistance is required. Furthermore, robots supporting healthcare infrastructure such as surgery can quickly examine data for safe, quick, and accurate processes. If these devices depend on spreading data to the cloud platform before building decisions, the outcomes could be disastrous.

3. **Secure Solutions:** Since it's essential to retort to threats within no time, security infrastructure can also profit from the edge model. Security solutions can detect potential dangers and alert end users to rare doings in real-time.

4. **Smart Devices:** These can increase the capability to construe voice commands locally to execute basic commands. Making automatics calls, turning electric components on or off, regulating device settings, even with low bandwidth and discontinued internet connectivity would be possible.

5. **Retail Industry:** Targeted advertisements and data for the retail industry are based on significant factors – demographic data and set

on field devices. The EC model can support and protect user security and privacy in the retail industry.

6. **Virtual Assistance:** By employing the EC model, we can bring software nearer to clients or participants to reduce several problems.

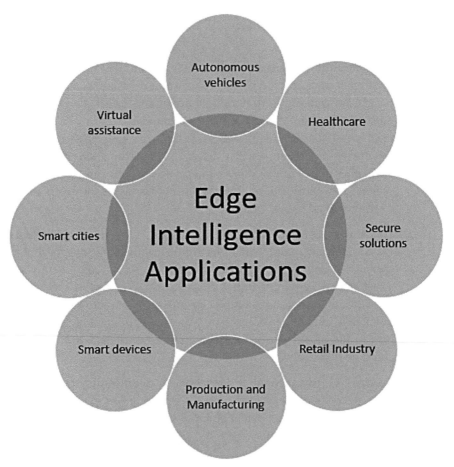

FIGURE 2.3   Applications of edge intelligence.

2.5 SIGNIFICANCE OF EDGE INTELLIGENCE (EI) IN HEALTHCARE

Several healthcare organizations have embraced CC infrastructure to provide reasonable and scalable healthcare solutions aiming to process and store huge volumes of data chronicled via many biosensors. Though, since cloud-driven healthcare processes frequently contain mobile nodes or devices, network infrastructure, data centers, and servers, there are frequently long distances concerning the systems' components, which increases a high latency concern in these systems [7, 8]. Consequently, real-time health demands cannot depend on cloud-driven healthcare organizations. Besides, the massive amounts of archives formed by sensors need to frequently be transported to the cloud to process and store, which involves high energy consumption and cost. Likewise, most chronic patients need low-cost smart mobile infrastructure, which is not sustained by cloud-driven solutions [9, 10]. The significance of EI is represented in Figure 2.4.

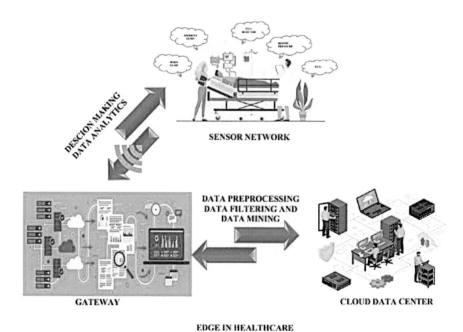

FIGURE 2.4   Significance of edge intelligence in healthcare.

Several applications of EI in healthcare are:

- Drug discovery;
- Efficient diagnostics;
- Electronic health record maintenance;
- Robotic surgery;
- Clinical trials;
- Healthcare maintenance;
- On-device intelligence.

A comprehensive view of several EI applications is given in Figure 2.5.

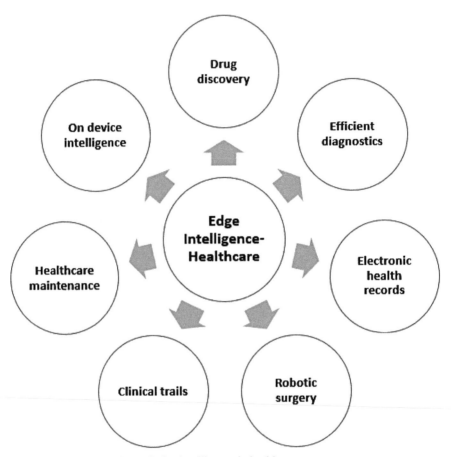

FIGURE 2.5   Applications of edge intelligence in healthcare.

2.6   CONCLUSION AND RESEARCH DIRECTIONS

This research highlights how the EC model, along with AI practices, can improve the performance of the smart healthcare infrastructure and systems. Data processing locally and nearby, EC model advances smart healthcare infrastructure and systems by decreasing network latency, system burden, and energy consumption. The combination of AI and EC technology creates the modules of smart healthcare infrastructure and systems smarter with many advantages. Further research is continuing toward next-generation smart and intelligent industry applications to address the growing day-to-day demands.

KEYWORDS

- **cloud computing**
- **edge computing**
- **edge intelligence**
- **healthcare**

REFERENCES

1. Zhou, Z., et al., (2019). Edge intelligence: Paving the last mile of artificial intelligence with edge computing. *Proceedings of the IEEE, 107*(8), 1738–1762.

2. Hayyolalam, V., Aloqaily, M., Özkasap, Ö., & Guizani, M., (2021). Edge intelligence for empowering IoT-based healthcare systems. In: *IEEE Wireless Communications* (Vol. 28, No. 3, pp. 6–14). doi: 10.1109/MWC.001.2000345.

3. Plastiras, G., Terzi, M., Kyrkou, C., & Theocharides, T., (2018). Edge intelligence: Challenges and opportunities of near-sensor machine learning applications. In: *2018 IEEE 29th International Conference on Application-Specific Systems, Architectures and Processors (ASAP)* (pp. 1–7). doi: 10.1109/ASAP.2018.8445118.

4. Liu, Y., Peng, M., Shou, G., Chen, Y., & Chen, S., (2020). Toward edge intelligence: Multiaccess edge computing for 5G and internet of things. In: *IEEE Internet of Things Journal* (Vol. 7, No. 8, pp. 6722–6747). doi: 10.1109/JIOT.2020.3004500.

5. Amin, S. U., & Hossain, M. S., (2021). Edge intelligence and internet of things in healthcare: A survey. In: *IEEE Access* (Vol. 9, pp. 45–59). doi: 10.1109/ACCESS.2020.3045115.

6. Zhang, J., & Letaief, K. B., (2020). Mobile edge intelligence and computing for the internet of vehicles. In: *Proceedings of the IEEE* (Vol. 108, No. 2, pp. 246–261). doi: 10.1109/JPROC.2019.2947490.

7. Dong, P., et al., (2020). Edge computing based healthcare systems: Enabling decentralized health monitoring in internet of medical things. In: *IEEE Network* (Vol. 34, No. 5, pp. 254–261). doi: 10.1109/MNET.011.1900636.

8. Oueida, S., Kotb, Y., Aloqaily, M., Jararweh, Y., & Baker, T., (2018). An edge computing based smart healthcare framework for resource management. *Sensors, 18*, 4307. https://doi.org/10.3390/s18124307.

9. Li, X., Huang, X., Li, C., Yu, R., & Shu, L., (2019). EdgeCare: Leveraging edge computing for collaborative data management in mobile healthcare systems. In: *IEEE Access* (Vol. 7, pp. 22011–22025). doi: 10.1109/ACCESS.2019.2898265.

10. Velichko, A., (2021). A method for medical data analysis using the LogNNet for clinical decision support systems and edge computing in healthcare. *Sensors, 21*, 6209. https://doi.org/10.3390/s21186209.

PART II
Edge-Intelligence Implementations for Smart Healthcare

CHAPTER 3

An IoT-Based Smart Healthcare System with Edge Intelligence Computing

PURANAM REVANTH KUMAR and B. SHILPA

Department of Electronics and Communication Engineering, IcfaiTech (Faculty of Science and Technology), IFHE, Hyderabad, Telangana, India

ABSTRACT

In response to the technology revolution and the population explosion, the need for real-time, inexpensive, and efficient smart healthcare services is developing tremendously. As a result, many healthcare systems are unable to provide a specialized resource service for patients with specific needs. An intelligent approach is needed in order to deal with the rising demands on this crucial infrastructure. To solve this issue, edge computing (EC) technologies can minimize latency and energy usage by physically relocating activities closer to data sources. Using EC, this system can monitor and evaluate the physical health of its users. As a result, each user's risk level for health problems is taken into account while allocating computing resources over the whole network of the EC. The purpose of this study is to demonstrate the advantages of implementing edge intelligent technology, as well as the application of artificial intelligence (AI) in smart healthcare systems, in order to improve patient outcomes. In addition, a new smart healthcare model has been developed to increase the use of AI and edge technologies in smart healthcare. Finally, we talk about possible problems and future research directions that could arise when these different technologies are combined.

Reconnoitering the Landscape of Edge Intelligence in Healthcare.
Suneeta Satpathy, Sachi Nandan Mohanty, and Sirisha Potluri (Eds.)
© 2024 Apple Academic Press, Inc. Co-published with CRC Press (Taylor & Francis)

3.1 INTRODUCTION

In recent years, healthcare has increasingly relied on information technology (IT) to create smart systems that attempt to accelerate the diagnosis and treatment of patients' illnesses. It is possible to reduce physician visits and improve patient care quality by using these technologies, which provide intelligent services for health monitoring and medical automation in various settings (hospitals, offices, homes, on-the-go, etc.) [1].

A healthy society is built on improved healthcare systems. As the world's population continues to expand and new diseases emerge, the demand for effective healthcare systems is increasing dramatically [32]. Technology advancement and the advent of the internet of things (IoT) have also resulted in the development of smart healthcare or connected healthcare systems (IoT) [2]. Wearable technologies and enhanced communication protocols will be used to connect patients, healthcare providers [33], and medical institutions in real time as part of a new healthcare paradigm termed "smart healthcare" (also known as "smart health") [3] (Figure 3.1).

Smart healthcare systems use a wide variety of smart devices and IoT technology to expand healthcare facilities and meet the needs of a rapidly growing population. Medical records generated by smart devices provide an enormous number of heterogeneous data that must be analyzed and evaluated in accordance with the system's requirements [5]. In order to achieve minimal reaction times for emergency situations in Realtime health requirements, good communication between various entities of the smart healthcare community and data centers is required [34]. Due to the fact that slow reaction times and excessive latency in data centers are major risks in smart healthcare systems and might result in irreversible crises [6].

As a result of these considerations, edge computing (EC) and artificial intelligence (AI) are the ideal solutions. When these two technologies are used together, it opens the scope to a number of possibilities for smart healthcare. Some procedures are moved closer to the data sources in order to limit the amount of data that must be sent [7]. Instead of transferring all information to cloud data centers, smart healthcare systems can execute certain procedures and store some data close to the end users [8]. Only a small amount of raw data and the outcomes of operations are required to be sent to cloud data centers in faraway locations. There are several advantages to using cutting-edge technology in the field of smart healthcare that include big data analysis, low delay in processing sensitive medical data, decreased energy usage and network congestion, as well as faster response times.

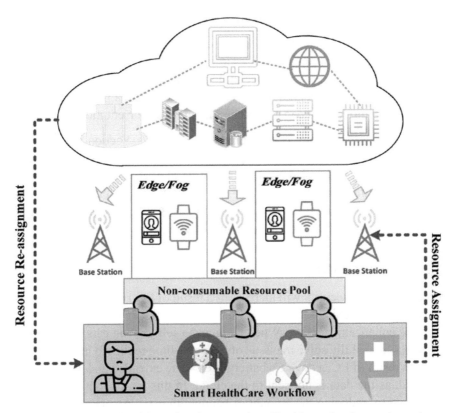

FIGURE 3.1   A flowchart illustrating the processing of healthcare data by an edge node.

Source: Reprinted from Ref. [5]. © 2018 by the authors. (http://creativecommons.org/licenses/by/4.0/).

AI can also speed up the estimation process by simulating human cognition in the analysis of data using complicated algorithms. On the basis of patient data, AI studies the relationships between illness treatment, prevention, and detection methods. Innovative and lightweight solutions are required at the edge setting because of the limited resources available [35]. To train the system for decision-making, actuation, and learning, machine learning (ML) and deep learning (DL) as subsets of AI are recommended. AI and EC together offer a new idea called "edge intelligence (EI)," which is driving a new wave of innovation in healthcare technology [9]. Smart healthcare systems that use AI approaches like DL, deep neural networks (DNNs) and reinforcement learning (RL) have been proposed by researchers.

This chapter's contributions may be summarized as follows:

- Smart healthcare solutions aided by AI are classified into three categories: application cases in IoT smart healthcare, AI deployment site at the edge, and AI technology employed.
- AI and edge technologies can be used to create a new smart healthcare model that can overcome the limits of current models.

The rest of the chapter is structured out as follows. Section 3.2 give brief discussion on some of the most important related work in cloud intelligence (CI) computing. A detailed presentation of AI in edge-enabled smart healthcare system are discussed in Section 3.3. Section 3.4 presents the proposed system design. Section 3.5 describes the research challenges and future directions. Finally, Section 3.6 provides the conclusion of the work.

3.2 LITERATURE SURVEY

Data quality and security will increase as a result of EC, one of the most recent technologies. Latency reduction in time-sensitive goods is the most essential of these enhancements [10]. When it comes to self-driving cars, for example, EC can successfully solve the issue of near real-time replies to incoming data. Since a result of EC, a device's battery life can be extended and its energy use reduced, as the data is not sent to the cloud. In this way, battery life may be improved by reducing the amount of bandwidth used. As 5G networks have been introduced and advanced, they are more compatible with EC systems than 4G networks. EC networks will benefit from 5G's ability to reduce latency between devices [11]. Data is collected and shared via a network of interconnected devices, collectively referred to as the IoT [12]. IoT gadgets include the Apple Watch and other wearable fitness devices, as well as remote lighting and thermostats [13]. Data is collected and analyzed by their company or a database server since they are all online and transmitting data back and forth. EC is a better fit for IoT systems than cloud computing (CC) [14]. EC provides minimal latency and lower energy consumption when utilized in conjunction with IoT devices. IoT devices' quality of service (QoS) and user experience will improve as a result of increased use of EC, according to [15]. With the present cost of bandwidth, it will be impossible for the average user to rely on the cloud when using a variety of IoT devices. As a result, the number of data breaches and probable security flaws increases. Moreover, the quantity of data transactions raises the danger. Data security breaches can be reduced by computing data on the edge, as demonstrated in Ref. [16].

To make life easier for citizens, smart cities employ cutting-edge technology and sensors, as well as AI algorithms. Everyday chores that take up a lot of time may be made more efficient with the help of these apps and devices. Examples given in Ref. [18] include rice cookers that begin cooking as soon as a user returns from work, heaters, and air conditioners that turn on before a person enters their house, CCTV cameras that recognize and report suspicious people roaming around houses, and many more [19]. This prevents pollution and decreases the use of increasingly precious resources by ensuring that people can monitor their gadgets at home and enable better control of energy usage. EC is a vital tool in addition to the previous examples. Adding EC to a smart city system will only enhance the system's ability to reduce emissions and pollution. In light of the rising cost of power due to the increasing number of electric devices in use, EC is more important than ever before [20].

3.2.1 ARTIFICIAL INTELLIGENCE (AI) IN EDGE DEVICES

Human activity recognition using Docker's technology on edge devices and AI approaches has been described in Ref. [21]. In the suggested concept, which includes a sensor network and a cloud server in control of sensors, EC will function as a bridge between the two. It is used in EC to detect sensor data using the RELM (a regularized extreme learning machine). An edge-assisted smart healthcare architecture that makes use of AI methods has also been presented by Feng et al. [22]. They've used DL data compression in mobile edge devices in order to reduce bandwidth and battery consumption. It is possible to extract data hierarchically using stacking auto-encoders (SAEs). ML algorithms were employed to categories data in order to achieve high reliability and quick response in finding or anticipating irregularities in the detection of epileptic seizures. According to [23], cutting-edge technology and AI methodologies might be used to develop a system that could antici-pate human action. The suggested system's edge device (laptop) performs feature extraction from sensor data. A recurrent neural network (RNN) is then trained on the features using the edge device. The RNN's capacity to be taught is tied to its ability to make predictions about human behavior. It is possible to recognize real-time stress levels using edge technology and DL by taking physical activity into account, according to [24]. Wristband sensors are used in the proposed system to acquire the necessary data. On the other hand, DNN is also used on the most cutting-edge gadgets. The sensor data is sent into the input layer of the DNN. The data and stress levels are analyzed in hidden layers, and the findings are saved in the cloud at the end of the process. It is used to improve the training approach, while logistic regression is used to categorize the suggested architecture's stress levels. For edge-aided smart healthcare systems that leverage AI technologies to secure user privacy in emergency care and telehealth advisory applications, by Rani et al. [25] developed an offloading model. The suggested approach uses an RL-based offloading method to preserve healthcare data. An AI-based real-time geriatric monitoring system was created by Tuli et al. [26]. The shimmer device is used to collect data in the proposed system, and compressed sensing (CS) is used to compress the data once it has been gathered. Using Bluetooth, the compressed data is sent to the edge gateway, where it is decompressed. This device serves as an edge gateway for decompressing and classifying compressed data in order to detect abnormal occurrences [27].

3.3   ARTIFICIAL INTELLIGENCE (AI) IN EDGE ENABLED SMART HEALTHCARE SYSTEM

Edge-enabled smart healthcare systems can benefit greatly from using AI, and this section gives an overview of the technology and its advantages. Then, various connected research papers are thoroughly explored. According to Figure 3.2, as there are three distinct ways to categories the examined works. Finally, in this part, a brief explanation is offered in conjunction with Table 3.1, which includes a summary of the chapter that were inspected.

The first categorization is based on the location of AI deployment in EC. Edge device deployment and edge server deployment articles are subdivided into two categories. The second classification divides the research into five distinct categories based on the context in which it is being used in smart healthcare (see the application case column in Table 3.1). Among the five groups listed are:

- Disorders of the nervous system;
- Real-time monitoring of activities;
- Detection of abnormalities in behavior;
- Disorders of the heart and blood vessels;
- An epidemic of disease.

DNN algorithms are used in edge devices for behavior recognition, for example. Three publications (CNN, SVM [29], K-means [30], and HTM [31]) have not been allocated to any of the application case categories since their application healthcare cases have not been explained by the authors, as can be seen in table. Additionally, Figure 3.2 shows a third classification

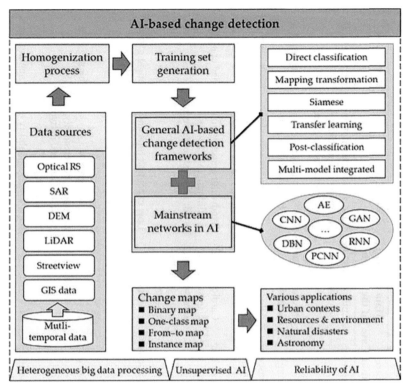

FIGURE 3.2   The use of AI tools to classify current state-of-the-art solutions.

Source: Adapted from Ref. [36]

depending on the AI approach used, which includes ML, DL, and hybrid techniques as subcategories. There are supervised, unsupervised, and RL, ML-based methodologies, as well as ML-DL and ML-heuristic hybrid technologies.

3.4   SYSTEM DESIGN

This section covers a new smart healthcare system that makes use of edge technologies while also applying various AI approaches such as deep rein-forcement learning (DRL). Figure 3.3 depicts the suggested system model with three primary levels, namely the sensor layer, the edge layer, and the cloud layer, which are shown in figure.

There are a variety of end-users in this paradigm, including patients in health institutions, elderly persons, and healthy individuals who are concerned

TABLE 3.1 Artificial Intelligence (AI)-based, Edge-Enabled Healthcare Solutions

Algorithm	AI Contribution	AI Deployment Place	Healthcare Application Case	Main Objective of the System	AI Benefits	References
DL (SAE) + ML	Compression of data (feature extraction), categorization of data.	Access to edge servers (smartphone)	Brain disorders	Epileptic seizure detection.	Bandwidth consumption is minimal; availability is good; and costs are cheap.	Azar et al. [28]
DL (RNN)	Predicting the outcomes of actions.	Access to edge servers (laptop).	Motion monitoring.	Predicting human behavior.	Real-time assistance as well as a high rate of accuracy.	Alhayani et al. [1]
CS, ENN/ KNN	Data reduction and data categorization.	Edge gateways and sensors.	Cardiovascular disorders.	Allocation of resources.	Bandwidth consumption is minimal; availability is good; and costs are cheap.	Zhang et al. [8]
RASPRO, SVM	Categorization, integration, and compression of large amounts of data.	Edge gateways and sensors.	Cardiovascular disorders.	Cardiovascular disease severity assessment and early warning systems.	Bandwidth consumption is minimal; availability is good; and costs are cheap.	Riad et al. [9]
FKNN	Classification of data.	Access to edge servers.	Infection outbreak.	Control the spread of the Chikungunya virus.	Low execution time and low latency are essential for real-time assistance.	Shigang et al. [17]
CNN, SVM	The process of extracting and classifying data.	Access to edge servers	Brain disorders.	Data investigation.	A high degree of accuracy and sensitivity, as well as reduced network congestion.	Shigang et al. [19]
K-means	Dissemination of data	Access to edge servers	Brain disorders	Data investigation	Superior dependability and precision.	Anumanthappa et al. [3]

about their health. A health expert, a health institute, a mobile ambulance, family members, or a pharmacy are all examples of caregivers. Different AI approaches, such as DRL, are incorporated into the suggested system, which is dispersed across sensors and the cloud in order to support smart healthcare services. Feature enables the framework to generate a solution map for each problem that arises. Cloud-to-cloud or cloud-to-edge activities can be distributed depending on how big of an issue is and how much data can be collected. As a result, the proposed system allows for the deployment of several DRL layers. There is no need to run some procedures on the cloud if the aim of the system is to track the health of a healthy person. As a result, the system's sensors and edge layer may perform processing tasks. End-users have the option of storing their findings either on the edge or in the cloud, depending on their preference. When it comes to healthcare, the system is able to select the proper location for DRL's input and output layers. Data from the end-user is often collected and sent to edge devices or edge servers, either via sensors or directly through a network connection. Reduce network congestion and edge-layer computing complexity by compressing sensors at their source. With the use of AI techniques like compressive sensing, sensor data may be compressed.

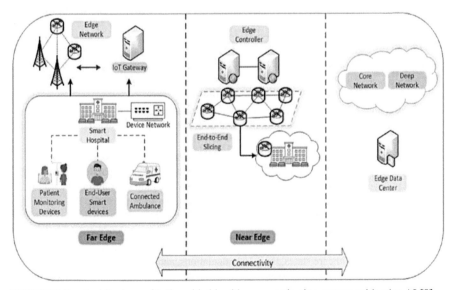

FIGURE 3.3 Architecture of IoT-enabled healthcare monitoring system with edge AI [8].

Source: Reprinted with permission from Ref. [8]. Copyright © 2021 Elsevier Ltd.

The edge layer is comprised of edge devices and edge servers that host AI methods. AI and edge technology have been used in several research projects in the realm of smart healthcare. However, there are a few issues that have yet to be resolved. As an example, DL requires a massive amount of data to train its algorithms. Tele-surgery is an example where there is not enough data to train on. In addition, the DL-trained data cannot be used for another condition of a similar nature, therefore the data must be re-trained. As a self-teaching system, RL should also make a number of tiny decisions in order to reach a complex goal. For example, in the case of chronically ill patients who are constantly moving, it may be impossible for an RL algorithm to learn from all states and regulate the reward route because of the unstable context information provided by the moveable patient. It is possible that AI approaches combining estimation and state mapping will be able to overcome these challenges. The proposed framework may make use of either a real-time self-training model or dataset training, depending on the situation. When it comes to monitoring, this function may be used for a range of purposes, from remote monitoring and self-monitoring to clinical monitoring. Table 3.2 lists the advantages and disadvantages of the most widely used AI methods in smart healthcare.

TABLE 3.2 The Advantages and Disadvantages of Commonly Used AI Algorithms in the Field of Smart Healthcare

AI Technique	Benefits	Disadvantages
Machine learning	Improves and adjusts without human involvement over time.	It takes a lot of time and effort to learn, and the chances of making a mistake are rather significant.
Reinforcement learning (RL)	Adaptable, dynamic, and able to learn from small amounts of data.	The information is not easily understandable and does not take past knowledge into account.
Deep learning	Large volumes of data can be handled by high-dimensional systems (those with several layers).	Medical data is very ambiguous and varied, thus difficulties like data sparsity, redundancy, or missing value may arise during the training phase. It's also difficult to apply this method to other situations because it only offers estimated statistics and doesn't produce exact findings.
Deep reinforcement learning (DRL)	Sophisticated smart healthcare states, the most accurate model, tremendous scalability, and complex decision-making are all achieved with this model.	Complexity states, off-policy learning, costly calculations, and constant data modification are all possible.

As a consequence, based on the findings of Table 3.2 and the discussion, DRL is considered to be the best option since it is capable of handling the scenarios listed above. Depending on the issue magnitude, the system can either map all the states or employ estimate. Real-time alerts can be extremely helpful in life-threatening situations. Timely delivery of medical care is critical in saving a patient's life. In smart healthcare systems, minimizing the time it takes to make a choice is essential. By spreading data and processes over several devices or hidden layers of DRL, DRL may be implemented on the edge layer in a parallel fashion. When compared to an unrivaled approach, the distributed parallel model provides significantly more to the reduction of latency and the speed of decision making. The power usage can be significantly reduced since the procedures are completed more quickly than in the past. Consequently, battery-powered gadgets' lifespans will be prolonged.

> **Summary:** The suggested system model's intelligent elements use sensors to collect data on the real-time state of patients while fully integrating physical items. Cloud-based system collects and analyzes all data generated by sensors, and all components are linked to it. Modeled as a digital twin, the technology can be used to predict sickness in advance or save lives in crucial situations by using real-time data from the actual environment. There are no sophisticated algorithms in the suggested system model, therefore it has a suitable level of complexity. Based on the health condition and the amount of data available, the suggested system model's total complexity can vary greatly. However, it can't be more difficult than DRL itself.

3.5 RESEARCH CHALLENGES AND FUTURE DIRECTIONS

An open problem and a set of hurdles in the implementation of AI in edge-assisted smart healthcare solutions have been identified. Based on our analysis, the following are some of the issues that researchers in this field face in the future.

3.5.1 BIG DATA MANAGEMENT

There is a massive amount of data that needs to be analyzed and protected because of a massive healthcare system and real-time data capture. An edge mining technique can significantly reduce cloud service delivery of long-term and continuous data from medical sensors, but further reduction is needed. It is not always necessary to minimize this data, but to study it in bulk numbers, which might be exabytes in size. This necessitates the development of new data analysis methods based on data attributes.

3.5.2 PATIENT INFORMATION PRIVACY

Even if edge-enabled healthcare devices improve patient experience and offer new sources of income for healthcare providers and 5G network operators, privacy issues will only grow in relevance as these devices become more extensively deployed and used. HIPAA does not yet encompass edge-enabled healthcare monitoring systems. Many stakeholders, such as research institutes and insurance companies, value healthcare providers' and networks' patient data and would take legal action if such data were compromised. These regulations and limits on the preservation of patient data differ from nation to country and area.

3.5.3 SENSOR USAGE

Patient comfort is the most critical factor in the adoption of sensors. Implantable or wearable sensors are also viable options. People over the age of 60 may find it challenging to use wearable devices. Implanted sensors may not be adopted by everyone. Because of this, it is impossible to assume that a patient's perceived level of comfort would be the same for all patients.

3.5.4 PRIVACY AND SECURITY

Because edge technology keeps data so near to the users, they have complete ownership and control over it. For this reason, they are unable to take use of advanced privacy and security protection methods. With the help of cutting-edge technology and AI, smart healthcare systems may still be improved in terms of privacy and security. This problem could be solved using a lightweight AI method.

3.5.5 AUTOMATIC NETWORK MANAGEMENT

In light of the important nature of smart healthcare systems, real-time, and automated network administration is essential. Smart healthcare systems can benefit from the use of lightweight AI approaches like lightweight RL to control network traffic. ML-based intrusion detection systems (IDS) may also be employed in the smart healthcare system to avoid security flaws and learn the network for autonomously decreasing any potential risks. The implementation of autonomous network management relies heavily on software-defined networking. For a self-regulated, smart healthcare system, learning algorithms can assist govern the virtualization of network components and operations.

3.6 CONCLUSION

This chapter explains how AI and edge technologies may improve healthcare systems. By lowering latency, network load, and power consumption at the edge, edge technology helps smart healthcare systems perform better. The system gains intelligence as a result of the use of AI. By combining AI with cutting-edge technology, smart healthcare systems become more intelligent and provide several benefits. Smart healthcare frameworks that use many AI algorithms in parallel using edge technologies are introduced here. The suggested approach distributes the processes across sensors and cloud servers. The latency, complexity, and network burden of some operations can be reduced by employing a lightweight AI approach on sensors. Adopting flexible AI methods for parallel processing at the edge layer allows for faster reaction and decision-making, as well as transmitting real-time notifications to healthcare providers, which are critical in smart healthcare services.

KEYWORDS

- **artificial intelligence**
- **automatic network management**
- **big data management**
- **edge computing**
- **healthcare system**
- **internet of things**
- **patient information privacy**
- **smart healthcare system**

REFERENCES

1. Alhayani, B., Kwekha-Rashid, A. S., Mahajan, H. B., et al., (2022). 5G standards for the industry 4.0 enabled communication systems using artificial intelligence: Perspective of smart healthcare system. *Appl. Nanosci.*

2. Yin, Z., Chi, J., Binglei, Y., Jiafu, W., & Mohsen, G., (2022). Information fusion for edge intelligence: A survey. *Information Fusion, 81,* 171–186.

3. Anumanthappa, J., Muaad, A. Y., Bibal, B. J. V., Chola, C., Hiremath, V., & Pramodha, M., (2022). IoT-based smart diagnosis system for healthcare. In: Karrupusamy, P., Balas, V. E., & Shi, Y., (eds.), *Sustainable Communication Networks and Application: Lecture Notes on Data Engineering and Communications Technologies* (Vol. 93). Springer, Singapore.

4. Mohindru, V., Vashishth, S., & Bathija, D., (2022). Internet of things (IoT) for healthcare systems: A comprehensive survey. In: Singh, P. K., Singh, Y., Kolekar, M. H., Kar, A. K., & Gonçalves, P. J. S., (eds.), *Recent Innovations in Computing: Lecture Notes in Electrical Engineering* (Vol. 832). Springer, Singapore.

5. Oueida S, Kotb Y, Aloqaily M, Jararweh Y, Baker T. An Edge Computing Based Smart Healthcare Framework for Resource Management. Sensors. 2018; 18(12):4307.

6. Min, C., Wei, L., Yixue, H., Yongfeng, Q., & Iztok, H., (2018). Edge cognitive computing based smart healthcare system. *Future Generation Computer Systems, 86,* 403–411.

7. Luca, G., Gennaro, P., Pierluigi, R., Francesco, T., & Mario, V., (2020). Trends in IoT based solutions for health care: Moving AI to the edge. *Pattern Recognition Letters, 135,* 346–353.

8. Vipin, K. R., Nikhil, K. R., Shubham, M., Bhavya, A. G., Prayag, T., Amit, K. J., & Shamim, H. M., (2021). An edge AI-enabled IoT healthcare monitoring system for smart cities. *Computers & Electrical Engineering, 96*(Part B), 107524.

9. Zhang, W. Z., Elgendy, I. A., Hammad, M., Iliyasu, A. M., Du, X., Guizani, M., et al., (2020). Secure and optimized load balancing for multi-tier IoT and edge-cloud computing systems. *IEEE Internet of Things Journal.*

10. Riad, K., Huang, T., & Ke, L., (2020). A dynamic and hierarchical access control for IoT in multi-authority cloud storage. *Journal of Network and Computer Applications, 160,* 102633.

11. Gouse, B. M., Shitharth, S., & Puranam, R. K., (2020). Integrated machine learning model for an URL phishing detection. *International Journal of Grid and Distributed Computing, 14*(1), 513–529.

12. Anuradha, M., Jayasankar, T., Prakash, N., Sikkandar, M. Y., Hemalakshmi, G., Bharatiraja, C., et al., (2021). IoT enabled cancer prediction system to enhance the authentication and security using cloud computing. *Microprocessors and Microsystems, 80,* 103301.

13. Aburukba, R. O., AliKarrar, M., Landolsi, T., & El-Fakih, K., (2020). Scheduling internet of things requests to minimize latency in hybrid fog–cloud computing. *Future Generation Computer Systems, 111,* 539–551.

14. Ali, B., Pasha, M. A., Ul Islam, S., Song, H., & Buyya, R., (2020). A volunteer supported fog computing environment for delay-sensitive IoT applications. *IEEE Internet of Things Journal.*

15. Wang, M., & Zhang, Q., (2020). Optimized data storage algorithm of IoT based on cloud computing in distributed system. *Computer Communications, 157,* 124–131.

16. Fuentes, H., & Mauricio, D., (2020). Smart water consumption measurement system for houses using IoT and cloud computing. *Environmental Monitoring and Assessment, 192*, 1–16.

17. Shigang, F., Qianrui, Q., Jun, Z., et al., (2016). Research on independent innovation ability training of intelligent robot practice course. *Comput. Educ., 12*(10), 45–48.

18. Xuren, W., Hua, W., Quan, Z., et al., (2009). Further improve the practice curriculum system of "intelligent robot" and promote practical teaching. *Comput. Educ., 2*(11), 116–118.

19. Wan, J., Li, X., Dai, H. N., Kusiak, A., Martínez-García, M., & Li, D., (2020). Artificial-intelligence-driven customized manufacturing factory: Key technologies, applications, and challenges. *Proc. IEEE, 3*(2), 25–33.

20. Xiaoping, C., & Wenjian, L., (2011). Research on practical innovation training system based on robot experiment. *Postgrad Educ. Res., 5*(3), 48–52.

21. Lu, Y., Chen, C., Chen, P., Chen, X., & Zhuang, Z., (2018). Smart learning partner: An interactive robot for education. In: *Proceedings of the International Conference on Artificial Intelligence in Education* (pp. 447–451). Cham: Springer.

22. Feng, Y., Hong, Z., Li, Z., Zheng, H., & Tan, J., (2020). Integrated intelligent green scheduling of sustainable flexible workshop with edge computing considering uncertain machine state. *J. Clean Prod., 246*, 119070.

23. Ji, W., Liang, B., Wang, Y., Qiu, R., & Yang, Z., (2020). Crowd V-IoE: Visual internet of everything architecture in AI-driven fog computing. *IEEE Wirel. Commun., 27*(2), 51–57.

24. Abdellatif, A. A., et al., (2019). Edge computing for smart health: Context-aware approaches, opportunities, and challenges. *IEEE Network, 33*(3), 196–203.

25. Rani, S., Ahmed, S. H., & Shah, S. C., (2018). Smart health: A novel paradigm to control the Chickungunya virus. *IEEE Internet of Things J., 6*(2), 1306–1311.

26. Tuli, S., et al., (2020). Healthfog: An ensemble deep learning based smart healthcare system for automatic diagnosis of heart diseases in integrated IoT and fog computing environments. *Future Generation Computer Systems, 104*, 187–200.

27. Pathinarupothi, R. K., Durga, P., & Rangan, E. S., (2018). IoT-based smart edge for global health: Remote monitoring with severity detection and alerts transmission. *IEEE Internet of Things J., 6*(2), 2449–2462.

28. Azar, J., et al., (2019). An energy efficient IoT data compression approach for edge machine learning. *Future Generation Computer Systems, 96*.

29. Al-Rakhami, M., et al., (2019). A lightweight and cost-effective edge intelligence architecture based on containerization technology. *World Wide Web*, 1–20.

30. Hosseini, M. P., et al., (2020). Multimodal data analysis of epileptic EEG and Rs-fMRI via deep learning and edge computing. *Artificial Intelligence in Medicine, 104*, 101813.

31. Shu, C., et al., (2019). Mobile edge aided data dissemination for wireless healthcare systems. *IEEE Trans. Computational Social Systems, 6*(5), 898–906.

32. Sallow, A. B., Sadeeq, M., Zebari, R. R., Abdulrazzaq, M. B., Mahmood, M. R., Shukur, H. M., et al. (2020). An investigation for mobile malware behavioral and detection techniques based on android platform. *IOSR Journal of Computer Engineering (IOSR-JCE), 22*, 14–20.

33. Mohiuddin, I., & Almogren, A., (2019). Workload aware VM consolidation method in edge/cloud computing for IoT applications. *Journal of Parallel and Distributed Computing, 123*, 204–214.

34. Gill, S. S., Tuli, S., Xu, M., Singh, I., Singh, K. V., Lindsay, D., et al., (2019). Transformative effects of IoT, blockchain and artificial intelligence on cloud computing: Evolution, vision, trends and open challenges. *Internet of Things, 8,* 100118.

35. Abdullah, P. Y., Zeebaree, S. R., Jacksi, K., & Zeabri, R. R., (2020). An HRM system for small and medium enterprises (SME) s based on cloud computing technology. *International Journal of Research-Granthaalayah, 8,* 56–64.

36. Shi W, Zhang M, Zhang R, Chen S, Zhan Z. Change Detection Based on Artificial Intelligence: State-of-the-Art and Challenges. Remote Sensing. 2020; 12(10):1688.

CHAPTER 4

Edge Computing for Smart Healthcare Monitoring Platform Advancement

NIDHI AGARWAL[1] and PRAKHAR DEEP[2]

[1]*Department of Information Technology, KIET Group of Institutions, Delhi-NCR, Uttar Pradesh, Ghaziabad, India*

[2]*Project Manager, Tech Mahindra, NSEZ Noida, Uttar Pradesh, India*

ABSTRACT

The whole world's countries are constantly facing various COVID waves. Since the last two years, there has been no time when COVID is not prevalent in any of the countries. Sometimes, it is aggressive in one country and sometimes in another one. In such a scenario and otherwise also, virtual healthcare is an imperative aspect of a patient's life. Many international patients are there, who can't move frequently to meet their consulting doctors because of COVID restrictions and various other reasons. With the advent of new digitized healthcare techniques, unnecessary clinic visits of the poor will be reduced. It will help them in early detection of diseases with the comfort of their homes. For senior citizens who face many challenges in visiting out for diagnosis and treatments, this technology is a boon. There has been a lot of advancement in the healthcare-based medicinal platforms' tools and technologies in the recent past. Even remote surgeries are carried out now-a-days with high micro-mini second level-based precision. Interactive video-audio services also play a critical role in making telemedicine services a reality. But this domain is still facing many challenges, especially its precise implementation related to privacy, security, and time-effective aspects. One of the most challenging issues which deals with providing a high level of security while transferring the real time data to cloud-based

Reconnoitering the Landscape of Edge Intelligence in Healthcare.
Suneeta Satpathy, Sachi Nandan Mohanty, and Sirisha Potluri (Eds.)

architecture will also be dealt with in detail. Medical data security is a matter of prime concern for both patient and doctor. Some issues also pertain to the effective tool selection and its implementation. If the Net-Medi (internet based medical system) system needs to be implemented successfully, so that even distant patients are also able to get its full benefits, then we need to make this system completely flawless.

4.1 INTRODUCTION

Nowadays, patients are inclined more and more towards the most sophisticated and latest techniques for healthcare systems. They rely on technologies which can be personal to them and are matching the pace for modern life. In such a scenario, the edge computing (EC) environment meets their demands to the utmost extent. This all has been accelerated in the recent past with the help of various 5th-generation and other modern computing technologies. With the advent of new techniques, the healthcare architecture was dependent on fog and sensor techniques. The main disadvantage with these techniques was the non-optimization of the algorithms, such as that for encrypting and authenticating the data and then classifying various devices used for EC architecture. The advent of modern tools and techniques has led to the personification of data. The data which is more focused towards the critical health monitoring signals related to various vital organs. There are various other techniques which also keep track of the abnormalities of the critical diseases. But the greatest disadvantage with these techniques has been the proper transmitting, encrypting, authenticating, classifying, and predicting the actual disease symptoms based on underlying factors. The various challenges which still lie in the path of EC to make it more universally accepted can be met with the help of improved fog and cloud architectures. In addition to them we need highly efficient computational techniques which can update the data in real time and maintain the secrecy and security of the patient's data.

As we need the devices involved in EC to be highly responsive with even micro- and milliseconds consideration, this increases many basic requirements of these devices. First of all, they should have high storing capacity locations and should be highly energy efficient to compute the data. Till now the technology which is providing the most accurate results with such a demand is the fog architecture which is also called edge computer movement as it involves all the computations towards the edge or corner of the network. Mobile cloud computing (MCC) was also classified by highly accurate data storage timings but limited area cover. Another disadvantage with them is high transmission cost and longer responsive timings. Other techniques called cloud-let and local-cloud were also used but they provided reduced quality of service (QoS) for the newer devices. The elevated costs attached with transmitting data arrived mainly from higher network traffic which impacted the transmission timings for mobile CC technique and also failed to provide security to the mobile devices because of limited Wi-Fi availability. There are various works available in literature which have provided a clear comparative analysis of cloud based and edge-based computing and concluded that only edge-based computing can meet the needs of the users. The various work done till now is discussed in the section below. It covers the various techniques which are used by the research community till now with their advantages and disadvantages. It also emphasizes how EC can be an answer or a solution to the various pertaining problems.

4.2 WORK DONE TILL NOW

The fog computing (FC) was proposed first by Juhu et al. [3] and was called so because the fog refers to the movement of computations at the edge of the network. As already discussed, the technology before FC called mobile CC was used which had certain drawbacks related to the response time efficiency and the QoS. Various research in Refs. [4–10] show that FC is fully able to satisfy the modern requirements based on latency, responsive time efficiency and energy efficiency. In one of the works [5], only the cloud computation was used for video analysis which consequently took half responsive time as compared to client only computing. This improvement in the responsive time using edge computation as compared to the traditional cloud computation was because of the various tools and technologies used with it. These tools and technologies were based on various latency reduction, time reduction, and improved efficiency of devices installed with the monitoring of vital organ data. The study was also concentrated on a large data set of people mostly belonging to the senior citizen age group so that the results can be predicted more efficiently. Also, the importance of results for senior citizens can be more fruitful based on the similarity of conditions. Moreover, the sophistication with respect to the various health monitoring devices, sensors' proper placement, real time minute tracking, etc., were also taken care of especially related to the vital organs data. The sensors used were placed in such a manner that they were able to collect the real time, even micro- and millisecond data of the patients whether they are hospitalized or at their home. Constant monitoring of the patients was done which proved to be beneficial both for the patients who were getting treated as well as for those who were using the predicted data based on their conditions. Healthcare monitoring nowadays is becoming a very important issue especially at the time of coronavirus when patients especially elderly people cannot go out and meet their doctors physically as and when required. If sophisticated devices are used which are able to monitor their conditions with respect to each and every aspect whether they are hospitalized or at their home and a 24-hour monitoring is done using proper and most sophisticated instruments then even the doctors can remotely treat the patients. The rest of the chapter discusses the various topics as under:

- Healthcare monitoring systems background;
- Details of various healthcare monitoring techniques used till date;
- Major Parameters for healthcare monitoring systems;
- Benefits of edge-computing architecture based on current computational requirements;
- Conclusion, issues still pertaining in the EC architecture, their resolution.

4.3   HEALTHCARE MONITORING SYSTEMS BACKGROUND

In this section we will discuss the various requirements for a healthcare based remote system and the various motivations which lead the researchers to develop this system. We will also emphasize the need for a central cloud computation-based system and how it switched to a distributed system. The distributed architecture acts as the base for the edge and the fog computations. This drift from the traditional to the edge-based technology is required so that people's problems can be dealt with remotely and with greater efficiency. The section will also cover various matrices which are required to be taken care of for developing quality systems for example QoS, energy efficiency, etc.

4.3.1   TYPES OF HEALTHCARE APPLICATIONS

There are various categorizations for remote healthcare applications based on the device, on the data type, on the age group of patients, studies of various age group patients, etc. The various healthcare domains can be discussed as follows.

- Real time-based healthcare systems;
- Emergency based healthcare systems;
- Mobile device-based healthcare systems;
- Information gathering healthcare systems.

The real time-based healthcare monitoring system involves a lot many domains at one time. If we take an example of the system which monitors the vital organ aspects through the mobile phone or censoring device or both, then all the things have to be incorporated together. Emergency based healthcare systems need some type of trigger or alarm with respect to the patient's critical aspects so that appropriate action can be taken timely. With the development of mobile devices now the various diagnostic features are well updated on the basis of various critical aspects. If we talk about the normal information gathering of healthcare devices then a lot of software's, web pages maintained either on centralized or on personal laptops or desktops can be used together by monitoring the data of patient illness and various other attributes of vital organs. The data would be more useful if elderly people are involved in that and all the modern healthcare devices like smart watches, etc., are used in facilitating the digital remote healthcare system. The devices can detect various fluctuations in blood pressure (BP), body temperature, heartbeat, and various other factors. The data can even be maintained for various other tests whose results are not updated at that very moment but take some time in obtaining the test results. These tests may include the uric acid level of the blood and various other test results like various infections in the body related to urine, stool, etc. All this data can be maintained in the above-mentioned fourth category. Here we collect information about the various diseases. All this data collected in real time or after getting the results can be proven to be very helpful for the elderly as well as other patients who are looking for virtual medical advice.

4.3.2   CLOUD-BASED APPLICATIONS

Cloud based applications consist of mobile devices, cloud base servers and networks. All these devices may have a great distance among themselves which can enhance the problem of higher latency. If one compares the traditional monitoring equipment with the cloud or fog based, then this has been found as a common problem. All this increases the retrieving time of data in real time to a great extent, which may actually reduce the purpose of going for virtual medical assistance. Why patients want to go for a virtual medical assistant is the quick response time. Enhanced response time has been found as a major drawback of this system. Humongous data which is generated by the sensors is also a big problem. A typical type of cloud-based application has higher latency and does lower sustainable performance as compared to the distributed architectures where many nodes are available at various locations on the earth.

4.3.3   FOG AND EDGE-BASED HEALTHCARE APPLICATIONS

The fog based and the edge-based applications help in switching the data processing network from the traditional to the network edged system. It helps in increasing the response time and in enhancing the efficiency of the system. As compared to the traditional architecture the data and the computing resources are expected to move at the edge or at the corner of the system so that various advantages can be achieved. For example, if you look at the response time, latency time, the involved cost efficiency, location updating ability then this system is expected to improve all these factors. As the information gets distributed across the fog and at the edge of the network so security is also easily implemented. The enhanced usability of the device and the user-friendliness are also ascertained. The system is also able to deal with the humongous data which is received either in real time or in the form of compiled data later on. This system is expected to fulfill the various specified technical requirements for the implementation of such a system.

4.3.4   TRADE-OFFS IN EDGE-BASED HEALTHCARE APPLICATIONS

Though EC improves the healthcare system by making it more and more remote. It is expected to reduce the patients' visits to the hospitals and to the doctors' clinics especially when scenarios like coronavirus are there. Remote healthcare is also important for elderly patients or patients suffering from chronic diseases. It will not only help the elderly people, rather will also prove to be a boon for the chronic patients. The sensor devices which are attached at the edges of the healthcare system help in tracking the various vital organ details of the patient. When a large amount of data is encountered then the cost also gets enhanced in maintaining and retrieving that humongous data. Though EC offers a lot many advantages but there is certain trade off or disadvantages also in its full applicability. Various types of domains are used then these challenges increase more when a decentralized technique is used. The diverse domains and servers being used increases the chances of network connections, stream management, information management and the nodal reliability. When we need to integrate various different types of sensors and nodes then additional resources in the form of management techniques on the edges are required to be implemented. This multiple interfacing with the help of various programming languages and codes further increases the trade off and the extra efforts to implement such a system. To develop such a system, one should be ready to scale the various parameters. With more and more demand and adoption of this system more and more data would be adding to the already existing data set. We should be able to manage this ever increasing and ever-growing data in real time as well as, need to store at various remote locations in a distributed manner. In such a scenario, the optimization of the various techniques which are used to maintain and retrieve the data would also be involved. Thus, we can see that a lot of manufacturers get involved gradually to implement EC for healthcare systems to a wider extent. The applicability and fruitfulness of the system can only be implemented if we are ready to incorporate and phase all these challenges and solve the basic underlying shortcomings which can pose a threat to edge related adoption to the utmost extent.

4.4   DETAILS OF VARIOUS HEALTHCARE MONITORING TECHNIQUES USED TILL DATE

In order to monitor health, generally various devices, consisting of a user device, IoT device, a smartphone with computing capabilities, or CC nodes are used. The computing performed by these devices is often distributed between the user device and the node. The important aspect of the architecture of these devices is the relationship between edge and cloud. The fast interventions are carried out by the edge, while the cloud helps by storing data in the long-term. However, challenges arise in this relationship, like load balancing, edge routing and cloud servers. An IoT layer in addition to a fog and cloud layer has also been included in the recent proposed architecture, and thus is a common setup for a fog or edge healthcare system. The IoT layer helps in the operation of all medical sensors. This is performed over an IoT network where each device has its own unique identifier. Now in order to compute and aggregate the data, it is transferred to a fog layer via Bluetooth, ZigBee, or Wi-Fi. A data center layer or Cloud are used to store this medical data. This setup results in lower latency values for computing. Now let's take a look at individual components of a common FC environment.

4.4.1   USER DEVICES

User device is at the very edge of the network. They manage to perform some computing even before some more power-intensive tasks, which are to be performed in a separate edge or node. User devices are generally of three types – smart devices, legacy medical instruments, and IoT-based sensor kits. In the early days of EC. Low-cost devices, such as Nokia mobile phones or PDAs were used. However, with the production of smart devices in bulk by companies, smartphones such as the Samsung Galaxy S311 became more affordable to be used for healthcare applications. In order to generate health data such as heart rate or to measure detailed heart sounds, built-in sensors or microphones of mobile phones are used. Thus, the smartphone-based sensors offer ease of usage to patients. However, it is limited in the variety of sensors that can be embedded in its hardware. In order to generate and handle larger sensor data, dedicated medical sensors are used, which lead to more accurate diagnoses. For monitoring health, several common uses of sensors are heart and respiration rate, BP, and glucose levels. Additional sensing capabilities include determining motion states, such as activity type, number of steps, or sleep cycle. The use of IoT devices is the latest trend for health EC. Legacy healthcare sensors lack interconnectivity, which is not the case with these IoT devices. Machine-to-machine (M2M) protocols are used to communicate with multiple devices placed across the body. However, an aspect that has been explored in recent times is the optimal placement of these sensing devices. User devices, such as the wireless capsule endoscope (WCE), or specialized prototype device, can also be used as an edge user device. To provide users with an acceptable level of visualization on their device is another advantage of the healthcare system. For example, an application can be developed for women that are soon-to-be mothers that would keep the tracks of lost resources. By providing customizability the usability of application can be increased. Another issue is to ensure that information provided to patients over an application is clearly understandable to non-professionals. Providing a clear menu for navigation, using graphs and other visual aids must also be taken into consideration while building an application.

4.4.2   COMMUNICATION PROTOCOLS

Short-range communication protocols, such as IEEE 802.15.1 or 802.15.4 are used to communicate between a device and a fog node. Wireless 802.11

protocol is often used to connect a sensor node to additional computing devices or cloud services. IEEE 802.15.1 or Bluetooth are used by many applications as a protocol for communication between a medical device and a smartphone. Data is transferred to a doctor or an additional server once a small amount of computing is finished on the smart device. This is done via a mobile communication service such as 4G or 5G.

4.4.3   NETWORK

The information is sent to the near end and far end of the network to be stored or, in some cases, additionally processed, after it has been gathered by the sensors. A fog node healthcare system provides us greater computing power, but smaller handheld devices do not. Data operations, such as classification or compression, in an EC architecture, are completed at the edge of the network. These edge nodes are often small servers that allow for the fast processing of data that mobile device cannot achieve. Edge or fog nodes can be a multitude of devices, deployed at different distances between the Cloud and edge user device, depending on the operating range. Commercially available products such as Raspberry Pi, Arduino served as edge gateways. Due to low cost and simple programming, these are popular solutions. Graphics processing unit (GPU) is used to compute when pictures are the data input. Other popular nodes for ambient sensing are Telos Mote and Intel Edison. Telos is a collection of sensing devices developed by the University of California Berkeley for wireless sensor network research that utilizes WPAN/IEEE 802.15.4.87 Intel Edison, although now discontinued, it is similar to the Telos mote, except that it is compatible with IEEE 802.11 and IEEE 802.15.1. After computing, additional computation or storage might be necessary, which is why information is sent further away from the user to the Cloud. The Cloud utilizes multiple servers for parallel computing and further analysis as a result it has a higher computing capacity than fog or edge nodes. The cloud is highly scalable which is a major advantage over node.

4.5   MAJOR REQUIREMENTS FOR HEALTHCARE MONITORING SYSTEMS

Measuring certain key performance indicators (KPIs) are focused upon more by current researchers. These are important for the progression of health services, such as response time, energy efficiency, and bandwidth cost. Main focus of a chapter is to optimize the KPIs related to a particular section of the EC architecture. The six basic operations discussed in this section are retrieval, encryption, classification, authentication, data reduction, and prediction. The trade-off between low latency and high security within protocols is discussed since security is a major focus for healthcare because of sensitive personal data.

4.5.1   TRANSMISSION AND RETRIEVAL

Latency in healthcare applications is due to data retrieval. For example, if we use cloud service for transferring data latency of the system increases by 2.71 seconds. However, using a smartphone for distributed computing, the latency in transmission decreases to 0.13 seconds. Some techniques focus on using data selection to choose which information is to be sent to the server or Cloud for further computing while some use a Nash bargaining approach for selecting anomalous data that is to be transferred to the Cloud for further storage. This approach helps in decreasing latency and power consumption. As compared to a baseline IoT system, an approach, called HiCH, gives a lower data dissemination delay. A common medical procedure, electrocardiography (ECG), in which the electrical activity of the heart is analyzed over a period of time, is a popular test for EC devices. In some cases, ECG data is transferred to an Amazon cloud server for computing and the round-trip time is compared for sending the same information to an edge gateway. As compared, the edge gateway transmission has a much lower round-trip time as compared with the Cloud.

4.5.2   ENCRYPTION

Energy efficient encryption techniques used on edge devices. A device having a lower energy encryption scheme, a higher percentage of available energy is able to be utilized for computing. Elliptic-curve cryptography (ECC) is a very popular encryption technique used on smart edge devices. For example, a key generated using ECC on the edge device and a key agreement is performed using the Diffie-Hellman (DH) scheme. ECC primarily requires a much lower key size, which is optimal for a smartphone with relatively limited storage and computing resources. Sources of encryption can also be hardware based, such as the lightweight KATAN ciphers on field FPGAs. A framework called the privacy-preserving fog-assisted information sharing scheme (PFHD) is a scheme that has privacy preservation on both the fog and cloud layers. The encryption scheme of PFHD when compared with traditional ciphertext policy attribute-based encryption (CP-ABE) in terms of cost results in a lower cost. For the same number of attributes, proposed personal access policy is found to have a lower energy consumption. Another technique, fully homomorphic encryption (FHE) is used in many works. It has the ability to analyze data in an encrypted form. Encryption is an important factor because it is another security concern for healthcare systems. Enhanced value substitution (EVS) can achieve a high level of privacy. Anonymity of patient files is governed by the privacy management framework. It does so by storing health profiles at the user side of a fog node. A pseudonym is used by each internet-of-health-things (IoHT) device to reduce linkage to real health data for each patient. Also, a clustering technique ensures privacy by a two-stage concealment process that disfigures data structures in patient health data.

4.5.3   AUTHENTICATION

Another requirement for a secure healthcare computing system is Authentication. It is closely related to encryption, so it has also been a focus for fog and EC technologies in healthcare. Guarantor of privacy for healthcare applications is authenticated key agreement (AKA). Authentication provides a novel way of generating a message authentication code by calculating values of interest from a patient's ECG signal and comparing the value to previously stored values. This saves the device from having to generate a key and, instead, simply sends the patient data that are verified or rejected by the server based on the data characteristics. There's also a certificate revocation scheme used for increased energy efficiency. It outperforms two other schemes, namely, certificate revocation list (CRL), and online certificate status protocol (OCSP), in terms of packet size reduction and communication overhead. Other fog node authentication schemes deviate from the quantitative cost analysis and instead provide attack immunity explanations. The node authentication in this work is immune to attacks such as replay, user impersonation, and session key disclosure attacks.

4.6   BENEFITS OF EDGE-COMPUTING ARCHITECTURE BASED ON CURRENT COMPUTATIONAL REQUIREMENTS

Most of the EC solutions for healthcare are tested in small-scale environments. The proposed system has an average delay of about half a second and about

0.003 kWH of power consumption for 1,50,000 users using 50 cloudlets. This accounts for a large number of users and considers a decision-making model that could help public health workers notice trends in disease spread. Similar prototype systems 86,116 simulate a medical service that can handle a large number of fog nodes. However, even though both of these studies use a large number of users, they still do not compare to the actual needs of a large medical community. A healthcare system will need to accommodate a huge number of patients being treated in a hospital. The number of staffed beds in registered hospitals in the United States was 8,94,574 in 2006. The hospital admission for the same year stood at 35,158,934. These numbers do not include smaller specialized hospitals such as gynecology, ENT, and rehabilitation hospitals. Edge-enabled healthcare systems will help reduce the glaring disparity between the existing infrastructure and hospital requirements for simultaneous record storage and patient monitoring.

4.6.1 BIG DATA MANAGEMENT

A large-scale healthcare system combined with real-time data acquisition guarantees that a large amount of data needs to be analyzed and secured. This issue is partially addressed in edge mining techniques, which significantly reduces the amount of data sent to cloud services; however, further reduction is needed for long-term and continuous data collection from medical sensors. Often, this data does not necessarily need to be reduced, but analyzed in bulk quantities, sometimes as large as exobytes. This means that new analysis techniques that rely on data features must be developed.

4.6.2 PATIENT INFORMATION PRIVACY

While edge-enabled healthcare devices enable better quality of life for patients and open revenue avenues for healthcare providers and 5G network operators, there are considerable concerns related to patient information privacy that will be exaggerated with large-scale deployment. Currently, existing HIPAA laws are not sufficiently established to be applicable on edge-enabled healthcare monitoring systems. As several stakeholders such as research organizations and insurance companies view patient information as a valuable asset, any data breach will be accompanied by legal implications for both the health provider as well as the network operator. To complicate matters, these laws and restrictions on patient data storage vary depending on the country and region. For example, Italy and Germany have no such restrictions. Current patient information privacy protocols focus on safeguarding personal details, such as name, address, and social security number In their work on ensuring healthcare privacy, Cavoukian et al. reveal that "any information, if linked to an identifiable individual, can become personal in nature, be it biographical, biological, genealogical, historical, transactional, locational, relational, computational, vocational, or reputational." Additionally, as patients acquire and own their own medical data through IoT devices, methods of patient permission-based authorization are needed. One such method is described in a blockchain-based MEC framework and is immune to unauthorized access and single point of failure. In light of the stated facts, sophisticated privacy and anonymization structures are prerequisites for large-scale healthcare systems. Computational complex cryptographic techniques jeopardize computation efficiency, but anonymization may also have risk of breach or theft. The distribution of the workload between sensor nodes and EC platforms without any compromise on privacy and security also remains an investigable challenge.

4.7 ISSUES STILL PERTAINING IN THE EDGE COMPUTING (EC) ARCHITECTURE AND THEIR RESOLUTION

4.7.1 INTEGRATED AI-5G FOR MEC-ENABLED HEALTHCARE

Current network deployments do not have the capabilities or capacity to handle large-scale allocated sensor-based medical monitoring and reporting. Converging telecommunications and IT services from the centralized cloud platform to the edge is essential but dependent on the success of multiple enabling technologies. One of the key enablers is virtualization techniques including virtual machines (VMs) and containers. While VMs provide its users a fully functional machine, regardless of the underlying hardware architecture, container environments such as Docker facilitate EC devices by offering lightweight virtualization solutions at user devices. Similarly, network function virtualization (NFV) decouples network functions and services from proprietary hardware, allowing colocation of multiple service instances over the same VM and consequently saving in the operator's capital and operational expenditures. In an MEC-based healthcare environment, NFV provides the operator the ability to transfer system processes from one edge platform to another when required, for instance, when there is congestion due to flash crowd events. Another crucial enabling technology is software-defined networks (SDNs). The main principle behind SDN is the decoupling of control and data plane, and introduction of a logical centralized control through which multiple virtual network instances can be initiated and offered via edge to the users. Coordination of dynamic provisioning of distributed services at the network edge is a challenge with existing network architectures. SDNs are expected to play a key role in providing network connectivity and service management across heterogenous MEC platforms. In addition to this, network slicing allows partitioning of one network into multiple instances, each optimized for a particular application/use case. For instance, we may have different 5G network slices for mobile broadband, automotive communication, and massive IoT. Because enhanced mobile broadband in 5G requires high capacity, several other related technologies deployed in the RAN would enable shorter transmission time intervals (TTI), pipelined packet processing, efficient radio resource control (RRC), and support of larger bandwidth. Some of these supporting technologies include user-centric architectures, massive MIMO (mMIMO), and transmission in millimeter wave (mmWave) spectrum. While 5G deployment is a key enabler to large-scale MEC-based healthcare infrastructure deployment, integration of artificial intelligence (AI) is essential to provide the most appropriate and timely services to the users. AI will leverage many factors, such as user mobility patterns, device usage patterns, patients' vital monitoring records, and existing medical conditions to provide timely diagnosis of health problems. Recent breakthroughs in ML, and in particular deep learning (DL), have enabled advancements in several areas from face recognition to medical diagnosis, and natural language processing (NLP). However, they involve complex processing of huge data sets in centralized and remote data centers and require massive amounts of storage and computing power. As the entire premise behind shifting processing at the edge hinges on ultra-reliable and low-latency communication (URLLC), it is imperative that distributed, low-latency, and reliable edge ML models are trained on local data. Edge ML provides dual benefits of low cost and reduced latency, which is important for mission critical IoT sensor devices on patients. An AI-integrated 5G infrastructure for a distributed healthcare system may include any combination of the three major ML categories, i.e., supervised learning, unsupervised learning, and reinforcement learning (RL). More details about these techniques in relevance with edge platforms can be found in a recent survey. When it comes to neural networks, there are some architectures that are more suited for MEC deployment. These include

(i) auto encoders (AEs) and (ii) generative adversarial networks (GANs). An AE is a stack of two feed-forward neural networks. The first phase called encoding involves compressing the original data into a short code representation, whereas in the second phase the compressed representation is decompressed in the same dimension space as the original input. Auto encoders learn distinct features of the data set, which are vital for anomaly detection, or from the perspective of healthcare MEC, for diagnosis of rare occurring diseases. To overcome the issue of nonavailability of huge data sets for localized learning in edge ML, GANs generate new data samples given by the estimated distribution of the input data samples. This is done from two NNs, a generator that produces fake data samples, and a discriminator that tries to identify the fake data samples created by the generator from the data set. The training reaches a Nash equilibrium when the discriminator is unable to distinguish between real and fake data points within the data set. The AI implementation at the edge can be implemented using a helper-device (h-d) split, where each device individually builds a learning model from the local data and then transfers the local model to a helper that aggregates all the models uploaded from multiple devices. In case a local model is exceeding a device's memory constraints, the model can be split and distributed between multiple devices. The intermediate model, in this case, will be transferred between devices during forward and backward training operations. Similar to its application in self-organizing network-enabled 5G wireless networks, the use of AI in healthcare systems is common in literature, as outlined in the previous section on classification and prediction. AI can take in several inputs such as patient variables (age, gender, medical conditions) and use these to give more insights on abnormal values for classification, as doctors do when diagnose a patient. This ensures a context-aware health system, which is important for personalized results [16]. AI techniques in literature have shown to be more useful than simple threshold-based methods. One of these describes a task involving the diagnosis of lung cancer in which IBM Watson achieved a higher precision in diagnosis than the average hospital. Similarly, other works for smart healthcare using EC have demonstrated higher accuracy for a voice disorder assessment and high prediction of pain emotion detection to allow the caregivers to proactively attend to patients' needs. Despite all the research and IoT device advancements, there is still much work to be done in improving the energy efficiency aspect of highly complex AI methods. In particular, the trade-off between performance and data computational efficiency must be proactively managed. Researchers should focus on developing low-latency decentralized training models on the edge devices that can use diverse input data from health sensors (voice, gait, etc.) and yield accurate individualized inferences. Moreover, in the field of healthcare social concerns about the use of AI, must be addressed.

4.8   CONCLUSION

EC is an interesting domain of the future cellular networks that aims to support multitude of IoT devices through low-latency processing [1–55]. From the multitude of use cases, our focus in this survey paper was its application in healthcare systems. Through this chapter work, we attempted to fill the gap in current healthcare surveys, which tend to focus on architecture and application types as opposed to maximum QoS for data operations. Moreover, we have presented the associated architecture, data operations, and the consumer perspective as detailed in the reviewed studies. We have also surveyed the studies from the perspective of qualifiers of EC that include cost, latency, security, location awareness, and energy efficiency. Based on our extensive literature review, we recommend further research to address the challenges related to large data volume, information security, compatibility with ultrareliable low-latency communication, and AI complexity-accuracy trade-offs. It is difficult to directly compare much of the research because experiments are done on a variety of platforms and with different data sets. However, even with these limitations, detailed comparative analysis of each data operation presented in this chapter can help researchers/health professionals choose the best authentication, data reduction, encryption, classification, or prediction method for a particular EC deployment use case in a healthcare setting.

KEYWORDS

- **authentication**
- **big data management**
- **communication protocols**
- **encryption**
- **healthcare applications**
- **healthcare monitoring systems**
- **user devices**

REFERENCES

1. Liu, L., Yang, Y., Zhao, W., & Du, Z., (2015). Semi-automatic remote medicine monitoring system of miners. In: *Adjunct Proceedings of the 2015 ACM International Joint Conference on Pervasive and Ubiquitous Computing and Proceedings of the 2015 ACM International Symposium on Wearable Computers (UbiComp/ISWC).* Osaka, Japan.

2. Kumar, K., & Lu, Y. H., (2010). Cloud computing for mobile users: Can offloading computation save energy? *Computer, 43*(4), 51–56. https://doi. org/10.1109/MC.2010.98.

3. Bonomi, F., Milito, R., Zhu, J., & Addepalli, S., (2012). Fog computing and its role in the internet of things. In: *Proceedings of the First Edition of the MCC Workshop on Mobile Cloud Computing (MCC).* Helsinki, Finland.

4. Maitra, A., & Kuntagod, N., (2013). *A Novel Mobile Application to Assist Maternal Health Workers in Rural India.* Paper presented at: 2013 5th International Workshop on Software Engineering in Health Care (SEHC); San Francisco, CA.

5. Yi, S., Hao, Z., Zhang, Q., Zhang, Q., Shi, W., & Li, Q., (2017). LAVEA: Latency-aware video analytics on edge computing platform. In: *Proceedings of the Second ACM/IEEE Symposium on Edge Computing (SEC).* San Jose, CA.

6. Jackson, K. R., Ramakrishnan, L., Muriki, K., et al., (2010). *Performance Analysis of High-performance Computing Applications on the Amazon Web Services Cloud.* Paper presented at: 2010 IEEE Second International Conference on Cloud Computing Technology and Science; Indianapolis, IN.

7. Bhunia, S. S., (2015). *Sensor-cloud: Enabling Remote Health-Care Services.* In: Proceedings of the 2015 on MobiSys PhD Forum (PhDForum); Florence, Italy.

8. Thiyagaraja, S. R., Dantu, R., Shrestha, P. L., Thompson, M. A., & Smith, C., (2017). Optimized and secured transmission and retrieval of vital signs from remote devices. In: *Proceedings of the Second IEEE/ACM International Conference on Connected Health: Applications, Systems and Engineering Technologies (CHASE).* Philadelphia, PA.

9. Althebyan, Q., Yaseen, Q., Jararweh, Y., & Al-Ayyoub, M., (2016). Cloud support for large scale e-healthcare systems. *Ann. Telecommun., 71*(9, 10), 503–515.

10. Miettinen, A. P., & Nurminen, J. K., (2010). Energy efficiency of mobile clients in cloud computing. In: *Proceedings of the 2nd USENIX Conference on Hot Topics in Cloud Computing (HotCloud).* Boston, MA.

11. Cao, Y., Hou, P., Brown, D., Wang, J., & Chen, S., (2015). Distributed analytics and edge intelligence: Pervasive health monitoring at the era of fog computing. In: *Proceedings of the 2015 Workshop on Mobile Big Data (Mobidata).* Hangzhou, China.

12. Bhargava, K., & Ivanov, S., (2017). *A Fog Computing Approach for Localization in WSN.* Paper presented at: 2017 IEEE 28th Annual International Symposium on Personal, Indoor, and Mobile Radio Communications (PIMRC); Montreal, Canada.

13. Yoon, J., (2017). *Leveraging Sensor Data Content to Assure Sensor Device Trustworthiness in Mobile Edge Computing.* Paper presented at: 2017 Second International Conference on Fog and Mobile Edge Computing (FMEC); Valencia, Spain.

14. Chung, K., & Park, R. C., (2017). Cloud based u-healthcare network with QoS guarantee for mobile health service. *Cluster Computing.* https:// doi.org/10.1007/s10586-017-1120-0.

15. Bhunia, S. S., Dhar, S. K., & Mukherjee, N., (2014). *iHealth: A Fuzzy Approach for Provisioning Intelligent Health-care System in Smart City.* Paper presented at: 2014

IEEE 10th International Conference on Wireless and Mobile Computing, Networking and Communications (WiMob); Larnaca, Cyprus.

16. Varshney, U., (2007). Pervasive healthcare and wireless health monitoring. *Mob. Netw. Appl., 12*(2, 3), 113–127. https://doi.org/10.1007/s11036- 007-0017-1.

17. Postolache, O., Girão, P. S., & Postolache, G., (2013). Pervasive sensing and m-health: Vital signs and daily activity monitoring. In: *Pervasive and Mobile Sensing and Computing for Healthcare: Technological and Social Issues* (pp. 1–49). Berlin, Germany: Springer-Verlag Berlin Heidelberg.

18. Aun, N. F. M., Soh, P. J., Al-Hadi, A. A., Jamlos, M. F., Vandenbosch, G. A. E., & Schreurs, D., (2017). Revolutionizing wearables for 5G: 5G technologies: Recent developments and future perspectives for wearable devices and antennas. *IEEE Microw. Mag., 18*(3), 108–124. https://doi.org/10.1109/ MMM.2017.2664019.

19. Elayan, H., Shubair, R. M., & Kiourti, A., (2017). *Wireless Sensors for Medical Applications: Current Status and Future Challenges.* Paper presented at: 2017 11th European Conference on Antennas and Propagation (EUCAP); Paris, France.

20. Thakar, A. T., & Pandya, S., (2017). *Survey of IoT Enables Healthcare Devices.* Paper presented at: 2017 International Conference on Computing Methodologies and Communication (ICCMC); Erode, India.

21. Kumar, N., (2017). *IoT Architecture and System Design for Healthcare Systems.* Paper presented at: 2017 International Conference on Smart Technologies for Smart Nation (SmartTechCon); Bangalore, India.

22. AbdElnapi, N. M. M., Omran, N. F., Ali, A. A., & Omara, F. A., (2018). *A Survey of Internet of Things Technologies and Projects for Healthcare Services.* Paper presented at: 2018 International Conference on Innovative Trends in Computer Engineering (ITCE); Aswan, Egypt.

23. Baker, S. B., Xiang, W., & Atkinson, I., (2017). Internet of things for smart healthcare: Technologies, challenges, and opportunities. *IEEE Access, 5*, 26521–26544. https://doi. org/10.1109/ACCESS.2017.2775180.

24. De Mattos, W. D., & Gondim, P. R. L., (2016). M-health solutions using 5G networks and M2M communications. *IT Professional., 18*(3), 24–29. https://doi.org/10.1109/ MITP.2016.52.

25. Mahmoud, M. M. E., Rodrigues, J. J. P. C., Ahmed, S. H., et al., (2018). Enabling technologies on cloud of things for smart healthcare. *IEEE Access, 6*, 31950–31967. https://doi.org/10.1109/ACCESS.2018.2845399.

26. Abbas, N., Zhang, Y., Taherkordi, A., & Skeie, T., (2018). Mobile edge computing: A survey. *IEEE Internet Things J., 5*(1), 450–465. https://doi.org/ 10.1109/ JIOT.2017.2750180.

27. Wang, S., Zhang, X., Zhang, Y., Wang, L., Yang, J., & Wang, W., (2017). A survey on mobile edge networks: Convergence of computing, caching and communications. *IEEE Access, 5*, 6757–6779. https://doi.org/10.1109/ACCESS.2017.2685434.

28. Yu, Y., (2016). Mobile edge computing towards 5G: Vision, recent progress, and open challenges. *China Communications, 13*(suppl 2), 89–99. https://doi.org/10.1109/ CC.2016.7833463 20 of 25 Hartmann et al., Hartmann et al., 21 of 25.

29. Mao, Y., You, C., Zhang, J., Huang, K., & Letaief, K. B., (2017). A survey on mobile edge computing: The communication perspective. *IEEE Commun. Surv. Tutor., 19*(4), 2322–2358. https://doi.org/10.1109/COMST.2017.2745201.

30. Taleb, T., Samdanis, K., Mada, B., Flinck, H., Dutta, S., & Sabella, D., (2017). On multi-access edge computing: A survey of the emerging 5G network edge cloud architecture and orchestration. *IEEE Commun. Surv. Tutor., 19*(3), 1657–1681. https://doi.org/10.1109/COMST.2017. 2705720.

31. Yu, W., Liang, F., He, X., et al., (2017). A survey on the edge computing for the internet of things. *IEEE Access, 6*, 6900–6919. https://doi.org/ 10.1109/ACCESS.2017.2778504.

32. Vallati, C., Virdis, A., Mingozzi, E., & Stea, G., (2016). Mobile-edge computing come home connecting things in future smart homes using LTE device-to-device communications. *IEEE Consumer Electron Mag., 5*(4),77–83. https://doi.org/10.1109/MCE.2016.2590100.

33. Shi, W., Cao, J., Zhang, Q., Li, Y., & Xu, L., (2016). Edge computing: Vision and challenges. *IEEE Internet Things J., 3*(5), 637–646. https://doi.org/10. 1109/JIOT.2016.2579198.

34. Rauf, A., Shaikh, R. A., & Shah, A., (2018). *Security and Privacy for IoT and Fog Computing Paradigm.* Paper presented at: 2018 15ᵗʰ Learning and Technology Conference (L&T); Jeddah, Saudi Arabia.

35. Salman, O., Elhajj, I., Kayssi, A., & Chehab, A., (2015). *Edge Computing Enabling the Internet of Things.* Paper presented at: 2015 IEEE 2ⁿᵈ World Forum on Internet of Things (WF-IoT); Milan, Italy.

36. Mouradian, C., Naboulsi, D., Yangui, S., Glitho, R. H., Morrow, M. J., & Polakos, P. A., (2018). A comprehensive survey on fog computing: State-of-the-art and research challenges. *IEEE Commun. Surv. Tutor., 20*(1), 416–464. https://doi.org/10.1109/COMST.2017.2771153.

37. Smith, W., Wadley, G., Daly, O., et al., (2017). Designing an app for pregnancy care for a culturally and linguistically diverse community. In: *Proceedings of the 29ᵗʰ Australian Conference on Computer-Human Interaction (OZCHI).* Brisbane, Australia.

38. Jacobs, M., (2015). Designing personalized technology to augment patient-centered care. In: *Adjunct Proceedings of the 2015 ACM International Joint Conference on Pervasive and Ubiquitous Computing and Proceedings of the 2015 ACM International Symposium on Wearable Computers (UbiComp/ISWC).* Osaka, Japan.

39. Thiyagaraja, S. R., Vempati, J., Dantu, R., Sarma, T., & Dantu, S., (2014). *Smart Phone Monitoring of Second Heart Sound Split.* Paper presented at: 2014 36ᵗʰ Annual International Conference of the IEEE Engineering in Medicine and Biology Society; Chicago, IL.

40. Chandrasekaran, V., Dantu, R., Jonnada, S., Thiyagaraja, S., & Subbu, K. P., (2013). Cuffless differential blood pressure estimation using smart phones. *IEEE Trans Biomed Eng., 60*(4), 1080–1089. https://doi.org/10.1109/TBME.2012.2211078.

41. Al Hamid, H. A., Rahman, S. M. M., Hossain, M. S., Almogren, A., & Alamri, A., (2017). A security model for preserving the privacy of medical big data in a healthcare cloud using a fog computing facility with pairing-based cryptography. *IEEE Access, 5*, 22313–22328. https://doi.org/10. 1109/ACCESS.2017.2757844.

42. Giri, D., Obaidat, M. S., & Maitra, T., (2017). *SecHealth: An Efficient Fog-based Sender Initiated Secure Data Transmission of Healthcare Sensors for E-medical System.* Paper presented at: 2017 IEEE Global Communications Conference (GLOBECOM); Singapore.

43. Tang, W., Zhang, K., Ren, J., Zhang, Y., & Shen, X., (2017). *Lightweight and Privacy-Preserving Fog-assisted Information Sharing Scheme for Health Big Data.*

Paper presented at: 2017 IEEE Global Communications Conference (GLOBECOM); Singapore.

44. Lin, H., Shao, J., Zhang, C., & Fang, Y., (2013). CAM: Cloud-assisted privacy preserving mobile health monitoring. *IEEE Trans, Inf, Forensics Secur., 8*(6), 985–997. https://doi.org/10.1109/TIFS.2013.2255593.

45. Soldani, D., Fadini, F., Rasanen, H., et al., (2017). *5G Mobile Systems for Healthcare.* Paper presented at: 2017 IEEE 85th Vehicular Technology Conference (VTC Spring); Sydney, Australia.

46. Hu, R., Pham, H., Buluschek, P., & Gatica-Perez, D., (2017). Elderly people living alone: Detecting home visits with ambient and wearable sensing. In: *Proceedings of the 2nd International Workshop on Multimedia for Personal Health and Health Care (MMHealth).* Mountain View, CA.

47. Muhammed, T., Mehmood, R., Albeshri, A., & Katib, I., (2018). UbeHealth: A personalized ubiquitous cloud and edge-enabled networked healthcare system for smart cities. *IEEE Access, 6,* 32258–32285. https://doi.org/10.1109/ACCESS.2018.2846609.

48. Lv, Z., Xia, F., Wu, G., Yao, L., & Chen, Z., (2010). *iCare: A Mobile Health Monitoring System for the Elderly.* Paper presented at: 2010 IEEE/ACM Int'l Conference on Green Computing and Communications & Int'l Conference on Cyber, Physical and Social Computing; Hangzhou, China.

49. Garibaldi-Beltrán, J. A., & Vazquez-Briseno, M., (2012). *Personal Mobile Health Systems for Supporting Patients with Chronic Diseases.* Paper presented at: 2012. IEEE Ninth Electronics, Robotics and Automotive Mechanics Conference; Cuernavaca, Mexico.

50. Wu, W., Cao, J., Zheng, Y., & Zheng, Y., (2008). *WAITER: A Wearable Personal Healthcare and Emergency aid System.* Paper presented at: 2008 Sixth Annual IEEE International Conference on Pervasive Computing and Communications (PerCom); Hong Kong.

51. Alrawais, A., Alhothaily, A., Hu, C., & Cheng, X., (2017). Fog computing for the internet of things: Security and privacy issues. *IEEE Internet. Comput., 21*(2), 34–42. https://doi.org/10.1109/MIC.2017.37.

52. HHS.gov. (2017). HIPAA for individuals.

53. Maddumabandara, A., Leung, H., & Liu, M., (2015). Experimental evaluation of indoor localization using wireless sensor networks. *IEEE Sensors J., 15*(9), 5228–5237. https://doi.org/10.1109/JSEN.2015.2438193.

54. Khin, O. O., Ta, Q. M., & Cheah, C. C., (2017). *Development of a Wireless Sensor Network for Human Fall Detection.* Paper presented at: 2017 IEEE International Conference on Real-time Computing and Robotics (RCAR); Okinawa, Japan.

55. Jamthe, A., Chakraborty, S., Ghosh, S. K., & Agrawal, D. P., (2013*). An Implementation of Wireless Sensor Network in Monitoring of Parkinson's Patients Using Received Signal Strength Indicator.* Paper presented at: 2013 IEEE International Conference on Distributed Computing in Sensor Systems; Cambridge, MA.

CHAPTER 5

Application of Wearable Devices in the Medical Domain

FATIMA FARIAH,[1] SHALINI MAHATO,[2]
CHINMAYA RANJAN PATTANAIK,[3] and SACHI NANDAN MOHANTY[4]

[1]*Department of Computer Science and Information Technology, Amity Institute of Information Technology, Amity University, Jharkhand, India*

[2]*Department of Computer Science and Engineering, Indian Institute of Information Technology, Ranchi, Jharkhand, India*

[3]*Department of Computer Science and Engineering, Ajay Binay Institute of Technology, Cuttack, Odisha, India*

[4]*School of Computer Engineering, VIT-AP University, Andhra Pradesh, India*

ABSTRACT

Wearable sensing device development is growing due to significant advancement in technology and engineering. Diagnoses and monitoring of disease are expensive. Due to the development of wearable devices, real time monitoring has become cheap and accessible. Wearable devices have led to complete clinical transformation in healthcare promising better medical solution. These devices are thought to have a big influence on the healthcare sector and improve patient's lives. In this chapter, the study focuses on latest advancement in different types of wearable sensor technologies its application to monitor health status.

Reconnoitering the Landscape of Edge Intelligence in Healthcare.
Suneeta Satpathy, Sachi Nandan Mohanty, and Sirisha Potluri (Eds.)
© 2024 Apple Academic Press, Inc. Co-published with CRC Press (Taylor & Francis)

5.1   INTRODUCTION

Global population aging is ubiquitous, severe, and long-term, resulting in an increase in the requirement for chronic and geriatric care at home. Patients may now engage in their healthcare in new and interesting ways due to mobile health. Even a routine medical check-up costs a lot of money, which may be conserved by using wearable devices, because wearable gadgets are small, portable, and provide findings in seconds.

Wearable devices are becoming increasingly significant because of the growth of coronavirus disease (COVID-19), which requires individuals to stay home and not go outside. They can use an oximeter to check their breathing or oxygen levels, or a corona kit to test oneself without going to the hospital, as it is harmful and will spread to anybody who comes into touch with it.

Wearable devices capture health data from users, which may then be analyzed to offer information about their health state. People may now test and monitor their glucose, heartbeat, and other psychological markers while sitting at home, because of technological improvements. Wearable technology and their applications can help people manage ailments without having to rush to the hospital.

In this study, the chapter would focus on various wearable devices and how they detect and monitor different diseases along with the psychological parameters has been discussed.

5.2   CLASSIFICATION OF WEARABLE DEVICES

Wearable devices can be further subdivided into following types as shown in Figure 5.1.

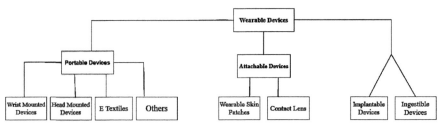

FIGURE 5.1   Classification of wearable devices.

5.2.1 PORTABLE DEVICES

"Devices that can be worn or paired with human skin to constantly and precisely monitor and individual's actions, without interrupting or restricting the user's motions" is the most applicable definition of wearable electronics. Micro-sensors completely integrated into fabrics, consumer electronics incorporated in stylish garments, computerized watches, bracelets, belt-worn personal computers (PCs) with a head mounted display and glasses in worn on different parts of the body all intended for broadband operation today (Figure 5.2). All the devices have the following characteristics: Location (geospatial coordinates), sensing (sensors that create alert warning signals), and connectivity (ability to connect with other devices and share information) are all used to establish positive identification of the user [1].

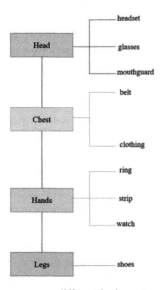

FIGURE 5.2 Portable devices worn on different body parts.

5.2.1.1 WRIST-MOUNTED DEVICES

Commercially available wrist-mounted physiological monitoring systems have improved battery life and hardware simplification for raw signals to explainable data in real time. The wrist-mounted device is used to monitor patients and quantify everyday activities such as motion, gesture, rotation, and acceleration. Biometric sensors are replacing simple accelerometer-based "smart pedometers" into fitness bands and smart watches. One of the most essential metabolic signs of a person's overall health is blood pressure (BP) monitoring.

Lee's team created a wearable device containing a Hall gadget capable of detecting minute variations in the permanent magnet's magnetic field and gather pulse wave data. This device, which is a pulsimeter without a cuff, can be worn on the wrist [1]. Ishikawa created a bracelet-style PPG heart rate sensor that scans variations in heart rate and with ordinary tasks, exhibits the capacity to overcome motion artifacts.[1]

One of the most widely used wearable device is smart watches. The Food and Drug Administration (FDA) has certified the first commercially approved asymptomatic, painless blood glucose monitoring gadget, GlucoWatch® biographer. It obtains glucose concentration information electrochemically from skin interstitial fluid collected by reverse iontophoresis [1]. Bella beat leaf is a fashionable accessory that can be worn as necklaces, bracelet, or clips., everyday activities, breathing, and menstruation cycles are all monitored using just 3D accelerometers and haptic vibration motors [2].

Apple released the Apple Watch Series 4 in December 2018, which for the first-time integrated ECG and watch functionalities. A bipolar ECG was also included on the dial to help detect hidden atrial fibrillation (AF). In terms of monitoring arrhythmia, atria, and ventricle blockage, and QRS duration extension, this equipment is comparable to standard 12-lead ECG recordings [16]. A team from the University of Pisa employed reconstruction of hand posture technology to rebuild hand movements using an adapted wearable glove, providing monitoring and feedback on a patient's hand function rehabilitation in real time.[16]. The Oura Ring is a metallic ring with microscopic systems that detect It measures vital signs including pulse rate, skin temperature, and respiratory rate. These characteristics may be checked for diseases such as the common cold, the flu, and even the newly discovered coronavirus 2019 (SARS-CoV-2). SARS-CoV-2 is the third and most current coronavirus. With 66 million cases, SARS-CoV-2 has now become a worldwide pandemic and 1.54 million fatalities over the world. The criteria are used by Oura Ring to detect SARS-CoV-2 symptoms in residential settings. With 90% accuracy, the wearable ring identifies typical SARS-CoV-2 symptoms as fever, cough, tiredness, and trouble breathing. Furthermore, the ring's battery lasts 4–7 days, depending on usage, and it only takes 20–80 minutes to recharge [15]

5.2.1.2   HEAD-MOUNTED DEVICES

Smart wearable eyeglasses are a type of head-mounted computer that displays information. Nichola 's Constant smart's glasses are pulse-detecting spectacles with a photoplethysmography (PPG) on the nasal patch that constantly measures respiratory rate [1]. MicroOpticalTM (Micro-Optical Corporation, USA) is a head mounted display used in orthopedic surgery to see intraoperative fluoroscopy pictures throughout the procedure [3]. Google Glass is powered by Android 4.04 Ice Cream Sandwich It is self-contained, with its own processing unit, random access memory, and flash memory. Glass (a trademark of Google Inc.) has a high-resolution display that, when viewed from eight feet away, is comparable to a high-definition screen of 25 inches. It's placed on a titanium structure with nose cushions that can be adjusted over the right eye. It has cameras that can take pictures and movies, GPS positioning, as well as the implementation of Technology such as virtual reality (VR), augmented reality (AR), and mixed reality (MR), making it appropriate for telehealth, clinical training, and operative navigation [16].

To offer surgeons who can remove cancer with clean, image-guided margins, Shao [3] utilized a head-mounted display device with the Google Glass (Google Inc., USA). The margins were detected and rendered apparent on the Glass using an *ex-vivo* tissue model that had been infused with fluorescence. This was utilized to detect remaining tumor foci and, as a result, lower the likelihood of recurrence disease after surgery. Following cancer resection surgery, this surgical navigation system has the potential to enhance clinical performance and outcomes. Mitsubayashi developed a glucose sensor in mouthpiece utilizing microelectromechanical systems (MEMS), which is made up of Silver/Silver chloride and Platinum electrodes besides a glucose oxidase enzymatic film mounted [1].

5.2.1.3   E-TEXTILES

Textiles that are referred to as smart clothes, are made up of conductive devices or electrodes and fabric are examples of sensors which are incorporated into textile-based diagnostic devices, which are connected to or woven into garments. The concept of "smart clothes" was described to gather signals from different physiological parameters were used to create a source data center for comprehensive health monitoring in smart textiles, three crucial components must be included: a control unit, an actuator, and a detector.[2]. The Life Shirt (*Vivo* Metrics Inc., USA) was used to test its suitability for tidal volume, oxygen saturation, and pulmonary frequency are all things that can be measured. It's also been utilized to correctly assess ECG in animal investigations without limiting mobility. The medical experts may be able to utilize the device to diagnose sleep problems, heart illness, pulmonary diseases, and pre- and post-operative monitoring [3].

The Georgia Tech Wearable Motherboard, for example, is a vest with plastic fiber optics and other unique fibers woven into the fabric and a system that allows connecting to vital signs sensors implanted at various body regions [12]. Its flexible data bus transmits sensors collect data to a controller, which interprets the signals before electronically transmitting them to the desired locations (Figure 5.3). Intel has also produced a smart t-shirt for those who exercise regularly, in collaboration with AIQ, a maker of electronic-based textiles. The shirt's conductive fibers detect the wearer's heart rate and may send the data to a smartphone. The electronics are stored in a small box that is coupled to a side bag that can be withdrawn to wash the shirt [13]. Caldara [5] have created smart wearable textiles that continually monitor pH levels. Sol-gel techniques are used to create the smart fabric, which uses an ecologically benign halogenated dye (litmus). The electrical device has low power dissipation, high-sensitivity color sensors, embedded processing, and a Bluetooth port. Wicaksono have also created a pleasant electronic textile suit (E-TEC's). The E-TECS uses inertial tracking to provide skin temperature sensing with an accuracy of 0.1°C, as well as pulse and breathing rhythms with a precision of 0.00122. In addition, wash ability and biodegradability tests for the E-TECS were conducted, with good rigidity and verification of no particles or staining after 10 cycles of washing, indicating that it is suitable for everyday use [15].

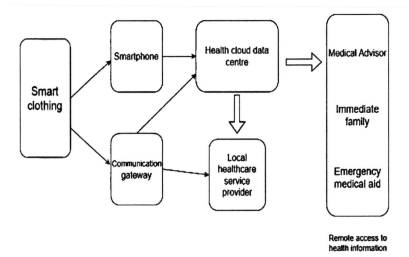

FIGURE 5.3   Smart clothing in sharing and communicating data.

5.2.1.4 OTHERS

A shoe with an electrical component has been designed to assess walking abilities, such as laterally ground reaction forces, foot impact, toe tension, and ground response forces, which all contribute to the identifying of gait stages [1]. Omega Wave is a digital chest strap with tracking electrodes that offers ECG and direct current data for the measurement of cardiac and central nervous system performance [1]. EQ02 Life Monitor (Equivital Inc., USA) belt has also been found to accurately monitor respiratory and heart rhythms, temperature, demographics, movement, sleep, fitness, and psycho-physiology in animal and human testing [3]. It has various advantages over other sensing devices like the BioHarness, including the design to sense and maintain core temperature as well as multicast temperature at multiple locations. It also allows data to be collected and communicated with a range of devices, allowing for data analysis. Godfrey [16] employed wearable devices to assist older individuals live independently by measuring gait and fall risk, evaluating the sustainability of everyday activities for elderly adults in an unattended home context, as well as identifying crucial forms of movement such as walking, standing, sitting, laying. Jung [16] designed a wearable system for the detection that detects falls by promptly uploading data on the whereabouts of senior citizens to a medical center and ensuring immediate assistance and treatments toward others.

5.2.2 ATTACHABLE DEVICES

The next generation of portable electronic healthcare gadgets for remote medical advancement is attachable monitoring devices. Skin-like adaptability and adaptability, which provides precise yet efficient sensing leaving no effects on a user's natural mobility and comfort, is a key attribute that defines an attachable device. Because of their remarkable qualities, ease of manufacture, and compressibility, elastic thermoplastic materials such as PC, PET, and synthetic polymers are utilized to create flexible materials [1]. Attachable devices can be built using the recent advancements in the innovation of sensors, physiotherapy, microsystems, data analysis, and connectivity.

5.2.2.1 WEARABLE SKIN PATCHES

Skin patches that can be worn are becoming more common in the wearable device industry. Electronic devices that are soft, flexible, and stretchy are linked to muscle tissue to develop a better framework for robotic feedback and management, tissue regeneration, and endless health insurance. Because skin pads may be hidden by clothes and capture data that is more exact without being hampered by movement, they are ideal wearables. Wearable patches are being used as vital signs, perspiration, tension, and temperature sensors on humans. A wearable patchwork sensor with an adaptable piezoresistive sensor (FPS) and epidermal ECG sensors has been developed for measuring BP without cuffs, as reported in Advanced Functional Materials [1].

Sheng Xu and company proved the starting operation of a conformal ultrasonic skin patch for monitoring BP waveforms in deep arteries and veins in recent research [1]. Ultrasonic waves may infiltrate further into biomechanical cells, allowing for 3-Dimensional identification of electronic gadgets that are currently worn. Wearable ultrasonic systems enable direct, precise interaction with the curved skin surface, enabling for constant CBP analysis for heart illness with no pain or inconsistency that other conventional approaches cause. The PDMS dermal pad is a microfluidic monitoring program that utilizes thermal blast technology to allow non-invasive regulate and capture glucose and other compounds within interstitial fluids without the need for separation.[1]. Kim's group had developed a graphene and gold-based wearable patch-type sensor for sweat analysis-based diabetic treatment [1]

5.2.2.2 CONTACT LENS

With the help of smart contact lenses, the physiological information of the eyes, can be analyzed non-invasively. For monitoring components such as lactate and glucose, conductivity of tear fluid, as well as the transdermal gases in the eye's mucosal surface, optical, and electrical approaches have been used to develop contact lens for it. Photonic crystals were innovated by Alexeev, which are comprised of colloidal particles and are arranged cubically facing the center and are encapsulated in hydrogel for non-invasive sensitive detection of tear fluid [1].

An optical sensor connected to commercial contact lenses was created to monitor glucose in physiological circumstances. It was manufactured on the surface of hydrogel network which is glucose-sensitive using a basic imprinting process. The sensor has a feature in which it can record the reflectance and diffraction of light with the help of smartphone applications, demonstrating the advantages such as high and low sensitivity, time of rapid reaction and saturation time. Sensimed, a Swiss company, fits glaucoma sufferers with a contact lens-like medical device that monitors their intra-ocular pressure 24 hours a day, seven days a week. Changes in intraocular pressure are the most important factor in diagnosing glaucoma, and continual intraocular pressure measurement can help to delay the onset of glaucoma. These contact lenses contain sensors and antennae that measure the user's intraocular pressure, send, and record the information in real time to a smart device, and thus save it on the doctor's computer via Bluetooth [8].

5.2.3 IMPLANTABLE DEVICES

There has been an improvement in the quality and efficiency of healthcare by the increasing development of implantable gadgets that uses tiny sensors and biomedical devices for diagnosis and prognosis over the last several decades, due to remarkable advances in electrical, biocompatible materials, and nano-materials. For cardiac patients, the most well-known surgically implanted device which is used for treating arrhythmias or irregular heartbeats is a pacemaker. By delivering low-energy electrical pulses, the device can restore normal rhythm of the heart. For necessitating stereotactic surgery towards the neurological structure, deep brain stimulation electrode transplants are used [1]. An implanted pulse generator (IPG) provides electrical signals to regulate movement through the specific electrodes for deep brain stimula-tion. To provide energy to the targeted neurological system, The IPG, which is comprised of a battery, generates an electrical stimulation, and operates electronic circuitry [1].

5.2.3.1 E-TATTOO

Tattoos are intriguing tools for keeping track of emotions and vital indi-cators. Electronic tattoos (e-tattoos) may be customized to fit a variety of skin textures, allowing for non-invasive and effective skin attachment. The structure of the tattoo adhesive layer is extremely flexible, allowing it to move with any skin movement and giving the patient with natural daily wear as well as exact data. To measure the amounts of lactate in sweat of an individual in a painless manner, a Tattoo biosensor has been developed to detect electrochemical signals that are enzymes generated [1].

The tattoo-based blood sugar tracking system uses an oxidized enzyme Prussian blue converter. The system is made up of reverse osmotic pressure-derived epileptic glucose and a measuring and recording sensor which is completely enzyme-based [1]. After a patient eats, the changes in BP are recorded by the verification technique which involves placing a sensor on the patient's skin.

For an effective control of diabetes and non-invasive monitoring of components, the study has found out that iontophoresis and biosensing tattooing systems will be the better apart from glucose in the interstitial fluid.

Ameri demonstrates an amazing tattoo-based ECG monitor [15]. It's constructed up of a graphene/polymethylmethacrylate (Gr/PMMA) bilayer with small electrical components placed on top. The graphene electronic tattoo (GET) has a thickness of 4,63,30 nm, an optical transparency of 85%, and a stretchability of more than 40%, and was created using a wet transfer, dry patterning technique. It can be deposited on skin like a tattoo due to its extreme stretchability and optical transparency. It uses Van der Waals forces to bind to the skin, making it practically undetectable to the wearer. The GET is an epidermal electronic device that can monitor ECG, EMG, and EEG, among other biopotentials. This wearable device, like bulk gel-based electrodes, produces a clear ECG with a high signal-to-noise ratio.

5.2.4 INGESTIBLE DEVICES

Using an ingestible sensor to obtain the fluid you wish to detect is a safe and non-invasive option. This orally administered sensor may pass through the digestive tract's lumen and reach organs in the belly. As a result, the ingestion sensor captures biometric data from the organs' inherent genital components and intercellular fluid, as well as enzymes, hormones, electrolytes, associated microorganisms, and metabolites surrounding the organs [1].

Proteus Digital Health from Redwood City, CA, USA has created edible medicines, which are also called smart pills, tracks the moment of consumption with accuracy. When the patient takes in the pill, it reaches the stomach and there it is energized by a chemical interaction with the stomach juice. During the process, it transmits the signal about the ingestion to the patch placed in the body. In addition to interacting with the pill. Heart rate, BP, pH, and temperature are some of the parameters that is analyzed by the patch [1]. My/treatment/medication (MyTMed) is an ingestible biosensor system. It is a method for checking drug adherence directly [1]. MyTMed which is composed of an electronic particle emits a radio frequency when it interacts with an acidic pH 2. To forward the radio frequency to the cloud server it meets the Hub for gathering the frequencies, thus helping both patients and the doctor to have a communication in both ways. In terms of drug intake information and adherence, the gadget can be controlled in a timely manner.

5.3 SENSORS BASED ON PHYSICAL QUANTITY MEASUREMENT

BP, heart rate and body temperature are the most important physical characteristics that needs to be monitored to identify different chronic diseases and maintain them. Monitoring them all are crucial in medical wellness.

5.3.1 MONITORING BLOOD PRESSURE (BP)

One of the most crucial physiological indicators of a person's health is tracking BP. Traditional arterial pulse sensors utilize cuffs to measure BP and optical pressure. It also includes sensors such as electrocardiogram (ECG). A thin, adjustable patch sensor that tracks BP is created using a structure of ferroelectric film that is layered, it consists of specially built electrodes, and adaptable electronic circuits that allows synchronous ECG and Ballistocardiogram (BCG) circumferences on the abdomen of the patient without distress. [1] To detect the pulse arrival time, Zheng used a wearable sleeveless gadget based on optical technology (the pulse transit time first from heart towards the peripheral blood vessels) to monitor BP fluctuations. This device is used for the treatment of hypertension [16] For BP estimation, a traditional cuff-based BP meter measures pulse-transit-times (PTT) and other characteristics obtained from PPG and ECG [17]. It collects the two signals from the user's fingertips after calibration with a traditional BP meter. From the connections between characteristic points in each cardiac cycle, systolic, and diastolic pressures (SBP and DBP) are calculated. To improve mobility, a Bluetooth link for transmitting the two signals to a PDA has been introduced, allowing real-time pre-processing and transfer of BP-related information to a distant interface. A low-cost wearable piezoelectric device for continuous SBP and DBP monitoring of vital signs from beat to beat has been presented by Wang and Lin [17] Using a piezoelectric pressure sensor in this device, the change in voltage between the subsequent systolic and diastolic function points of a pressure pulse wave was immediately converted to pressure differential.

5.3.2 MONITORING HEART RATE

The development of effective and continuous heart status monitoring might help improve healthcare delivery for the most common cause of death worldwide—cardiac illness. In a living thing, the cardiovascular system is a continuous cycle in which the heart pumps carry oxygen and other nutrients into the body through arteries while carbon dioxide diffuses through the lungs. The number of heart contractions (beats) per minute determines the frequency of the ventricular contraction which is known as the heart rate or pulse (bpm). Any alteration in a human's physical or mental condition causes their heart rate to alter. The Holter monitor is the most well-known medical equipment, which is used to record a patient's heart response during typical activities for up to 24 hours. Electrodes are attached to a small, battery-powered recording equipment that is worn on the patient's chest. Patients must keep records of their activities, which is then examined by their therapists in conjunction with the data, by linking any abnormal heart rate with the patient's activity on a regular basis.

The next stage was to use wearables for application areas, which involved merging physiological monitoring with an alert system [3]. Tison's team employed smart devices to create an algorithm for detecting AF using data from the PPG sensor and the accelerometer's step count. AF is the most prevalent risk factor for stroke, and those patients who are at a higher risk of suffering from a heart attack can know it by tracking AF on a frequent basis.[1] Park offers a self-powered, extensible piezoelectric pulse sensor which is based on high-quality zirconate titanate (PZT) filament, for an authentic arterial pulse tracking system. The created sensor was linked to a wireless Bluetooth transmitter and an Android-based smartphone that displayed the collected information in real-time [1]. Aingeal is a wireless wearable device which was originated in Intelesens Ltd., Northern Ireland that continuously records the respiratory and heart rates of the patient, as well as the temperature of the surface of skin. It's capable of detecting arrhythmias and alerting medical personnel to the danger of cardiac arrest [3]. Colantonio [16] created a wearable device that employs by monitoring the patient's breathing rate, respiratory sound, blood oxygen saturation, and ECG, a wireless sensor network system can assess the therapeutic impact of COPD medications. It is also used for the treatment of various pulmonary diseases. BioHarness (Zephyr Technology Corp., USA) detects respiration and heart rate via a thoracic pressure sensor connected to a chest band. Its excellent accuracy and user-friendliness have been confirmed in numerous studies, and it can also be linked with a smartphone to see live physiological data wirelessly or on a central display monitor [3]. Dae used a piezoelectric sensor that powers itself for uninterrupted and authentic detection of the arterial pulse. The pulse in the arteries, which is a component of cardiac output, is a measurement of the heart's contraction rate (heart rate stroke volume). The pressure generated by arterial pulses is converted into electrical pulses by a piezoelectric sensor. The identification of anomalies in atrial pulses in real time might help to avert major heart illnesses. The measurement of arterial pressure might aid in the detection of heart and blood diseases [15].

5.3.3 MONITORING BODY TEMPERATURE

It's crucial to keep an eye on skin temperature when it starts to have some changes in the early stages of the condition's diagnosis and therapy. An ultra-thin sensor that are somewhat skin type was developed by Roger and his colleagues that can be freely placed to the skin surface for constant and precise measurement of heat [1]. First, the skin-like characteristics are effectively separated from the strain imposed by the sensor systems and are securely adhered to the skin without causing discomfort. Second, the device has a very reduced temperature mass as well as a very higher moisture permeability, which helps with reaction times and thermal load. To build ultra-thin photonic devices, chromogenic temperature indicators were combined with wireless flexible electronics [1]. On a thin elastomer substrate, the device was built of thermochromic liquid crystals in a massive two-dimensional array. Monitoring it constantly in daily life will avoid any bad effects on the society and healthcare. As a result, researchers developed an elastic human stress measuring patch with a contact to the lower skin area and improved adhesive wear. The human stress tracking pad is 25 mm x 15 mm x 72 mm in size and is subdivided into three sensors that can measure surface temperatures, skin conductance, and heart waves. Hong [15] created a wearable temperature sensor using single-wall carbon nanotubes that are electrically linked through integrated interconnects. The sensor has a response time of 1.8 seconds at a highest temperature of 45°C. Based on the data obtained, the sensor can be used to create virtual skin.

5.4 SENSORS BASED ON CHEMICAL QUANTITY MEASUREMENT

Because diabetes and other chronic diseases are on the rise, it's more vital than ever to keep track of the factors that affect one's health. It is now simpler to monitor glucose, body fluids, and other chemical quantities for determining the health condition of specific individuals diagnosed with various diseases at home, due to improvements in wearable devices.

5.4.1 MONITORING GLUCOSE

Diabetes is a category of metabolic disorders defined by hyperglycemia induced by insulin secretion abnormalities or biological actions that are compromised. Improvements in the ability of diabetic patients to self-monitor and self-manage their blood glucose levels have helped to reduce diabetes-related morbidity and death. Liu built a glucose and lactate monitoring device using electrodes based on oxidizing agents and lactate oxidase in a cloth to monitor glucose and lactate with excellent accuracy [1]. Pillalamarri [16] created a portable insulin pump that intelligently regulates the rate and volume of insulin injections while maintaining blood glucose levels using biomedical MEMS technology. Yao [5] have developed a dual-electrode glucose sensor that is both flexible and wearable. The two electrodes are used as functioning and opposing electrodes in a reverse transdermal method to collect interstitial fluid from the skin and identify glucose in the interstitial fluid. Binghamton University at Novel York State University researchers have created a novel sensor patch that is self-powered, biodegradable, and portable that may detect hypoglycemia linked with exercise by monitoring glucose in human perspiration [1]. A glucose/oxygen enzymatic fuel cell is put in vertically in a traditional Band-Aid glued pad inside this glucose detecting sensor. Without the usage of any separate power supply or complex reading technology, the sensors are installed on to the skin to check glucose levels. Lin [15] created a smart contact lens that uses tears to diagnose and monitor diabetes over time. The lens is comprised of phenylboronic acid (PBA), a non-enzyme, and hydroxyethyl methacrylate (HEMA), a monomer. For detection of medical conditions such as diabetes, the contact lens based on reversible covalent binding of the PBAHEMA is used. As the glucose level rises, the thickness of the contact lens starts to grow at a constant speed. The need for internal power circuits or extra photosensors are not required by the contact lens. To detect the changes in the thickness of contact lens, the lens depends solely on a smartphone. The collection of reflection of light emitted by the diodes on the smart lens is done by the smartphone. Using built-in algorithms for the identification of glucose levels, the images are processed. The MiniMed 670G from Medtronic combines blood glucose tracking and an insulin pump into a single device. The device can be placed around the waistline of the patient, and daily monitoring and injection intervals can be configured [16].

5.4.2   MONITORING FLUIDS (SWEAT)

Sweat and other epidermal biofluids are significant indicators of changes in the human body, as a result, it can be employed in biological and chemical sensing as a metric. Sweat contains a wide range of indicators, including metabolites (sugar, lactate, ammonia, and many others), proteins, nucleotide, and electrolytes (chlorine, salinity, and some others), all of which have important clinical implications. Sweat which is widely dispersed with more than 100 glands per centimeter on the surface of the skin is easily detectable chemically. As a result, sweat may be utilized to extract various chemical and biological data utilizing wearable devices to offer monitoring and diagnostics. Koh [4] created a microfluidics-based flexible, soft, and stretchy device for colorimetric sweat biomarker detection. This HWD can measure electrolytes including ions of chloride and hydronium, which are important for cystic fibrosis monitoring. CF is a hereditary condition that causes shortness of breath. In addition to pH, perspiration rate, and overall sweat loss, the microfluidic hardware device may enable for the measurement of sugar and lactate levels, which is important for diabetics. Sweat is pumped into microprocessor compartments as perspiration begins, where biomarkers such as sugar oxide mixtures and horseradish peroxide (HRP) are responded by the chromogenic reagents for glucose. The HWD monitors the concentrations of the electrolytes on a continual basis, and the results are in great agreement with sweat laboratory analysis. The soft lithographic method is used to create the microfluidic device, which is made of PDMS. For activating epidermal examination of biodegradable fluid, the extensible cordless sweat sensor which is made of nanofibers is mounted on operational elastomeric surfaces [1]. This perspiration sensor uses dielectric and colorimetric sensing to determine the amount of perspiration and its chemical characteristics. Tomczak created a sweat detecting system that is properly integrated, wearable, adjustable, and remote that can constantly and non-invasively monitor electrolytes during severe activity to determine hydration status [1]. The following are the device's primary distinguishing characteristics:

i. For efficiently gathering sweat those form on the skin at a faster frequency, A transdermal fluid system is used, and it detects sweat absorption. It extracts the sweat from the region which has been tracked by the program and reduces the physiological impacts caused by the sweat.

ii. Wearable, wireless sweat monitoring is enabled integrating Na+ and K+ ion sensitive electrodes with flexible microfluidic systems and low-noise technology.

A wearable bracelet for pH monitoring in sweating has been proposed by Pablo [5] A microfluidic cloth analytical device and the system's two main components are a micro-readout module and a power supply. The wearable bracelet enables for continuous sweat pH monitoring and wirelessly communicates the data to a smartphone through Bluetooth in real time. The sensor has a pH range of 6 to 8, with a CV of 3.6 to 6.0% at various pH levels. In a discontinuous sensing mode, the created device is predicted to last up to 2.63 days on a single charge, and it can be used in the realm of personal health assessment.

5.5   RECENT LITERATURE STUDY

There are many works done in this area here are few of the works I have discussed. Here, Table 5.1 consists of different types of wearable devices/sensors and how it detects and monitors various diseases as well as psychological parameters.

5.6   DISCUSSION

Thus, wearable devices can be used to detect or cure various acute and chronic diseases such as diabetes, hypertension, pulmonary disorders, and cardiovascular diseases. Various sensors embedded in wearable devices can be used to track physical and chemical data like heart rate, BP, body temperature, glucose, and physiological fluids. Wearable biosensors have achieved tremendous gains in terms of endurance and longevity as the complexity and downsizing of sensors, battery solutions, and material science have progressed, and further advancements will be necessary. Healthcare gadgets are expected to address a growing need for medical services among senior individuals who have limited mobility and lack access to professional healthcare, as well as the growing desire for remote hospital facilities that are not limited by space or time. Many factors impact the growth of the remote healthcare industry, such as the rising number of patients with chronic conditions including diabetes and cardiovascular problems. The present COVID-19 epidemic has emphasized the importance of remote healthcare delivery even more. Reliability, susceptibility, and biomedical applications with time, for example, must all be enhanced to fulfill regulatory bodies' minimum criteria for diagnostic equipment.

TABLE 5.1 Comparative Study of Various Wearable Devices

Sl. No.	Paper Name	Type of Wearable Device/ Sensor	Type of Disease	Physiological Parameter
1.	Evolution of wearable devices with real-time disease monitoring for personalized healthcare [1].	Wrist band/watch	Metabolic disorder	Heart rate, blood pulse, glucose, sodium
		Mouth guard, eyeglasses	Fitness tracking	Lactate, uric acid and glucose, lactate, and potassium, heart rate
		Electrode textiles, leg calf, footwear	Skeletal system disease	Glucose and lactate, heart rate and temperature, foot motion
		Ring necklace and clip, belt worn on chest	Sleep or test related disease	Sleep, daily activity, step count, sitting time, ECG, and direct current
		Patch	Respiratory diseases	Blood pressure and heart rate by ECG measure.
		Contact lens	Astigmatism	Glucose and lactate in tear fluid
		Tattoo	Skin disease and UV related	Monitoring respiration and pathogenic bacteria, detection with tooth enamel lactate, glucose, alcohol, and electrolytes
		Bio-ink	Cardiovascular disease	Glucose, pH, and electrolytes
2.	Wearable devices in medical internet of things: scientific research and commercially available devices [2]	Smart cloth	Myalgic encephalomyelitis (ME)	Photoelectric volume pulse wave signal measurement.
		Fitbit flex	Fitness tracker	Step counting and quality, small size, wrist worn
		Withing pulse	Fitness tracker	Measuring heart rate and percentage of optimal sleep hours.
		Jawbone	Fitness tracker	Tracking user sleep data, eating habits.
3.	A review of wearable technology in medicine [3].	MicroOpticalTM	Internal fracture fixations and spinal pedicle screw placement.	Orthopedic fluoroscopy
		Opti-vu HDVD	Muscle fatigue	Laparoscopy HMD
		ANC HD1080P CMOS	Cancer	Visual image guided cancer resection surgery.
		Google glass	Residual tumor	Evaluation in forensic medicine.
		BioHarness	Cardiovascular issues	Respiratory and heart rate.

TABLE 5.1 *(Continued)*

Sl. No.	Paper Name	Type of Wearable Device/ Sensor	Type of Disease	Physiological Parameter
4.	Wearable devices and healthcare: Data sharing and privacy [4]	Fitbit	Fitness tracker	All day activity, heart rate and sleep tracking.
		Omnipod®	Diabetes	Continuous insulin delivery.
		Pacemaker	Heart rhythm disorders	Heartbeat control
5.	Recent developments in sensors for wearable device applications [5]	Capacitive pressure sensor	Congenital diaphragmatic hernia (CDH)	Blood pressure, pulse
		Strain sensor	Kidney dialysis	Respiratory rate
		Electrochemical sensors	Diabetes	Glucose rate
		Fluorescence spectroscopy	Multisystem cancers	Glucose, lactic acid, pH, chloride Blood pressure
		Pressure sensor	Hypertension	Arterial pulse, respiratory rate
6.	Wearable devices in healthcare [6]	Peripheral sensors	Nerve injury	Sensing body temperature and muscle movements.
		Galvanic skin response sensors	Cardiac problem	Heart rate, respiration rate, emotional state and brain waves.
		Gluco Watch	Diabetes	Glucose
		LifeVest	Cardiac arrest	Abnormal heart rhythms
		Vital positioning system	Heart attack	Heart activity
		USBONE	Bone fracture	LIUS therapy sessions
		Holter monitor	Cardiac problems	Cardiac responses
		WAMAS	Balance disorders	Basic human motions
7.	Understanding the emergence of wearable devices as next-generation tools for health communication [7].	Wrist-worn sensors	Heart problems	Physical activities
		Pulse oximeter	Pulmonary diseases	Oxygen level
		Sensimed	Glaucoma	Measure their intraocular pressure

TABLE 5.1 (*Continued*)

Sl. No.	Paper Name	Type of Wearable Device/ Sensor	Type of Disease	Physiological Parameter
8.	Transformation in healthcare by wearable devices for diagnostics and guidance of treatment [9].	Apple watch	Arrhythmia	Heart rate
9.	Consumer adaptation and infusion of wearable devices for healthcare [10].	Virtual reality (VR)	Anxiety and stress	Pain and physical movements.
10.	Wearable technology for cardiology: An update and framework for the future [11]	Cardionet MCOTTM	Arrythmeia	Ambulatory ECG data
		Zoll's LifeVest	Cardiac arrest	Heart rate
11.	Wearable medical devices for tele-home healthcare [12]	Cygnus	Diabetes	Blood glucose
		Cuffless blood pressure meter	Irregularity of blood pressure	Blood pressure
		Finger-ring sensor for HR monitoring	Cardiac issues	Heart rate
12.	Wearable technology: if the tech fits, wear it [13]	OM signal's shirt	Fitness tracker	Heart and breathing rates, calorie burned and stress level
		Google glass	Alzheimer	Brain terminology
13.	Wearable devices in healthcare: Privacy and information security issues [14]	Pressure sensors	Asthma	Muscle function and co-ordination
		Heartrate sensors	Arrythmia	Heart rate, blood pressure and blood oxygen.

TABLE 5.1 *(Continued)*

Sl. No.	Paper Name	Type of Wearable Device/ Sensor	Type of Disease	Physiological Parameter
14.	Advances in healthcare wearable devices [15]	E-TeCS	Sleep disorders	Heart rate, respiratory rates, skin temperature
		Wearable EMG shirt	Muscle fatigue	EMG in upper limbs, muscle activity
		Electronic tattoo	Tachycardia and bradycardia	Heart signals
		Piezoelectric sensor	Cardiac and blood diseases	Arterial pulse
		Piezoelectric patch	Hypertension	Blood pressure
		Oura ring	Cold flu, novel corona virus (SARS-CoV-2)	Heart rate, body temperature, breathing
		Sensimed triggerfish	Glaucoma	Ocular volume changes
15.	Wearable health devices in healthcare: narrative systematic review [16]	Apple watch	Stroke heart failure	Irregular rhythms in heart rate
		Sports vest	Heart diseases	Rhythmic beats of heart
		Medtronic's MiniMed 670G	Diabetes	Blood glucose level

5.7 CONCLUSION

The study goes through the many types of wearable devices and how it monitors various physical and chemical quantities in a person's body. It also discusses how new and creative advancements in the wearable sector have simplified customized healthcare and how it treats various chronic diseases. Still wearable devices require a lot of progress in terms of design, measurement accuracy, operation, and battery consumption, storage capacity, etc. Devices' power consumption, including data capture and transmission, must be efficiently reduced, which is important for long-term operations. Thus, the more technological advancement in development of wearable devices is sooner going to change the face of medical sector and make the life of many patients easier with real time and cost-effective diagnosis.

KEYWORDS

- **blood pressure**
- **chemical quantity measurement**
- **devices**
- **diagnosis**
- **disease**
- **heart rate**
- **portable devices**
- **wearable sensor**

REFERENCES

1. Guk, K., Han, G., Lim, J., Jeong, K., Kang, T., Lim, E. K., & Jung, J., (2019). Evolution of wearable devices with real-time disease monitoring for personalized healthcare. In: *Nanomaterials* (Vol. 9, No. 6). MDPI AG. https://doi.org/10.3390/nano9060813.
2. Haghi, M., Thurow, K., & Stoll, R., (2017). Wearable devices in medical internet of things: Scientific research and commercially available devices. *Healthcare Informatics Research, 23*(1), 4–15. https://doi.org/10.4258/hir.2017.23.1.4.
3. Iqbal, M. H., Aydin, A., Brunckhorst, O., Dasgupta, P., & Ahmed, K., (2016). A review of wearable technology in medicine. In: *Journal of the Royal Society of Medicine* (Vol. 109, No. 10, pp. 372–380). SAGE Publications Ltd. https://doi.org/10.1177/0141076816663560.

4. Banerjee, S., (Sy), Hemphill, T., & Longstreet, P., (2018). Wearable devices and healthcare: Data sharing and privacy. *Information Society, 34*(1), 49–57. https://doi.org/10.1080/01972243.2017.1391912.

5. Cheng, Y., Wang, K., Xu, H., Li, T., Jin, Q., & Cui, D., (2021). Recent developments in sensors for wearable device applications. In: *Analytical and Bioanalytical Chemistry* (Vol. 413, No. 24, pp. 6037–6057). Springer Science and Business Media Deutschland GmbH. https://doi.org/10.1007/s00216-021-03602-2.

6. Glaros, C., & Fotiadis, D. I. (2005). Wearable devices in healthcare. In: Silverman B., Jain A., Ichalkaranje A., & Jain L., (eds.), *Intelligent Paradigms for Healthcare Enterprises: Studies in Fuzziness and Soft Computing* (Vol. 184). Springer, Berlin, Heidelberg. https://doi.org/10.1007/11311966_8.

7. Park, E., Kim, K. J., & Kwon, S. J., (2016). Understanding the emergence of wearable devices as next-generation tools for health communication. *Information Technology and People, 29*(4), 717–732. https://doi.org/10.1108/ITP-04-2015-0096.

8. Lee, S. M., & Lee, D. H., (2020). Healthcare wearable devices: An analysis of key factors for continuous use intention. *Service Business, 14*(4), 503–531. https://doi.org/10.1007/s11628-020-00428-3.

9. Mahajan, A., Pottie, G., & Kaiser, W., (2020). Transformation in healthcare by wearable devices for diagnostics and guidance of treatment. *ACM Transactions on Computing for Healthcare, 1*(1), 1–12. https://doi.org/10.1145/3361561.

10. Marakhimov, A., & Joo, J., (2017). Consumer adaptation and infusion of wearable devices for healthcare. *Computers in Human Behavior, 76*, 135–148. https://doi.org/10.1016/j.chb.2017.07.016.

11. Pevnick, J. M., Birkeland, K., Zimmer, R., Elad, Y., & Kedan, I., (2018). Wearable technology for cardiology: An update and framework for the future. In: *Trends in Cardiovascular Medicine* (Vol. 28, No. 2, pp. 144–150). Elsevier Inc. https://doi.org/10.1016/j.tcm.2017.08.003.

12. Hung, K., Zhang, Y. T., & Tai, B., (2004). Wearable medical devices for tele-home healthcare. In: *The 26th Annual International Conference of the IEEE Engineering in Medicine and Biology Society* (pp. 5384–5387). doi: 10.1109/IEMBS.2004.1404503.

13. Wright, R., & Keith, L., (2014). Wearable technology: If the tech fits, wear it. *Journal of Electronic Resources in Medical Libraries, 11*(4), 204–216. https://doi.org/10.1080/15424065.2014.969051.

14. Cilliers, L., (2020). Wearable devices in healthcare: Privacy and information security issues. *Health Information Management Journal, 49*(2, 3), 150–156. https://doi.org/10.1177/1833358319851684.

15. Iqbal, S. M. A., Mahgoub, I., Du, E., Leavitt, M. A., & Asghar, W., (2021). Advances in healthcare wearable devices. In: *NPJ Flexible Electronics* (Vol. 5, No.1). Nature Research. https://doi.org/10.1038/s41528-021-00107-x.

16. Lu, L., Zhang, J., Xie, Y., Gao, F., Xu, S., Wu, X., & Ye, Z., (2020). Wearable health devices in health care: Narrative systematic review. In: *JMIR mHealth and uHealth* (Vol. 8, No. 11). JMIR Publications Inc. https://doi.org/10.2196/18907.

17. Zois, M. T., James, I. R., Chris, R. B., & Hamideh, K., (2021). Flexible ferroelectric wearable devices for medical applications. *iScience, 24*(1), 101987, ISSN 2589-0042, https://doi.org/10.1016/j.isci.2020.101987. https://www.sciencedirect.com/science/article/pii/S2589004220311846 (accessed on 10 July 2023).

CHAPTER 6

Edge Computing for Smart Disease Prediction Treatment Therapy

PREETHI NANJUNDAN,[1] W. JAISINGH,[2] and JOSSY P. GEORGE[3]

[1]Assistant Professor, Department of Data Science, Christ University, Lavasa, Pune, Maharashtra, India

[2]School of Computing Science and Engineering, VIT Bhopal University, Bhopal, Madhya Pradesh, India

[3]Department of Data Science, Christ University, Lavasa, Pune, Maharashtra, India

ABSTRACT

Healthcare systems are increasingly seeking to match patients' pace of life and be personalized, as they are demanding more advanced products and services. The only solution for collecting and analyzing health data in real-time is an edge computing (EC) environment, coupled with 5G speeds and modern computing techniques. The technology in healthcare is currently being used to develop smart systems that can expedite the diagnosis of disease and provide precise and timely treatment. The automated hospital monitoring system and medical diagnosis system enable doctors to monitor and diagnose patients from a variety of locations, including hospitals, workplaces, and homes and provide transportation options. As a result, overall doctor visits are reduced as well as patient care is improved. More than 162 billion healthcare IoT devices are expected to be used worldwide by 2021 thanks to the internet of things (IoT) sensors and applications for general healthcare. With edge intelligence (EI), wearable devices with sensors, like smartwatches or smartphones, and gateway devices, such as

Reconnoitering the Landscape of Edge Intelligence in Healthcare.
Suneeta Satpathy, Sachi Nandan Mohanty, and Sirisha Potluri (Eds.)

microcontrollers, can form edge nodes: smart devices with sensors, as well as gateway devices with sensors, can act as edge nodes. Smart sensor devices are typically installed at a greater distance from personal computers (PCs) and servers, which can be utilized in fog computing (FC). In healthcare, EC and FC are used to deliver reliable, low-latency, and location-aware healthcare services by utilizing sensors located within users' reach. Recently, many researchers have proposed using hierarchical computing for the distribution and allocation of inference-based tasks among edge devices and fog nodes, which could lead to an increase in computing power and compute capability of edge devices. For disease prediction, this chapter discusses a variety of EC techniques.

6.1 INTRODUCTION

With the introduction of modern and next-generation healthcare services, new levels of computing power and response time had to be met. As a result, these new devices require more processing power and storage capacity than traditional cloud services can provide [1, 2]. One of the most promising technologies being developed by Bonomia [3] is fog computing (FC). Often referred to as edge computing (EC), the network's edge is populated with computers. Data transmission costs are high, response times are long, and the coverage area is limited as a predecessor to mobile cloud computing (MCC). Using Cloudlet and local clouds, two similar technologies, new devices suffer from inferior quality of service (QoS). Network traffic is high, which causes data transmission costs to be high. Cloudlet-based solutions have shorter latency than MCC solutions, but limited Wi-Fi coverage makes them unable to provide the mobility devices need. Several studies have examined the difference between CC and EC. Recent studies suggest that EC is the only technology that can meet modern requirements for latency [5], mobility [6], and energy efficiency [7]. Based on a study [5], public cloud-based video analytics had a response time more than two times faster than client-based video analytics.

By utilizing EC, healthcare applications can be more effective than traditional CC. Additionally, in addition to reducing the latency associated with traditional computers, edge-based solutions are capable of monitoring vital signs, detecting falls, and checking health trends [8]. Furthermore, caregivers are provided access to data such as blood pressure (BP), pulse rate, and glucose levels with the use of a connected system [9]. A new generation of EC systems makes it possible for healthcare providers to treat chronically ill people in their homes using wearable vital sign sensors combined with ambient sensors located in their homes [10]. They can be used both indoors and outdoors by healthcare workers to determine whether a patient is at risk based on their location. Individuals now have the option of receiving healthcare tailored to their needs through personalized healthcare. Edge devices and nodes must be energy efficient, have location awareness, and meet security standards in order to provide a robust real-time service. Research in this area aims to examine specific methods of information handling that can achieve quality performance in a healthcare system that is edge-based. These methods can be used to classify, authenticate, encrypt, and reduce the size of edge devices by identifying the most effective methods for reducing data.

6.2 A HEALTHCARE SYSTEM THAT INTEGRATES CUTTING-EDGE TECHNOLOGY

Many publications have published surveys about healthcare technology since the mid-2000s. Therefore, these older polls do not include developments like the internet of things (IoT), FC, and 5G, as well as their corresponding requirements. Another issue is the type of architecture as well as the platforms and communication standards used by these applications. In previous surveys, no specific approaches to computing were discussed. In addition to examining the latest research on the best EC platforms, the survey also examines how each of the healthcare requirements is addressed in the survey.

6.3 THE EVOLUTION OF COMPUTERS IN HEALTHCARE

The content in this section describes how healthcare computing functions, as well as why a more distributed architecture is more important than centralized CC, the foundation of edge and FC. The cost, energy efficiency, and overall quality of a hospital's edge healthcare are also considered.

6.3.1 TYPES OF APPLICATIONS IN HEALTHCARE

Healthcare applications can be categorized in several ways. Depending on the type of gadget, the data type, or the particular application case, they can be categorized. There are several healthcare classes based on use cases:

- Monitoring the progress of the population's health in real time;
- Management of emergency situations;
- Mobile devices with health-related capabilities;
- Providing healthcare information to the public.

Monitoring health in real-time can be done with multiple systems at the same time. A smartphone, a wearable sensor, or both can be used to monitor vital signs, for example [10], as shown in Figure 6.1. Unlike real-time health monitoring, emergency monitoring systems send out an alert if a patient's vital signs fall below a certain level. Now, patients can perform diagnostic tests on their mobile devices, thanks to improved devices. The internet provides a great deal of health information, and today mobile applications provide additional health information and counseling, especially for people with chronic illnesses [12]. There are many forms of healthcare available today to the end-user:

- Sensors are worn by humans – mobile devices;
- Sensors in the environment.

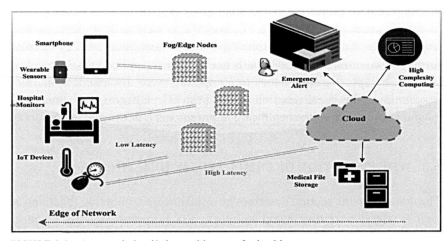

FIGURE 6.1   A general cloud/edge architecture for healthcare.
Source: Reprinted from Ref. [11]

In contrast to traditional methods of glucose testing like finger pricks, wearable sensors are able to detect aberrant body functions like heart rate, BP, and heat much faster. A sensor's data is frequently transferred over a long distance to a server from an EC application. Medical applications can be developed using smartphone sensors, such as microphones and gyros

[13]. Wearables and smartphones do not require the user to wear devices, but environmental sensors do. They are positioned throughout a room or a group of rooms to capture information about the user's location. Using this arrangement is more convenient and is commonly employed in applications such as fall monitoring or geriatric location tracking during dementia situations. Depending on their specialization, indoor ambient sensors can function independently, or can work alongside outdoor location sensors.

6.4 WEARABLE TECHNOLOGY USING EDGE COMPUTING (EC)

During the last few years, wearable technology has advanced rapidly. According to International Data Corporation [14], wearable shipments are projected to increase 12.4% annually over the next five years, from 396.0 million units in 2020 to 637.1 million units in 2024. Wearable gadgets, as opposed to smartphones, are always close to the body, allowing them to detect directly from it or interact with it without needing a lot of manual interaction. As compared to smartphones, wearable gadgets, such as smartwatches, wristbands, and smart glasses, greatly improve the quality of life. With the Mi Smart Band 5 [15], for example, the user's heart rate can be monitored throughout the day and vibrates to remind them of their health status. The device will vibrate to alert the user if the heart rate is abnormally high. Apple Watches use an accelerometer sensor to automatically record motion data when a user falls. The device will place an emergency call if the user remains immobile for more than a minute after detecting a fall. Wearables can be used while being worn, which is their distinguishing characteristic.

In contrast, wearables have the downside of being worn while being used. Wearable gadgets must fit well and be light in order for users to feel comfortable wearing them. The technology in wearables may have to be low-end to adhere to these size and weight constraints. Weaker batteries, for instance, use a lot of energy because they are small. For continuous service, the charging frequency should be every 18 hours (such as for Apple Watch Series 6 [16]). Due to their limited computing capabilities, most commercially available wearables cannot support delay-sensitive applications. Examples include fall detection using wearables and simultaneous localization and mapping (SLAM) in headsets.

The provision of external resources through communication technologies is a promising method of addressing the challenges for wearables. Through MCC, data storage and processing can be done on mobile devices directly from remote clouds [19], it would be possible to improve resource-constrained mobile devices without adding weight or size. There are many examples of MCC being used in mobile applications (e.g., MCC-based search [20], the payment service [21], and so on), but based on several unique character-istics of wearable devices and wearable applications, MCC is not suitable for many wearable applications. As a starting point, many applications for wearable devices must operate in real-time, such as monitors for users' health emergencies [22]. An MCC paradigm explains how data is uploaded to the cloud through inconsistencies in the internet connection, resulting in significant fluctuating speeds. The second advantage of smartwatch apps is that many use data provided by sensors continuously as input [23, 24]. This would place considerable strain on the Internet's bandwidth if such large volumes of data were uploaded to the mobile cloud.

The emerging paradigm of EC can address MCC's limitations while still giving wearables resources. A multi-access edge computing (MEC) applica-tion is described in this survey as EC. According to the European Telecom-munication Standards Institute (ETSI) [25], multi-access EC is a computing concept, which enables IT service environments and CC capabilities to be implemented on access networks. In this chapter, edge gateways will be referred to as devices that provide EC capabilities. Compared with central-ized cloud servers, the decentralized architecture of MEC allows wearables to be connected to the Internet via edge gateways, resulting in lower latency, jitter, and Internet overhead.

6.5   COMPUTING AT THE CUTTING EDGE OF DISEASE PREDICTION

A number of applications can be developed using EC, such as video analysis, content distribution, and smart city applications. Using traffic management, smart cars, personal digital assistants (PDA), surveillance, and augmented reality (AR) as examples, Ananthanarayanan et al. [26] identified five possible applications for video analysis. Edge gateways offer the potential for low latency data processing. Content distribution networks (CDNs) could also help achieve this. In order to reduce overall network latency, static resources are deployed on the intermediate server close to clients. There are many sensors in a smart city that generate significant amounts of data each day. A majority of raw data is processed at the edge [27] in order to reduce transmission overhead.

Contrary to CC, which generally only consists of a central cloud layer and a layer on the end device, EC is a more integrated approach. The second layer also has an edge gateway component. Information about each layer is provided in the following sections (Figure 6.2).

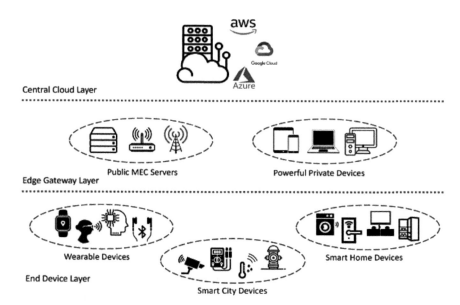

FIGURE 6.2 A diagram illustrating an edge-computing architecture.

Source: Reprinted with permission from Ref. [28]. Copyright © 2021 Elsevier Inc.

There is a wide range of end devices in the end device layer, including wearable devices, smart city devices, and smart home devices. They all have several characteristics in common. There are many devices that use sensors to continuously provide measurements of the physical world. Such sensors can generate data that can be used as input by many applications [26]. The majority of COTS wearables include accelerometers [29, 30], and most smart speakers come with microphones [38, 39]. As a second factor, these devices are usually built with fewer resources than general-purpose computers in order to enable widespread use at an affordable price. According to the report, the most widely used smart cameras have a single CPU core, run at speeds between 1 and 1.4 GHz, and have 64 MB to 256 MB of RAM.

A number of edge gateways are located near end devices, and they have some of the latest resources at their disposal. Several studies have examined how computation could be offloaded from end devices to edge gateways as resource-constrained end devices may not be able to process continuously generated sensor data in real-time. Within the edge gateway layer, MEC servers are classified into two types: public MEC servers such as network routers, base stations, and servers that support MEC, and powerful private devices such as smartphones, tablets, and laptops. Several findings have been documented regarding public MEC servers [34, 35], while others have focused on powerful private devices [34, 35].

6.6   THE IMPLEMENTATION OF A SMART REMOTE BMI MONITORING FRAMEWORK USING GAIT-BASED EDGE COMPUTING (EC)

According to [36], body mass is calculated as a ratio of height squared in meters to body mass in kilograms. An abnormal BMI is associated with increased risks as we age. Based on a report published by WHO [37], BMI class is categorized differently among different races and ages. However, an average rule of thumb measures BMI as follows: Below 18.5 Kgm^2 is "underweight," between 18.5 and 25 is "normal," between 25 and 30 is "overweight," and over 30 is "obese." Over the years, BMI has been linked to an individual's overall health and well-being. Death rates have been associated with BMI categories outside of the normal range [38]. Though there are a number of reasons why someone is underweight, including medical conditions, genetic disorders, and high metabolic rates, malnutrition, and excessive physical activity are the most common causes. Osteoporosis causes bones to become brittle and easily break in overweight people compared to underweight people. As a result of malnutrition, an underweight person may suffer dry skin, hair loss, poor dental health, irregular menstruation, early menopause, infertility, and weakened immunity [39]. While obesity tends to result from a combination of unhealthy eating habits and insufficient physical activity, as well as insulin and leptin resistance, a slowed metabolism, and the use of anabolic steroids, obesity is primarily caused by an unhealthy diet and a non-physical activity lifestyle. An increase in body weight is related to an increase in cardiovascular disease, hypertension, high blood sugar, various types of arthritis, sleep apnea, and breathing problems, among others [40]. Having an overweight BMI can affect your overall health and even your lifespan, so monitoring it is important [41].

Various biological signal processing techniques are used to analyze walking patterns, which is referred to as gait analysis. It is possible to determine the magnitude and other risk factors associated with any neuromusculoskeletal disorder through further examination of the gait pattern [42]. Body mass index (BMI) is one such health indicator that can be used for this purpose. We discovered that the BMI category can be calculated using gait after conducting an extensive investigation. It is possible to use a number of data gathering and processing methodologies in order to study this effect. Among the most widely used data collection strategies are video-based, sensor-based, and custom environments [43]. However, video-based technologies are computationally complex and require proper synchronization to be effective, making them difficult to implement. Customizing environments for gait tracking, on the other hand, is extremely accurate but very expensive and does not move with the wearer. A sensor-based technique can be implemented relatively quickly and requires little computational effort [44, 45]. Our experiment to detect BMI categories was conducted using a smartphone equipped with built-in accelerometers and gyroscopes.

Client-server-based health monitoring and device native monitoring have traditionally been used in remote health monitoring. Data collected by sensors on a local level is sent to a client-server, which analyzes it and returns the results. As a key disadvantage of this strategy, it fails to function without the internet, and it is also limited in its diagnostic capabilities when the latency is minimal. These systems have substantial maintenance costs since the server is responsible for the bulk of the processing. Most of these systems are centralized, so when there is a problem with the master node, the entire configuration ceases to work [46]. Additionally, server scalability limits their ability to handle an increasing workload. Scalability is also a concern since it limits the capacity of the servers to process increasing loads. As an alternative, a device native technique sees the model available on the device, but without using the server. The application has a lower latency and can be used without an internet connection, but it does not perform better over time when detecting new threats. EC was used to achieve this. The data gathered from the source is analyzed at the source, which reduces latency, and is synchronized across all the peer devices, allowing overall model performance to be improved. The model can also be updated at the device level to make EC more fault-tolerant, as can replication of the server. Therefore, the system still operates even if some nodes go down or if the internet is shut down on the data source devices [48].

Using deep learning (DL) or traditional machine learning (ML) techniques can help construct smarter decision-making systems. On the other hand, DL demands large amounts of data, as well as a lot of computing power in order to train the model. Sometimes it may be impossible to acquire this information or power. By contrast, ML models that are more conventional might be developed with fewer data points, but as the amount of training data points increases, they either grow more deficient or progressively slower [49]. ML methods that are incremental can therefore be used to solve this problem. These methods allow the model to be trained with a minimum amount of data in the shortest amount of time. By adding more and more training data points, the performance of the model will improve. A notable algorithm in this regard is stochastic gradient descent [50]. To minimize the contrast between the obtained and actual results, the cost function is iteratively optimized to find the global minima. Using these methods, a reliable framework can be created for a quick and fault-tolerant remote health monitoring system that can be enhanced over time without rewriting the model. A total of 30 healthy adult human participants provided their consent for the experiment. EC and incremental ML were used to process the data collected by an accelerometer and gyroscope. With very little load, models can be deployed and trained in live production environments without requiring a lot of data. As a result, fault tolerance and system performance are improved. In Figure 6.3, the workflow for the BMI category detection framework is summarized.

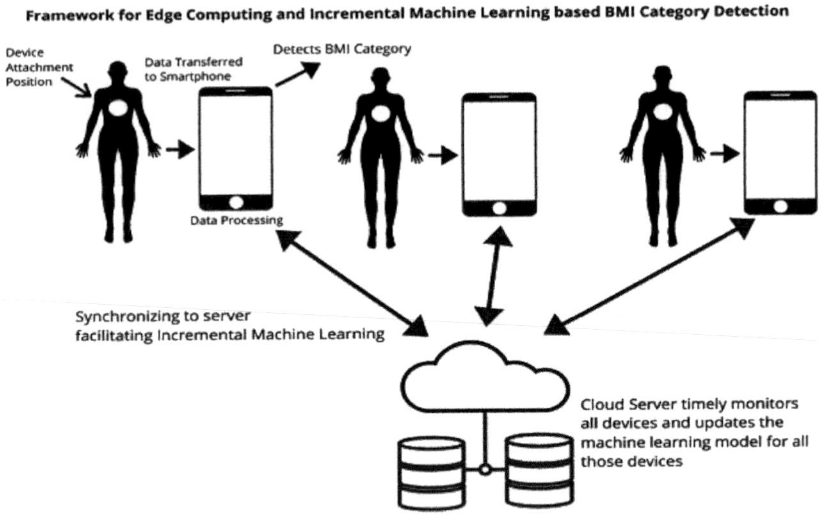

Framework for Edge Computing and Incremental Machine Learning based BMI Category Detection

FIGURE 6.3   Model for detecting categories of BMI using edge computing and incremental machine learning.

6.7 THE DEVELOPMENT OF A SMART HEALTHCARE SYSTEM THAT PREDICTS ACTIVITY LEVELS THROUGH WEARABLE SENSORS

In recent years, technologies (such as the IoT and the cloud of things) have played an increasingly significant role in healthcare. Consequently, they can develop smart healthcare solutions with smart services in various settings, such as the home, office, and hospital. The vast system would utilize many IoT devices and sensors. The cloud is used to process huge amounts of data collected by devices and sensors, to provide high-performance computing and extensive data storage. Using CC and the internet of things (Cloud-IoT), healthcare systems can be made more practical for real-time applications. Although huge amounts of data are generated by healthcare devices and sensors, handling them is still a major challenge. Recent research has suggested that edge-of-things (EoT) computing can reduce the burden on clouds by operating between sensors and clouds. As a result, the computation of sensor data is done locally on devices like smartphones, computers, and smart routers rather than in the cloud. EC and storage functions are mainly provided at a small scale. An edge device, such as a laptop or a personal computer, is used in this work to process various types of sensor data.

Various industries, including entertainment, security, and medicine, are beginning to adopt wearable sensors. Such sensors are capable of detecting people's conduct correctly. Consequently, the sensors may be used and investigated to provide a healthy living environment. Accordingly, wearable sensors could change our lives in a similar way to how personal computers (PCs) changed ours. A wearable sensor, known as a panic button, has been tested for commercial purposes and deemed successful [54]. It is essential the user is aware and physically capable of using the panic button.

The button should also be lightweight and comfortable to wear. Scientists in the medical field, especially those interested in monitoring physiological activity, have recently turned to wearable sensors. Monitoring vital signs such as body temperature and heart rate can be done with medical apps [54]. Wearable sensors should be light enough to allow them to be worn on the body for regular medical monitoring.

Using wearable sensors, patients who suffer from heart attacks and Parkinson's can receive appropriate therapy at home. Frequently, patients undergo a rehabilitation phase after surgery in which they must follow a strict regimen. With wearable sensors, the wearer can monitor all of the patient's physiological signals as well as their actions. Through the wearable sensors, rehabilitative services may be provided, such as auditory feedback. These services may be customized for each patient. Monitoring the patient's health and behavior is possible by doctors or caretakers [55].

With wearable sensors used to monitor behavior, much is currently being done to build smart systems, such as ones that detect older people falling at home [56]. Wearable gadgets are becoming more popular commercially. The number of electronics in gadgets such as heart rate monitors, smartwatches, and smart eyewear from Google, for instance, is rapidly increasing. Wearable technology may influence future innovations in medicine, for instance, by helping to better define the doctor-patient relationship and reduce healthcare costs. According to their rapid expansion, wearable technologies will continue to be adopted by various industries, including healthcare.

Context-aware systems have recently gained attention for applications in various domains [57]. People's activities may be better understood by better integrating perception and thinking. Several fields are becoming increasingly important to the study of human behavior, including ubiquitous and mobile computing, surveillance-based security, context-aware computing, health, and ambient assisted living. It is essential to recognize and improve health systems by understanding body postures and movements. Avci et al. evaluated several applications of activity pattern recognition to healthcare, wellness, and sports systems [58]. Examples of HAR integration with wearable sensors are healthcare monitoring and diagnosis, rehabilitation systems for determining the relationship between movement and emotion, and child and senior care. They also studied the benefits of assisted living and home monitoring systems for ensuring the safety, well-being, and medical care of children, the elderly, and those with cognitive disabilities. According to Preece et al., correlations were established between prevalent illnesses and physical activity levels using activity classification methods [57, 58]. Researchers are also investigating ways to better diagnose and treat neurological and respiratory illnesses by monitoring everyday activity patterns. By quantifying the degrees of physical activity, other methods provide users with feedback and motivation to reach physical fitness goals. Using smartphone sensors as a way to assess energy consumption in free-living situations by identifying physical activities, Guidoux et al. [59] described a method. Assistive technology and health systems can also make use of activity prediction to provide individualized care.

At present, there are two main methods for analyzing activity patterns: video and other sensors. Most video-based techniques are based on camera-captured image sequences [60]. The quality of the images determines the system's performance. People are frequently concerned about privacy when it comes to video surveillance.

Contrary to this, other sensor-based methods are often free of these challenges [61]. The disadvantages of these methods are numerous. Sensors, for example, can be inconvenient if they are worn for an extended period of time. Battery power consumption is another concern. Input data for wearable sensors, however, is often contaminated by noise due to faults in the sensors or environmental disturbances. Input data can therefore only be used for limited purposes. The use of solid and robust ML algorithms that can cope with noisy data is important for the creation of an activity prediction system.

Modeling time-sequential patterns in input data with Hidden Markov models (HMMs) is common [62]. DL algorithms have recently attracted the attention of experts in pattern recognition [63]. In the field of pattern recognition, deep belief networks (DBNs) were the first DL systems to show successful results [63]. In contrast to a traditional big artificial neural network, DBN training is much faster with RBM. Convolutional Neural Networks (CNN) are also popular due to their superior discriminative capabilities over DBNs. Convolutional neural networks (CNNs) are a type of DL that combines feature extraction and convolutional stacking to construct an abstract feature hierarchy. An effective CNN must perform convolution, pooling, tangent squashing, rectifier, and normalization [63]. DL based on CNNs is primarily used in visual applications, such as the recognition of objects in large images. Since CNN is best suited for decoding single image-based pattern recognition rather than time-sequential inputs, it is not widely applied to time-sequenced inputs. Recurrent Neural Networks (RNNs) however can offer better discrimination than DBNs or CNNs since they can store and learn temporal sequential information very effectively [64]. In order to simulate different activities in wearable sensor data, this study uses RNN.

Figure 6.4 illustrates a typical cloud-based healthcare service. A sink or edge device receives and transmits body sensor data to a broker for health services. Verifying the user's hospital authentication and extracting features from sensor data is done by the healthcare service broker. Following this, the characteristics are tested against the taught DL model, which associates with the user's state of health. A health service broker may suggest a family doctor, relatives, or an emergency department to the user, if necessary. The whole process involves many departments. In this way, an edge device that is computationally powerful can make judgments and process data, instead of just delivering it to the broker machine [65]. Especially when it comes to limited healthcare services, such as identifying daily activities and detecting falls, this might make the process quicker than usual. During the healthcare process, it also limits the possibility of the user's data being sent between multiple clouds.

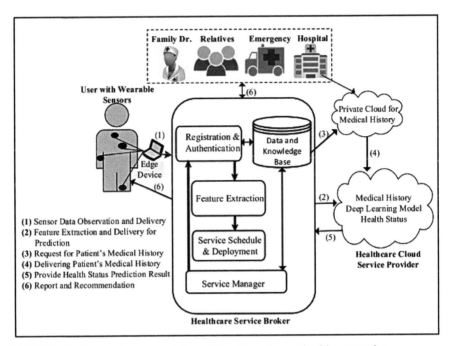

FIGURE 6.4   Schematic representation of cloud-based smart healthcare service.

Source: Reprinted with permission from Ref. [66]. Copyright © 2018 Elsevier Inc.

6.8   AN EDGE ENVIRONMENT FOR PREDICTING EARLY-STAGE ILLNESSES BASED ON MACHINE LEARNING (ML)

A new subfield of digital epidemiology healthcare has recently been pioneered by ML [67]. Researchers have explored epidemiology as a scientific method of predicting the chances of many causes causing disease [68]. Since medical data patterns are complicated and vast, epidemiologists typically handle a large amount of health data [67]. In healthcare applications, ML requires a high level of accuracy despite the fact that they are increasingly used in predictive healthcare systems. A creative original framework is needed to achieve high levels of accuracy for such predictive systems.

A number of current academic approaches have been developed and approved to improve the credibility of medical and healthcare apps [71]. It has long been thought that feature selection improves healthcare data mining accuracy. The computation of features (CFS) and medical features selection (MFS) have been shown, in particular, to lead to an increase in the capability of choosing prospective features while maintaining a reasonable level of accuracy [72]. Though MFS is positioned as a medical knowledge-driven method, future automated healthcare systems will need clear guidelines for how to utilize domain expert knowledge. Healthcare decision-making based on association rules and ontologies, on the other hand, has been studied and analyzed as one of the best methods to deploy and implement predictive healthcare systems [73].

Medical researchers and the general public recognize that there is a scientific link between illnesses and epidemiological characteristics [68], but there is still no foundation for effective predictive healthcare based on ML. A framework based on association rules can reduce this by applying epidemiological ontology. ML systems with adequate predictive abilities are still in their infancy in digital epidemiological healthcare [74]. The chapter thus provides a framework of ontologies that takes into account epidemiological aspects and helps future dependable systems predict the likelihood of getting a disease at an early stage based on epidemiological data.

6.9 BY OFFLOADING EDGE COMPUTING (EC) TASKS, MACHINE LEARNING (ML) CAN BE USED IN SMART HEALTHCARE

As technology becomes more widespread and sophisticated, ML can play an important role in smart healthcare, particularly in offloading EC tasks. Mobile devices with multifunctional abilities, such as smartphones, smartwatches, smart glasses, and health sensors, are gaining traction in the market [75, 76]. Intelligent IoT and IoT-based applications are affecting our lives in a number of different domains, like smart homes, smart cities, agriculture, food, and healthcare, factories, green energy, disaster management, emergency management, and aerospace. The types of challenges faced by these applications vary depending on their application area, such as scaling, privacy, security, usability, and energy efficiency.

Even though edge devices like smartphones are gaining computational power (such as when a coronavirus disease 2019 (COVID-19) was reported) [78], it is still necessary to offload tasks to other devices. A growing number of smart services are being offered on the market due to the proliferation of IoT applications. As a result of learning, intelligence is achieved, which is highly dependent upon the amount of data received by the computer [79]. The edge devices' energy is depleted when they are carrying a lot of data [80]. Additionally, there are some tasks that are too resource-intensive for modern smartphones or edge devices. Therefore, it becomes necessary to offload some functions from resource-constrained edge nodes to higher level computing devices, such as the cloud, fog, or a federation of edge devices called a Femto-cloud [78].

Cloud-based chores are usually the default option, but they have a number of drawbacks. Cloud service providers need large datacenters to reliably provide compute and storage resources. This means CC is more expensive at first. As a result of its wide availability across the public network, reaching out to the cloud compromises privacy as well [81]. There is no need to send all of the data over public networks, which consume a lot of bandwidth. Perform a number of functions locally to reduce the need for unnecessary communications across the main network.

A Using local nodes such as fog and edge has a number of drawbacks. By transmitting only, the essential data, offloading to fog or edge reduces communication costs. Cloud resources outpace those of fog and edge devices. When you need a lot of computing or storage power (like for complex machine-learning tasks, long-term data storage, or data security), you use the cloud.

The offloading of tasks will eventually depend on a system that is smart enough to know which tasks are best sent to the cloud, local fog, or a felt cloud. There are no offloading options for local tasks. The tasks that are concerned with privacy or cost and involve basic ML should be handled using locally available resources, such as household edge devices. And last but not least, the cloud is a good option for storing data and performing sophisticated ML operations. To demonstrate the importance of a system like this in this study, we use case studies from the healthcare industry. A system may be used in several locations, such as at home, on public transportation, and abroad, to perform machine-learning activities required for healthcare applications. IoT devices and cloud services are connected by middleware entities. As part of this work, (middleware) entities such as fog can serve as micro- or nano-datacenters, edge services, felt clouds, MEC, and cloudlets can also be used.

6.9.1 *POTENTIAL APPLICATIONS OF SMART HEALTHCARE POWERED BY MACHINE LEARNING (ML)*

Our goal in this chapter is to explain how we can use smart devices to improve healthcare services. Smart devices can opportunistically support health treatments that would otherwise be unavailable, lack privacy protection, or are not affordable. There is an average of 5.5 people in every home in the world [83] who are involved in healthcare services that are concerned about privacy. Africa and Asia, the world's most populous regions, have homes that may contain up to nine people [83]. The average person owns 6.58 gadgets, according to Statista(.com). By combining the resources of these devices, several applications can be developed for a home that otherwise would require the use of expensive high-end computers. Privacy remains an issue with healthcare applications. When household devices are used to enhance healthcare applications (such as evolutionary intelligence), a high level of privacy can be ensured (since personal data isn't transmitted over a public network) and customization is possible (as the application is tailored to the needs of each individual user).

6.9.2 CONVOLUTIONAL GRAPH NETWORKS WITH EDGE-VARIATIONAL PROPERTIES FOR DISEASE PREDICTION

As multimodal clinical data continues to increase, learning models that integrate imaging data with non-imaging measures (e.g., age, gender, and genomic data) are becoming increasingly necessary for computer-aided diagnosis (CAD) systems to improve the accuracy of disease prediction. Collaborations have taken place on an international scale, such as the International Neuroimaging Data-sharing Initiative (INDI) and the Alzheimer's Disease Neuroimaging Initiative (ADNI), to collect large cohorts of clinical, demographic, genomic, and behavioral data to discover effective biomarkers for better understanding disease mechanisms and predicting disease progression [86]. Various diagnostic applications can use image data to monitor pathology, assess the health of a subject, etc. Non-imaging data, on the other hand, can be used to identify relationships between different patients in a community, which may then be combined with imaging data for the purpose of predicting illness. A computational model that can jointly combine imaging and non-imaging data is crucial for using the growing amount of multi-modal medical data, which will ultimately lead to more accurate illness prediction.

Despite convolution neural networks (CNNs)' being powerful at learning representations and outperforming humans at many tasks related to natural and medical image analysis [88], combining and learning from both imaging and non-imaging datasets of a population is a challenging and time-consuming process. Combining several techniques (usually via concatenation) and then applying a deep neural network is a common method of achieving multimodal learning. The histopathologic characteristics based on histology pictures were correlated with the genomic features using VGG19 [90] and concatenation [89]. A multilayer perceptron (MLP) is used to classify Glioma cancer from its combined characteristics. A sequence of joint layers is created by concatenating the characteristics of the Cervi gram picture and several clinical tests of a person. Xu et al. [91] use the same method to predict cervical dysplasia. Unfortunately, this method does not explicitly model interactions and associations among individuals within the same population, which might provide additional insight into disease severity or explain data heterogeneity (by accounting for the location and protocol of data collection, for example).

By modeling population-based illnesses as graph nodes and edges, graph learning-based models provide another perspective on how to approach the problem of predicting population-based illnesses. Graph convolutional neural networks (GCN) have also been extended to work with irregular graph data [93] through recent research on GCN [92]. Contrary to this, graph convolutional networks have shown remarkable promise for the semi-supervised learning of node classification in transudative scenarios, when only a portion of the graph can be used to train the network. A high level of representation of graph data's node connections was developed by Kipf and Welling [94] using the Renormalization Trick. The graph convolutional network uses graph attention networks (GATs), which apply learned attention (weights) to the edges of a node in graph convolution. The technique is described by Velickovi c' et al. [95]. Rather than training embedded vectors for each node in order to yield node embeddings from unseen data, GraphSAGE [96] learns an aggregator function that aggregates characteristics of a node's immediate neighborhood in order to create new node embeddings. Since GraphSAGE is typically better at generalizing unweighted graph data, it can be used in high-throughput, production ML systems. This type of encoder-decoder architecture comprises an unpooling layer that matches the graph pooling layer that unpools the top k largest projected nodes, and an encoder-decoder architecture that makes encoder-decoder architecture such as U-Nets applicable to graph data. There is a novel form of graph pooling and unpooling layer proposed in Ref. [98] to resolve the gradient vanishing problem in graph U-Nets.

6.9.3 *SEVERAL ALGORITHMS USE MACHINE LEARNING (ML) AND DEEP LEARNING (DL) APPROACHES TO PREDICT CARDIO-VASCULAR DISEASES (CVD)*

Heart and blood vessel diseases (CVDs) are disorders that affect the human heart and blood vessels. Blood can also accumulate in the arteries of the kidneys, the heart, the eyes, and the brain. Across the world, cardiovascular disease is a leading cause of death among both industrialized nations and developing nations. The risk of developing it, however, can be greatly reduced by adopting a healthy lifestyle.

Cardiovascular diseases can be grouped into four categories. Coronary heart disease (CHD) results from a blockage of the blood flow to the heart muscle. This extra strain on the heart can lead to angina, heart attacks, and heart failure. A transient is chemic attack (TIA) is caused by a blockage of blood flow to the brain, resulting in a temporary disruption of blood flow to the brain. A peripheral arterial disease is characterized by the obstruction of blood flow to the limbs, which is caused by arterial blockage. A result of this is that legs become painful, hair falls out, limbs are weak, and ulcers form. One of the largest blood vessels is affected by the Aortic Disease, our final category.

Plaque, a waxy substance that forms inside the coronary arteries, is responsible for coronary artery disease (CAD) and CHD. In addition to causing major health problems, a heart attack can even kill you, because it is the leading cause of death worldwide.

There are a variety of ways in which CVD can develop even though its specific cause has yet to be identified. Numerous factors can increase the risk of CVD. Factors affecting BP, smoking, cholesterol, diabetes, obesity, and family history are among the most influential.

The key to preventing CVD is identifying those who are at risk. For disease prediction, scientists have shifted their focus to data mining, ML, and DL methodology due to the limitations of manual detection of cardiac disorders. The [2] have proved useful in assisting decision-making and forecasting from the massive amount of data generated by the healthcare industry.

CVD can be diagnosed using a variety of lab tests and imaging examinations. The most important aspects of diagnosis are the patient's medical and family history, risk factors, and physical examination. Statistical data can be used to correlate results and processes and predict the occurrence of illness. With DL and automation, doctors can make better decisions.

Disease prediction automation can enable the acquisition of structured data and efficient patient treatment from a single platform. This increases the standard of care for individuals. By using artificial intelligence (AI) and ML, computers can be trained to recognize patterns in which disease arises and translate them into structured data that can be used to predict disease.

Electronic health records (EHR), revenue cycle, and operations can be improved using this innovation. As it becomes more integrated with clinical workflows and current technologies, practitioners will be able to access real-time data at the point of care.

6.10 CONCLUSION

Global population growth is resulting in a rapid increase in the number of elderly people, increasing healthcare expenses. In the future, healthcare technology will allow people to monitor their health without requiring them to be hospitalized. A sensor device that continuously monitors human activity is now feasible thanks to advances in sensor technology. Smart wearable gadgets have gained popularity as a result of their unique ability to be worn while using them. Despite the criteria for small size and light weight, most wearable goods do not have sufficient on-device resources, which stymies wearable technology advancement. While staying within their weight and size limits, wearable devices can access more resources with EC. An edge device's graphics processing unit (GPU) is utilized to calculate experimental data quickly.

KEYWORDS

- **automated medical diagnosis systems**
- **cardio-vascular diseases**
- **deep learning**
- **edge computing**
- **healthcare system**
- **machine learning**
- **smart devices, sensors**
- **surveillance frameworks**

REFERENCES

1. Liu, L., Yang, Y., Zhao, W., & Du, Z., (2015). Semi-automatic remote medicine monitoring system of miners. In: *Adjunct Proceedings of the 2015 ACM International Joint Conference on Pervasive and Ubiquitous Computing and Proceedings of the 2015*

ACM International Symposium on Wearable Computers Ubicomp/ISWC'15 Adjunct. ACM; New York, NY, USA: 93–96.

2. Kumar, K., & Lu, Y. H., (2010). Cloud computing for mobile users: Can offloading computation save energy? *Computer, 43*(4), 51–56. doi: 10.1109/MC.2010.98.

3. Bonomi, F., Milito, R., Zhu, J., & Addepalli, S., (2012). Fog computing and its role in the internet of things. In: *Proceedings of the First Edition of the MCC Workshop on Mobile Cloud Computing MCC '12* (pp. 13–16). ACM; New York, NY, USA.

4. Maitra, A., & Kuntagod, N., (2013). A novel mobile application to assist maternal health workers in rural India. In: *2013 5th International Workshop on Software Engineering in Health Care (SEHC)* (pp. 75–78).

5. Yi, S., Hao, Z., Zhang, Q., Zhang, Q., Shi, W., & Li, Q., (2017). LAVEA: Latency-aware video analytics on edge computing platform. In: *Proceedings of the Second ACM/IEEE Symposium on Edge Computing SEC* (Vol. 17, pp. 15:1–15:13). ACM; New York, NY, USA.

6. Thiyagaraja, S. R., Dantu, R., Shrestha, P. L., Thompson, M. A., & Smith, C., (2017). Optimized and secured transmission and retrieval of vital signs from remote devices. In: *Proceedings of the Second IEEE/ACM International Conference on Connected Health: Applications, Systems and Engineering Technologies CHASE '17* (pp. 25–30). IEEE Press; Piscataway, NJ, USA.

7. Miettinen, A. P., & Nurminen, J. K. (2010) Energy Efficiency of Mobile Clients in Cloud Computing. *Proceedings of the 2nd USENIX Conference on Hot Topics in Cloud Computing, HotCloud'10,* Boston, 22–25 June 2010, 4.

8. Bhargava, K., & Ivanov, S., (2017). A fog computing approach for localization in WSN. In: *2017 IEEE 28th Annual International Symposium on Personal, Indoor, and Mobile Radio Communications (PIMRC)* (pp. 1–7).

9. Yoon, J., (2017). Leveraging sensor data content to assure sensor device trustworthiness in mobile edge computing. In: *2017 Second International Conference on Fog and Mobile Edge Computing (FMEC)* (pp. 147–152).

10. Chung, K., & Park, R. C., (2017). Cloud based u-healthcare network with QoS guarantee for mobile health service. *Cluster Computing.*

11. Morghan, H., Umair, S. H., & Ali, I. (2019). Edge computing in smart health care systems: Review, challenges, and research directions. *Transactions on Emerging Telecommunications Technologies.*

12. Smith, W., Wadley, G., Daly, O., et al., (2017). Designing an app for pregnancy care for a culturally and linguistically diverse community. In: *Proceedings of the 29th Australian Conference on Computer-Human Interaction OZCHI '17* (pp. 337–346). ACM; New York, NY, USA.

13. Thiyagaraja, S. R., Vempati, J., Dantu, R., Sarma, T., & Dantu, S., (2014). Smart phone monitoring of second heart sound split. In: *2014 36th Annual International Conference of the IEEE Engineering in Medicine and Biology Society* (pp. 2181–2184).

14. Worldwide Wearables Market Forecast to Maintain Double – Digit Growth in 2020 and Through 2024, According to IDC, https://www.businesswire.com/news/home/20200925005409/en/Worldwide-Wearables-Market-Forecast-to-Maintain-Double-Digit-Growth-in-2020-and-Through-2024-According-to-IDC (accessed on 10 August 2023).

15. *Mi Smart Band 5*, https://www.mi.com/global/mi-smart-band-5/specs/ (accessed on 10 July 2023).

16. *Apple Watch Series 6* – Technical Specifications, https://support.apple.com/kb/SP826 (accessed on 10 July 2023).

17. De Quadros, T., Lazzaretti, A. E., & Schneider, F. K., (2018). A movement decomposition and machine learning-based fall detection system using wrist wearable device. *IEEE Sens. J. 18*(12), 5082–5089.

18. Ben, A. A. J., Hashemifar, Z. S., & Dantu, K., (2020). Edge-SLAM: Edge-assisted visual simultaneous localization and mapping. In: *Proceedings of the 2020 ACM MobiSys* (pp. 325–337). ACM, New York, NY, USA.

19. Dinh, H. T., Lee, C., Niyato, D., & Wang, P., (2013). A survey of mobile cloud computing: Architecture, applications, and approaches. *Wirel. Commun. Mob. Comput., 13*(18), 1587–1611.

20. Kim, Y., (2015). *Mobile Terminal and Photo Searching Method Thereof.* https://patents.google.com/patent/US9043318B2 (accessed on 10 July 2023).

21. Belpaire, A., & Natu, A., (2017). *Cloud Based Payment Method.* https://patents.google.com/patent/US9672513B2 (accessed on 10 July 2023).

22. Gusev, M., Stojmenski, A., & Guseva, A., (2017). ECGalert: A heart attack alerting system, in: Trajanov, D., & Bakeva, V., (eds.), *Proceedings of the 2017 International Conference on ICT Innovations* (pp. 27–36). Springer, Cham, Switzerland.

23. Concone, F., Re, G. L., & Morana, M., (2019). A fog-based application for human activity recognition using personal smart devices. *ACM Trans. Internet. Technol., 19*(2), 1–20.

24. Samie, F., Bauer, L., & Henkel, J., (2020). Hierarchical classification for constrained IoT devices: A case study on human activity recognition. *IEEE Int. Things J., 7*(9), 8287–8295.

25. ETSI GS MEC 001 – V2.1.1. https://www.etsi.org/deliver/etsi_gs/mec/001_099/001/02.01.01_60/gs_mec001v020101p.pdf (accessed on 10 July 2023).

26. Ananthanarayanan, G., Bahl, P., Bodík, P., Chintalapudi, K., Philipose, M., Ravindranath, L., & Sinha, S., (2017). Real-time video analytics: The Killer App for edge computing. *Computer 50*(10), 58–67.

27. Arasteh, H., Hosseinnezhad, V., Loia, V., Tommasetti, A., Troisi, O., Shafie-khah, M., & Siano, P., (2016). IoT-based smart cities: A survey. In: *Proceedings of the 2016 IEEE EEEIC* (pp. 1–6). IEEE, New York, NY, USA.

28. Xinqi, J., Lingkun, L., Fan, D., Xinlei, C., & Yunhao, L. (2022). *A Survey on Edge Computing for Wearable Technology.* https://doi.org/10.1016/j.dsp.2021.103146.

29. Microsoft Hololens, https://www.microsoft.com/en-us/hololens (accessed on 10 July 2023).

30. *AirPods Max* – Technical Specifications – Apple, https://www.apple.com/airpods-max/specs/ (accessed on 10 July 2023).

31. Li, Y., Padmanabhan, A., Zhao, P., Wang, Y., Xu, G. H., & Netravali, R., (2020). Reducto: On camera filtering for resource-efficient real-time video analytics. In: *Proceedings of the 2020 ACM SIGCOMM* (pp. 359–376). ACM, New York, NY, USA.

32. Yousefpour, A., Ishigaki, G., Gour, R., & Jue, J. P., (2018). On reducing IoT service delay via fog offloading. *IEEE Int. Things J., 5*(2), 998–1010.

33. Wang, K., Tan, Y., Shao, Z., Ci, S., & Yang, Y., (2019). Learning-based task offloading for delay-sensitive applications in dynamic fog networks. *IEEE Trans. Veh. Technol., 68*(11), 11399–11403.

34. Al-Zinati, M., Almasri, T., Alsmirat, M., & Jararweh, Y., (2020). Enabling multiple health security threats detection using mobile edge computing. *Simul. Model. Pract. Theory, 101*, 101957.

35. Yang, Y., Geng, Y., Qiu, L., Hu, W., & Cao, G., (2017). Context-aware task offloading for wearable devices. In: *Proceedings of the 2017 IEEE ICCCN* (pp. 1–9). IEEE, New York, NY, USA.

36. Fryar, C. D., Kruszon-Moran, D., Gu, Q., & Ogden, C. L., (2018). Mean body weight, height, waist circumference, and body mass index among adults: United States, 1999–2000 through 2015–2016. *National Health Statistics Reports*, (122), 1–16.

37. *Body Mass Index* – Wikipedia. (2019). https://en.wikipedia.org/wiki/Body_mass_index (accessed on 10 July 2023).

38. Mestre, L., Pavela, G., Yi, N., Xun, P., & Allison, D., (2021). Assessing the association between relative BMI and mortality. *Current Developments in Nutrition, 5*(Supplement_2), 36.

39. Drosopoulou, G., Sergentanis, T. N., Mastorakos, G., Vlachopapadopoulou, E., Michalacos, S., Tzavara, C., et al., (2020). Psychosocial health of adolescents in relation to underweight, overweight/obese status: The EU NET ADB survey. *European Journal of Public Health, 31*(2), 379–384.

40. Asensio-Cuesta, S., Blanes-Selva, V., Conejero, J. A., Frigola, A., Portolés, M. G., Merino-Torres, J. F., et al., (2021). A user-centered chatbot (wakamola) to collect linked data in population networks to support studies of overweight and obesity causes: Design and pilot study. *JMIR Medical Informatics, 9*(4).

41. Fenger, K. N., Andersen, I. G., Holm, L. A., Holm, J. C., & Homøe, P., (2020). Quality of life in children and adolescents with overweight or obesity: Impact of obstructive sleep apnea. *International Journal of Pediatric Otorhinolaryngology, 138.*

42. Shih, H. J. S., Gordon, J., & Kulig, K., (2021). Trunk control during gait: Walking with wide and narrow step widths present distinct challenges. *Journal of Biomechanics, 114.*

43. Kasović, M., Štefan, L., & Štefan, A., (2021). Normative data for gait speed and height norm speed in ≥ 60-year-old men and women. *Clinical Interventions in Aging, 16*, 225.

44. Davis-Wilson, H. C., Johnston, C. D., Young, E., Song, K., Wikstrom, E. A., Blackburn, J. T., et al., (2021). Effects of BMI on walking speed and gait biomechanics after anterior cruciate ligament reconstruction. *Medicine and Science in Sports and Exercise, 53*(1), 108–114.

45. Dotan, I., Shochat, T., Shimon, I., & Akirov, A., (2021). The association between BMI and mortality in surgical patients. *World Journal of Surgery, 45*(5), 1390–1399.

46. Dong, P., Ning, Z., Obaidat, M. S., Jiang, X., Guo, Y., Hu, X., et al., (2020). Edge computing-based healthcare systems: Enabling decentralized health monitoring in internet of medical things. *IEEE Network, 34*(5), 254–261.

47. Pustokhina, I. V., Pustokhin, D. A., Gupta, D., Khanna, A., Shankar, K., & Nguyen, G. N., (2020). An effective training scheme for deep neural network in edge computing enabled internet of medical things (IoMT) systems. *IEEE Access, 8*, 107112–107123.

48. Ning, Z., Dong, P., Wang, X., Hu, X., Guo, L., Hu, B., et al., (2021). Mobile edge computing enabled 5G health monitoring for internet of medical things: A decentralized game theoretic approach. *IEEE Journal on Selected Areas in Communications, 39*(2), 463–478.

49. Smith, S., Elsen, E., & De, S. (2020). On the Generalization Benefit of Noise in Stochastic Gradient Descent. *Proceedings of the 37th International Conference on*

Machine Learning, in *Proceedings of Machine Learning Research. 119*, 9058–9067. Available from https://proceedings.mlr.press/v119/smith20a.html.

50. Deepa, N., Prabadevi, B., Maddikunta, P. K., Gadekallu, T. R., Baker, T., Khan, M. A., et al., (2021). An AI-based intelligent system for healthcare analysis using ridge-Adaline stochastic gradient descent classifier. *The Journal of Supercomputing, 77*, 1998–2017.

51. Garcia, S. A., Brown, S. R., Koje, M., Krishnan, C., & Palmieri-Smith, R. M., (2021). Gait asymmetries are exacerbated at faster walking speeds in individuals with acute anterior cruciate ligament reconstruction. *Journal of Orthopaedic Research.*

52. Subhrangshu, A., & Arindam, G., (2022). e-BMI: A gait based smart remote BMI monitoring framework implementing edge computing and incremental machine learning. *Smart Health, 24*, 100277.

53. Shi, W., Cao, J., Zhang, Q., Li, Y., & Xu, L., (2016). Edge computing: Vision and challenges. *IEEE Internet Things J., 3*(5), 637–646.

54. Malhi, K., Mukhopadhyay, S. C., Schnepper, J., Haefke, M., & Ewald, H., (2012). A Zigbee based wearable physiological parameters monitoring system. *IEEE Sens. J., 12*(3), 423–430.

55. Castillejo, P., Martínez, J. F., Rodríguez-Molina, J., & Cuerva, A., (2013). Integration of wearable devices in a wireless sensor network for an e-health application. *IEEE Wirel. Commun., 20*(4), 38–49.

56. Hassan, M. M., Uddin, M. Z., Mohamed, A., & Almogren, A., (2018). A robust human activity recognition system using smartphone sensors and deep learning. *Future Gener. Comput. Syst., 81*, 307–313.

57. Preece, S. J., Goulermas, J. Y., Kenney, L. P., Howard, D., Meijer, K., & Crompton, R., (2009). Activity identification using body-mounted sensors-a review of classification techniques. *Physiol. Meas., 30*, 1–33.

58. Avci, A., Bosch, S., Marin-Perianu, M., Marin-Perianu, R., & Havinga, P., (2010). Activity recognition using inertial sensing for healthcare, wellbeing and sports applications: A survey. In: *Proceedings of the 23rd International Conference on Architecture of Computing Systems* (pp. 1–10). Hannover, Germany.

59. Guidoux, R., Duclos, M., Fleury, G., Lacomme, P., Lamaudiere, N., Maneng, P., Paris, L., Ren, L., & Rousset, S., (2014). A smartphone-driven methodology for estimating physical activities and energy expenditure in free living conditions. *J. Biomed. Inform., 52*, 271–278.

60. Shoaib, M., Bosch, S., Incel, O. D., Scholten, H., & Havinga, P. J., (2015). A survey of online activity recognition using mobile phones. *Sensors, 15*, 2059–2085.

61. Ugulino, W., Cardador, D., Vega, K., Velloso, E., Milidiú, R., & Fuks, H., (2012). Wearable computing: Accelerometers' data classification of body postures and movements. In: *Advances in Artificial Intelligence—SBIA 2012* (pp. 52–61). Springer, Berlin, Germany; Heidelberg, Germany.

62. Cohen, I., Sebe, N., Garg, A., Chen, L. S., & Huang, T. S., (2003). Facial expression recognition from video sequences: Temporal and static modeling. *Comput. Vis. Image Underst., 91*, 160–187.

63. Kiranyaz, S., Ince, T., & Gabbouj, M., (2016). Real-time patient-specific ECG classification by 1-D convolutional neural networks. *IEEE Trans. Biomed. Eng., 63*(3), 664–675.

64. Sak, H., Senior, A. W., & Beaufays, F., (2014). *Long Short-Term Memory Recurrent Neural Network Architectures for Large Scale Acoustic Modeling* (pp. 338–342). Interspeech.

65. Alam, M. G. R., Haw, R., Kim, S. S., Azad, M. A. K., Abedin, S. F., & Hong, C. S., (2016). EM psychiatry: An ambient intelligent system for psychiatric emergency. *IEEE Trans. Ind. Inform., 12*(6), 2321–2330.

66. Md. Zia, U., (2019). A wearable sensor-based activity prediction system to facilitate edge computing in smart healthcare system. *Parallel Distrib. Comput., 123*, 46–53.

67. Roth, J. A., Battegay, M., Juchler, F., Vogt, J. E., & Widmer, A. F., (2018). Introduction to machine learning in digital healthcare epidemiology. *Infect. Control Hosp. Epidemiol., 39*(12), 1457–1462.

68. Hoshino, Y., & Kapikian, A. Z., (2000). Rotavirus serotypes: Classification and importance in epidemiology, immunity, and vaccine development. *J. Health Popul. Nutr.*, 5–14.

69. Mena, L. J., & Gonzalez, J. A., (2006). *Machine Learning for Imbalanced Datasets: Application in Medical Diagnostic* (pp. 574–579). In: Flairs Conference.

70. Char, D. S., Shah, N. H., & Magnus, D., (2018). Implementing machine learning in health care—Addressing ethical challenges. *N. Engl. J. Med., 378*(11), 981.

71. Remeseiro, B., & Bolon-Canedo, V., (2019). A review of feature selection methods in medical applications. *Comput. Biol. Med.*, 103375.

72. Nahar, J., Imam, T., Tickle, K. S., & Chen, Y. P. P., (2013). Computational intelligence for heart disease diagnosis: A medical knowledge driven approach. *Expert Syst. Appl., 40*(1), 96–104.

73. Shen, Y., Colloc, J., Jacquet-Andrieu, A., Guo, Z., & Liu, Y., (2017). Constructing ontology-based cancer treatment decision support system with case-based reasoning. In: *International Conference on Smart Computing and Communication* (pp. 278–288). Springer.

74. Lipton, Z. C., (2018). The mythos of model interpretability. *Queue, 16*(3), 31–57.

75. Perez, A. J., & Zeadally, S., (2018). Privacy issues and solutions for consumer wearables. *IT Prof., 20*(4), 46–56.

76. Adi, E., Anwar, A., Baig, Z., & Zeadally, S., (2020). Machine learning and data analytics for the IoT. *Neural Comput. Appl., 32*, 16205–16233.

77. Muangprathub, J., Boonnam, N., Kajornkasirat, S., Lekbangpong, N., Wanichsombat, A., & Nillaor, P., (2019). IoT and agriculture data analysis for smart farm. *Comput. Electron. Agric., 156*, 467–474.

78. Mukherjee, A., & De, D., (2016). Low power offloading strategy for femto-cloud mobile network. *Eng. Sci. Technol. Int. J., 19*(1), 260–270.

79. Hussain, F., Hussain, R., Hassan, S. A., & Hossain, E., (2020). Machine learning in IoT security: Current solutions and future challenges. *IEEE Commun. Surv. Tutor., 22*(3), 1686–1721.

80. Zeadally, S., Khan, S. U., & Chilamkurti, N., (2012). Energy-efficient networking: Past, present, and future. *J. Supercomput., 62*(3), 1093–1118.

81. Zeadally, S., & Badra, M., (2015). *Privacy in a Digital, Networked World: Technologies, Implications and Solutions.* Springer.

82. Aazam, M., Zeadally, S., & Harras, K. A., (2018). Offloading in fog computing for IoT: Review, enabling technologies, and research opportunities. *Future Gener. Comput. Syst.*

83. *Household Size and Composition Around the World 2017*, United Nations, (2017).

84. Di Martino, A., Yan, C. G., Li, Q., Denio, E., Castellanos, F. X., Alaerts, K., Anderson, J. S., Assaf, M., Bookheimer, S. Y., Dapretto, M., et al., (2014). The autism brain imaging data exchange: Towards a large-scale evaluation of the intrinsic brain architecture in autism. *Molecular Psychiatry, 19*(6), 659–667.

85. ADNI, (2019). *Alzheimer's Disease Neuroimaging Initiative.* http://ADNI.loni.usc.edu/ (accessed on 10 July 2023).

86. Trojanowski, J. Q., Vandeerstichele, H., Korecka, M., Clark, C. M., Aisen, P. S., Petersen, R. C., Blennow, K., Soares, H., Simon, A., Lewczuk, P., et al., (2010). Update on the biomarker core of the Alzheimer's disease neuroimaging initiative subjects. *Alzheimer's & Dementia, 6*(3), 230–238.

87. He, K., Zhang, X., Ren, S., & Sun, J., (2016). Deep residual learning for image recognition. In: *Proceedings of the IEEE Conference on Computer Vision and Pattern Recognition* (pp. 770–778).

88. Litjens, G., Kooi, T., Sánchez, C. I., et al., (2017). A survey on deep learning in medical image analysis. *Medical Image Analysis, 42*, 60–88.

89. Mobadersany, P., Yousefi, S., Amgad, M., Gutman, D. A., Barnholtz-Sloan, J. S., Vega, J. E. V., Brat, D. J., & Cooper, L. A., (2018). Predicting cancer outcomes from histology and genomics using convolutional networks. *Proceedings of the National Academy of Sciences 115*(13), E2970–E2979.

90. Simonyan, K., & Zisserman, A., (2014). *Very Deep Convolutional Networks for Large-Scale Image Recognition.* arXiv preprint arXiv:1409.1556.

91. Xu, T., Zhang, H., Huang, X., Zhang, S., & Metaxas, D. N., (2016). Multimodal deep learning for cervical dysplasia diagnosis. In: *International Conference on Medical Image Computing and Computer-Assisted Intervention* (pp. 115–123). Springer.

92. Wu, F., Souza, A., Zhang, T., Fifty, C., Yu, T., & Weinberger, K., (2019). Simplifying graph convolutional networks. In: *International Conference on Machine Learning* (pp. 6861–6871). PMLR.

93. Shuman, D. I., Narang, S. K., Vandergheynst, P., et al., (2013). The emerging field of signal processing on graphs: Extending high-dimensional data analysis to networks and other irregular domains. *IEEE Signal Processing Magazine, 30*(3), 83–98.

94. Kipf, T. N., & Welling, M., (2016). *Semi-Supervised Classification with Graph Convolutional Networks.* arXiv preprint arXiv:1609.02907.

95. Velic̆kovic, P., Cucurull, G., Casanova, A., Romero, A., Lio, P., & Bengio, Y., (2017). *Graph Attention Networks.* arXiv preprint arXiv:1710.10903.

96. Hamilton, W., Ying, Z., & Leskovec, J., (2017). Inductive representation learning on large graphs. In: *Advances in Neural Information Processing Systems* (pp. 1024–1034).

97. Gao, H., & Ji, S., (2019). *Graph u-Nets.* arXiv preprint arXiv:1905.05178.

98. Doosti, B., Naha, S., Mirbagheri, M., & Crandall, D. J., (2020). Hope-net: A graph-based model for hand-object pose estimation. In: *Proceedings of the IEEE.*

CHAPTER 7

IoT-Based Safety Measures and Healthcare Services for Transgender Welfare and Sustainability

SUGYANTA PRIYADARSHINI,[1] SUKANTA CHANDRA SWAIN,[1] SACHI NANDAN MOHANTY,[2] and NISRUTHA DULLA[1]

[1]School of Humanities, KIIT Deemed to be University, Bhubaneswar, Odisha, India

[2]School of Computer Engineering, VIT-AP University, Andhra Pradesh, India

ABSTRACT

The longstanding discrimination and violence against the community of transgender people are pervasive, preventing them from accessing healthcare facilities and equal opportunities for employment and education. These extreme limitations in employment for transgender people push them towards less potential jobs such as begging and sex work for their daily bread and butter. In this line of work, they are subjected to verbal and physical abuses resulting in a high rate of mental health issues and HIV. However, the rapid changes in the field of information and communication technology (ICT) have introduced e-health services and smart security solutions that can benefit this community in accessing greater healthcare and optimum security in times of crisis. The research work has focused on the use of electronic health intervention such as paper based reporting system for antiretroviral therapy, Medicom and Paab modules, Smart Card for ART by NACO, Telemedicine consultations, blended learning in the form of Broadcasting health content related to HIV/AIDS through radio and TV for HIV positive transgender patients; and use of Tele Psychiatry Services, Bibliotherapy,

Reconnoitering the Landscape of Edge Intelligence in Healthcare.
Suneeta Satpathy, Sachi Nandan Mohanty, and Sirisha Potluri (Eds.)

Telemedicine Technology and Self-Help Programs based on Tele-Cognitive Behavior Therapy for transgender patients dealing with mental problems; and use of smart security solutions such as Society Harnessing Equipment, ILA Security, Advanced Electronics System for Human Safety, VithU app and Smart Belt for their safety and security. The e-health services and e-security solutions through IoT devices have redesigned the healthcare systems to improve the quality of care for transgender patients generally ignored by healthcare professionals and help the victimized transgender people stuck in a perilous situation.

7.1 INTRODUCTION

The ubiquitous gender inequality in India is a barrier to its development, justice, social stability, and human potential. Widening the aspects of gender beyond the bilateral division of men and women, it is observed that inequality cuts deeper for the marginalized community of transgender. Discrimination against the transgender community is a persistent and long-run phenomenon that has characterized Indian society at every level. The incongruity between the sex assigned to them at birth and their personal opinion on their gender identity transgresses the stereotypical definition, construction, and formation of the bilateral division of gender identity predetermined by society. Consequently, they are socioeconomically ostracized and culturally criticized and are subjected to physical violence, verbal abuse, and sexual assaults. Despite entitling transgender people under the category of 'Third gender' by Indian Supreme Court in 2014, most of them are constantly denied the fundamental rights, directive principles, and fundamental duties violating their right to gender identity [1]. The ways in which discrimination and seclusion impact the life of transgender people are interconnected. Societal ostracization, lack of economic support system, and transphobic attitude of non-transgender people drive poverty, isolation, depression, and other compromised mental and physical health outcomes. Each context relates to and often aggravates the other [2].

The community of transgender prefers coming out at different stages of life and various degrees. It will be essential for some to come out as themselves publicly, whereas others prefer coming out only to themselves. Some of them come out early in their lives, whereas few come out in their later stages of life [3]. Transgender individuals who come out early to their family and relatives are mostly rejected by them. Suppose they are not cast out from their family. In that case, they are typically limited within their homes' four walls, resulting in a lack of educational opportunities and no attention to their mental and physical health. Those who express their true gender identity in the later stages of their lives are often rejected by mainstream society and subjected to constant humiliation and complete ostracization. The hostile environment surrounding transgender people fails to understand their feelings and necessities instead threatens their safety [4].

Consequently, in this hostile environment, transgender people have limited access to pursue education and face greater odds of getting employment, thereby experiencing homelessness [3] and poverty [4]. Transgender students who join schools with utmost difficulty also face prejudices and humiliation in the hands of administration and non-transgender teaching staff and peers resulting in higher drop-out rates [5], with few battling with threatening school environment but advancing towards higher education [6]. Further, previous research work related to the working environment for Transgender individuals reveals that the trans workers are the most marginalized working section who are significantly excluded from gainful employment facilities and also come across a wide range of discrimination in the employment process, including recruitment, provision of skillful perspective, training opportunities, promotion, increment, and other employee benefit plans [7]. Such an unwelcoming society's attitude towards the transgender community instills pessimism in them and further discourages them from accessing education and applying for jobs [8]. These extreme limitations in the field of employment for transgender people push them towards less potential jobs such as sex work, entertaining on streets, beautician, begging for their daily bread and butter [9]. These low-paying or risky jobs push them into the cycle of poverty. Unfortunately, the legitimate system often entrenches this ostracization, brings in inequality, and instills violence against the community of transgender [2]. For instance, they have to live in criminal contexts under the legislation that castigates purported prostitution, cross-dressing, and homosexual propaganda and makes them prey for indulging in fake extortion and violence cases [10].

Further, when the police pick them up for the crimes mentioned above under vague charges, their abuse continues in the hand of the police [11]. Consequently, being criminalized, they get discouraged from complaining to the police or seeking justice when subjected to forced sex, molestation, violence, and abuse, and rapes [12]. Few documents from the last decade reveal that most transgender people are subjected to violence and inhuman torture in the hands of non-transgender people due to perpetuating transphobia among them [13, 14]. Trans sex workers are often sexually exploited and raped by police, who are considered so-called protectors of Law. Unfortunately, the government turns a blind eye towards this brutality of police towards transgender people.

The aforementioned tragic rebuff by family, friends, relatives, and society puts transgender individuals at risk of numerous health problems, including a heightened risk of mental health disorder (depression and anxiety issues), HIV as well as addiction to drugs and alcohol [15, 16]. Unfortunately, most healthcare professionals and medical systems fail to extend their function outside the gender binary framework (men/women), keeping transgender patients outside the periphery [17]. Healthcare providers are generally unaware and untrained about facilitating suitable services for handling HIV-positive transgender patients or identifying or clarifying any other problems related to their sexual or reproductive health [18, 19]. Most HIV-positive transgender patients express their disinterest in visiting hospitals due to their past experience of humiliation at the hands of medical staff. Further, transgender dealing with mental problems like depression and anxiety issues when showing up in the hospitals for check-ups are generally mocked by the healthcare professionals and are not taken on a serious note, which discourages them from mentioning their healthcare problems in the future [20–22]. The financial instability and hostile social and legal environment limit transgender individuals from accessing healthcare facilities and further create health gaps resulting from an unresponsive, ignorant, and irresponsible public health system. Under such precarious circumstances, the lives of transgender people are at stake. ICS and IoT-based strategies can be primed to offer an efficient and reliable solution keeping in backdrop their significant potential to operate at a fine granular level and provide rich low-level information.

The very idea of developing smart devices for transgender people is that they should be very comfortable, easy to use, and cheaper in all aspects compared to infamous mobile apps used for tracking safety, security, and necessity and help. Taking into account the healthcare facilities and safety of the community of transgender people, an advanced system of a smart security solution can be introduced (GPS recovery, Pulse rate sensor, GSM) which can detect the location as well as the health condition of the individual and send a signal to the near and dear ones to take necessary actions [21]. Several sensors can be used to precisely detect the transgender individual stuck in any critical abusive situation or real-time health crisis. The pulse rate and heartbeat of individuals during these critical times are very high, which becomes helpful in decision making along with other supporting motion sensors that track the abnormal movement of the victimized transgender people. Further, the smartphones used by the victims will be well integrated with their smart devices, which makes it cheaper by using the GSM and GPS of the smartphone [22]. Further, it also enables low energy consumption and reduced use of power by getting connected through Bluetooth, which can be used for several days with a single charge shot.

Most transgender people are victimized to stigma, discrimination, bullying, rejection, and ostracization, which prevent them from accessing healthcare facilities and equal opportunities for employment and education. They are subjected to verbal and physical abuses resulting in a high rate of mental health issues. The above-mentioned factors affect the well-being of transgender people and place them at heightened for HIV. Further, the community of transgender is recognized with a bad name on the international podium for carrying the burden of HIV infection of approximately 20% of worldwide HIV prevalence [23]. Unfortunately, most HIV-positive transgender patients come across the lack of cultural competence by healthcare professionals, thereby facing discomfort and disgust in their hands, pushing them not to opt for medical treatment at regular intervals.

Further, treatment for HIV-positive transgender patients is not recorded in the conventional medical curriculum resulting in limited knowledge and experience of the healthcare providers [24, 25]. However, treatment for HIV requires constant evaluation and check-ups, which is generally found difficult for transgender people. Consequently, telemedicine and e-monitoring can be considered useful tools in providing regular healthcare facilities and monitoring their well-being [26]. One of the major hindrances to accessing treatment through anti-retroviral medication is the difficulty of finding the appropriate and au-fait data at the planning level 1. However, information and communication technology (ICT) has proved to be useful in addressing the mentioned bottleneck by putting forward the system of telemedicine and e-health applications. These projects are used in many pilot studies. It was analyzed that ART delivery can be channelized to marginalized sections like the community of transgender people by integrating local primary healthcare information with centralized databases to allow national monitoring [27, 28]. This research work analyzes the role of mobile technology, telemedicine, and other innovative IoT-based safety trackers for transgender healthcare and security, respectively. However, the hour needs to analyze and identify the possible ways in which IoT strategies can be used for extending a helping hand towards their healthcare and safety, keeping in mind transgender victimization towards stigma and violence. However, there are limited documents on IoT and ICT strategies' role in reaching the low- and middle-income transgender population victimized to health disorders and safety-related issues.

7.2   RESEARCH METHODOLOGY

computerized systematic literature survey was conducted in scientific databases like Cochrane Library Controlled Trial Registry, Science Direct, Medline, and PsycINFO Centre for Reviews and Dissemination. Following searched words included ART (anti-retroviral therapy), AIDS (acquired immune deficiency syndrome), HIV (human immunodeficiency virus), ICT (Information and Commination Technology), IoT (internet of things), e-health, telehealth, telecare, teleconsultation, mental healthcare service, video conference, Mediware Datamate Info Solutions, Unisolv, iDART, Pharm, ASSIST, AIDS-Drugs-Online.com, HIV Vaccine Translational Research Laboratory, Telemedicine consultations, Blended learning. The general search engine used for the searching database was 'Google.' The searches were limited to the articles published between 1995 and 2020. The study was conducted from January to August 2020. Few studies are translated and reported in the English language. Information about psychic health and violence on transgender people was collected from different newspaper articles and blogs. Several Project managers, telehealthcare professionals, and e-health stakeholders were contacted through telephonic conversation to collect details about the beneficiaries of telemedicine facilities.

7.3   DISCUSSION

Social seclusion, economic exclusion, political restriction, and cultural segregation have increased the issues faced by the disadvantaged and disenfranchised community of Transgender people. The multidimensional problems they face are interrelated and are considered the consequences of an orthodox mindset regarding the binary division of sex (male and female), excluding transgender people in every sphere. They are mostly excluded from social and cultural life, economic and political participation, and other decision-making processes. The framework (Figure 7.1) illustrates the multiple forms of issues faced by transgender people, which are interconnected and act as a barrier in their development. The unacceptance and intolerance of Indian society towards the transgender community date back to the 1800s after enforcing the Criminal Tribes Act, 1871.

Further, the limited knowledge of common masses regarding homosexual orientation and specifically the transgender community instills transphobia. After coming out, most transgender face social exclusion ranging from rejection in the hands of family and friends and restriction from accessing educational facilities and healthcare facilities. Consequently, the transgender child from a very tender age prefers running away from family, unable to resist discrimination by parents compared to the treatment provided to other siblings. Most of them find no way to enroll themselves in the 'Hijra' community. Thus, being dropped out from school after quitting home, most of them remain uneducated and fail to get prestigious jobs. Despite being qualified and skilled, few transgender people are denied employment. They have to face several verbal abuse and physical violence cases, which worsens their struggle for existence. Lack of livelihood options forces them to have minimal sources of income streams like begging and sex work. As a result of being indulged in the profession of prostitution, they are victimized by HIV/AIDS and other related health risks. Unfortunately, they face discrimination at the hands of healthcare professionals in healthcare settings. Most healthcare providers are ignorant about sexual diversities and are unfamiliar and misinformed about the health issues faced by the transgender community. Thus, they are subjected to several barriers in accessing sex reassignment surgery, hormonal treatments, HIV/AIDS, and anti-retroviral treatment.

Further, few transgender patients cannot get treated by healthcare professionals or pay the premiums for health insurance or life insurance due to financial constraints. Further, lack of legal recognition prohibits them from accessing government ration cards, passports, bank accounts, and other subsidies. However, the lack of legal validity of I'd card and voter I'd cards forbid them from political participation. It has been documented that transgender people have contested in the election in the past and were victorious but unfortunately, were overturned since they contested as female and was considered illegal. Further, when they face various verbal abuse and physical violence, it is observed that the Law and system do not support them rather indulge them in fake extortion and vague charges and further interrogate them looking into them from a criminal context.

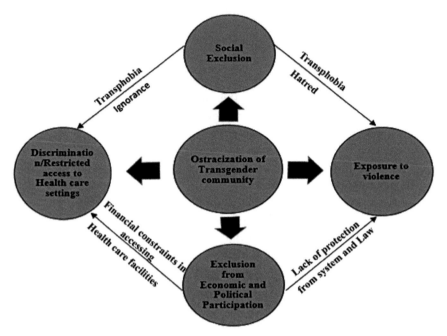

FIGURE 7.1   Framework of the issues faced by the transgender community.

7.3.1   *ELECTRONIC-HEALTH INTERVENTION FOR HIV POSITIVE TRANSGENDER HEALTHCARE*

Socio-economic exclusion leads to livelihood deprivation among the trans-gender community, resulting in poverty [29]. This results in the inability to access sex reassignment surgery for transition in sexual anatomy and other healthcare services [30]. Approximately 20% of the transgender population cannot meet gender-specific healthcare needs [31]. Economic marginaliza-tion has pushed 20 to 30% of transgender people in India to engage in begging and sex work as their primary occupation for their daily bread and butter, which puts them at heightened risk for HIV/AIDS. In India, the nationwide prevalence of HIV/AIDS is approximately 0.31% whereas, the frequency of HIV among the community of transgender is estimated to be 8.2% [32]. The stress associated with socio-economic isolation and rejection leads to a higher rate of consumption of drugs and alcohol, affecting the judgment of risk regarding the lesser use of condoms.

Further, the community of transgender people is 49 times more suscep-tible to the HIV epidemic than the general masses [33]. Unfortunately, due to a lack of adequate knowledge of healthcare professionals on sexual diversities, they cannot take proper care of transgender patients suffering from different sexual healthcare issues. Further, the persisting transphobia in hospital staff and healthcare providers behave differently with HIV-positive transgender patients while providing medical services. Some typical types of discrimination reported by transgender patients in the hands of hospital staff and healthcare providers include intentional use of gender abusive languages while addressing them, registering them under the category of 'males' and admitting them into male wards, verbal abuses by co patients and harassment by healthcare professionals due to their unique identity, little attention towards them during a critical situation, absence of sensitive and trained healthcare providers in healthcare settings and sometimes denial of medical services. Most transgender people face such humiliation and discrimination due to their unique sexual orientation, sex work, HIV status, or a combination of all these. Most doctors maintain distance or show discomfort in touching transgender patients in most healthcare settings.

Further, few doctors have a misconception about the sexual lives of transgender and believe that they are engaged with multiple sex partners, which limits their interaction with transgender patients. Further, if HIV-positive transgender patients visit hospitals, they face doubling the discrimination, making it difficult to continue their treatment. Moreover, visiting doctors at a regular interval is not quite possible from their end due to the financial constraints faced by them. Bias faced in the hands of doctors can influence their decision not to continue their treatment in hospitals and prefer homemade treatments that can be risky. Tired of constant humiliation and discrimination, most transgender patients express their hesitance in getting treatment in healthcare settings or visiting doctors when they are diagnosed with critical health issues like AIDS/HIV.

Further, there is a limited record of transgender people who have HIV/AIDS in India as most of them prefer not getting diagnosed in healthcare settings due to constant humiliation and discrimination in the hands of healthcare providers and lack of sufficient money in hand. However, in this case, electronic health intervention such as paper based reporting system for antiretroviral therapy, Medicom and Paab modules, Smart Card for ART by NACO, OpenMRS, ARV medication, Mediware Datamate Info Solutions, Unisolv, iDART, Pharm, ASSIST, **AIDS-Drugs-Online.com**, HIV Vaccine Translational Research Laboratory, Telemedicine consultations, Blended learning in the form of Broadcasting health content related to HIV/AIDS through radio and TV can play a significant role in recording and reporting the cases by keeping track of the affected transgender patients. Thus, it will help deliver accurate data effectively and efficiently, resulting in a bigger picture of the potential benefits of adopting an electronic health system. This would further result in better patient care, improved monitoring of the status of HIV-positive transgender patients, and a better policy framework for bringing HIV-positive transgender patients into the loop of proper attention and care. By using the up-to-date data, healthcare providers could directly check the patients using the recent real-time information in the last check-up without cross-questioning them, contact the patient in case of missed treatment and make a list of necessary out-of-stock ART drugs. The HIV patients who either fail to meet their healthcare professionals due to lack of finance or hesitance in physically appearing in healthcare settings could also opt for telemedicine consultations. Table 7.1 gives an overview of e-health systems for information handling and communicating with patients virtually.

TABLE 7.1   Digital Healthcare for HIV/AIDS Treatment for Transgender Patients

Sl. No.	e-Health Systems for HIV Treatment	Usefulness of ICT Systems for HIV Positive Transgender Patients
1.	Paper-based reporting system for antiretroviral therapy	• Data on HIV positive transgender patients can be recorded electronically, which can be used for estimating the total affected count.
		• Keeps in track the report summary (drug dosages, changes of treatment regimen, and assessment of treatment outcomes) such that the transgender patient will not be answerable to every doctor.
2.	Medicom and Paab modules through COP 2017 in three clusters (Andhra Pradesh, Maharashtra, and the Northeast)	• Strengthen strategies to trace out HIV cascade with a focus on hidden and difficult to find transgender.
		• Provide optimum attention and treatment for transgender detected with HIV.
		• Build intellectual and well-informed human capacity to scale innovations and ways for preventing HIV among transgender people.
3.	Smart Card for ART by NACO	• Benefit the mobile population of transgender suffering from HIV who find it difficult to proceed in accordance with treatment plans.
		• Improve drug adherence in case of HIV positive transgender patients in order to prevent the risk of resistance.
4.	OpenMRS (BAHMNI)	• EMR or retrieval systems can be used for treating HIV/AIDS affected transgender patients.

TABLE 7.1 *(Continued)*

Sl. No.	e-Health Systems for HIV Treatment	Usefulness of ICT Systems for HIV Positive Transgender Patients
5.	Anti-retroviral medication (Mediware Datamate Info Solutions)	• Provision of low-priced medicines for transgender who is facing financial constraints in accessing HIV medicines. • Availability of quality-assured medicines.
6.	Unisolv, iDART, Pharm ASSIST, AIDS-Drugs-Online.com	• Online Consultations from reputed doctors along with the provision of less priced and qualitative medicines.
7.	HIV Vaccine Translational Research Laboratory	• Designing a new broad-spectrum HIV vaccine will be the mandate of this new lab to reach the minority section (Transgender community) who remain unnoticed.
8.	Telemedicine consultations	• Access specialized care at a low cost. • Expert opinion and guidance. • Easy flow and better delivery of healthcare consultation to patients in remote areas.
9.	Blended learning in the form of broadcasting health content related to HIV/AIDS through radio and TV	• Transgender patients will be more cautious about their health through visual depiction or reference for a better understanding.

7.3.2 TELEMEDICINE FOR MENTAL HEALTHCARE OF TRANSGENDER PATIENTS

The Survey of Mental health documented that around one-fifth of the total world population suffers from a wide range of mental disorders which require clinical attention [34]. Transgender people are subjected to mental health disorder due to longstanding exposure to discrimination, stigma, violence, rejection, hatred, and other psychological distress [35]. Even after 1000 years of the existence of the transgender community in Hinduism, the Indian society is still intolerant towards this community for their unique gender identity, which stigmatizes and marginalizes them from the mainstream. However, previous studies have documented that the societal stigma, economic disadvantage, and transphobia among non-transgender people are significantly interconnected and have resulted in depression, anxiety issues, suicidal ideation, and many other mental health disorder [36]. Meyer's Minority stress theory has come up with the persistence of psychological stress in the community of transgender people being subjected to humiliation, discrimination, marginalization, prejudices, and stigma in the transphobic society [37]. Since most transgender people are engaged in sex work, they are subjected to physical violence, verbal abuse, and substance use, which exacerbate their vulnerability to mental health disorders. However, despite the high prevalence of mental illness in transgender people, there is a limited provision of adequate treatment of mental illness. Unavailability and inaccessibility of affordable mental healthcare treatment are rife in the case of transgender people suffering from a mental disorder.

Further, the attitude towards transgender people held by a psychiatrist can highly impact the decision of transgender people to continue treatment for mental disorders. Generally, in India, transgender people are considered abnormal. Most doctors have a misconception about the sexual lives of transgender people and believe that they are engaged with multiple sex partners, which limits their interaction with their transgender patients. Further, healthcare professionals are not trained in dealing with transgender patients, which is a matter of concern. However, the expenses of treating mental disorders are mostly beyond the range of affordability of transgender patients, which further discourages them from mental healthcare treatment.

Currently, the healthcare services are overburdened, and transgender patients feel ignored in their service. There is a shortage of staff which results in delays in treatment. Keeping all these factors into account, telepsychiatry service can be proved useful in improving the quality of mental healthcare service provided to transgender patients. Tele psychiatry service can be a blissful tool for transgender people as they mostly face minimal therapist support. Further, getting treated virtually can minimize the stigma related to transgender patients from the psychiatrist's end, showing a higher level of satisfaction. However, introducing ICT for managing mental health disorders is threefold: (i) to increase the accessibility of transgender patients who are unable to visit hospitals due to a remote location and persisting stigma; (ii) to check the potential spread of mental health disorders in the transgender community and relapse prevention; and (iii) to keep in the record the number of mental disorder cases in the transgender community who required clinical attention which can also be used for further research work. E-mental healthcare measures include Tele Psychiatry Services, Bibliotherapy, Telemedicine Technology, and Self-Help Programs based on Tele-Cognitive Behavior Therapy. These tools record the characteristics of the patient, their intense behavior, and the environment surrounding them, which can be the influential factors in detecting the source of the problem. Previous studies on the role of ICT in controlling mental health disorder has proved the success rate of the aforementioned ICT tools [38–40]. Tele Psychiatry Services, Bibliotherapy, Tele-medicine Technology and Self-Help Programs based on Tele-Cognitive Behavior Therapy can overcome the persisting drawbacks of face-to-face analysis of psychiatric issues faced by the transgender psychiatric patients through improved access in a remote location through video conferencing calls and telephonic conversation, providing primary care with behavioral healthcare for better outcomes, reducing meeting the psychiatrists in regular intervals in hospitals, reducing delay in providing emergency mental healthcare in crisis time, improved continuity of mental healthcare and keeping track of follow-up, reduce barriers of stigma in the hands of untrained and unskilled psychiatrists who have limited knowledge about techniques of dealing with transgender patients, reducing potential transport barriers such as long drives to meet the concerned the psychiatrist (Table 7.2).

TABLE 7.2 Digital Mental Healthcare for Mentally Disturbed Transgender Patients

Sl. No.	ICT-based Tools for Treating Mental Health Disorder	Technology	Usefulness
1.	Tele psychiatry services	Live and interactive communications.	• Medication management. • Patient awareness about their psychiatric disorder. • Psychiatric evaluation. • Recording the interaction and sending the same for better analysis of the disorder and saving it for later review. • Convenient, affordable, and readily accessible mental health services.
2.	Bibliotherapy	e-books, e-pamphlets, videotapes, computer programs.	• Therapeutic service used for addressing behavioral health problems. • Cost-effective method. • Treats mood related problems. • Interactive discussions to imbue positive thinking. • Using modalities such as play therapy and cognitive behavioral therapy. • Helpful in dealing with posttraumatic stress and improving self-esteem and self-awareness in facing any crisis.

TABLE 7.2 *(Continued)*

Sl. No.	ICT-based Tools for Treating Mental Health Disorder	Technology	Usefulness
3.	Tele-medicine technology	Video consultations, medical imaging, medical diagnosis	• Remote clinical services. • Address transgender going through hormonal therapies and psychic changes derived from it. • E-prescribed medication for psychic issues. • Discussing with the transgender patients about their emotions hidden deep inside resulting in depression and other anxiety issues.
4.	Self-help programs based on e-cognitive behavior therapy	Telephone cognitive behavior therapy	• Specialized treatment can be more accessible to transgender staying in a remote location. • Can be cured suffering from obsessive-compulsive disorder. • Cost-effective.

These electronic-health systems for reaching mentally disturbed transgender patients can be considered a new version of the organization comprising new healthcare processes and efficient roles assigned to human resources. This process is backed by supportive, caring, and trained psychiatric caregivers who will be efficient enough to provide necessary consultations and support patients in online clinical aspects, facilitate continuity of treatment, and keep track of the follow-up. Transgender patients most prone to depression and anxiety disorder can be treated with appropriate therapy by discussing their problems in a private online room, which will be confined to only the caregiver and the receptor and will remain confidential to maintain the comfort of transgender patients. Transgender patients targeted with depressive symptoms are counseled, keeping in backdrop their circumstances and history of mental disorder reports. Although traditional face-to-face interaction in psychotherapies for counseling cannot be replaced with Tele-psychiatry and other ICT tools in mental healthcare, it can surely be a valuable augmentation to it.

7.3.3 SMART SECURITY SOLUTION FOR TRANSGENDER THROUGH IOT

Violence against transgender people is rampant in India. They are subjected to societal stigma and economic disadvantage, thereby remaining unemployed due to lack of career training and education. Consequently, they enroll themselves in gig jobs like sex work for their survival. The nature of the job victimizes them towards verbal abuses, physical violence, rapes, assaults, and other harassments throughout their lives, which puts them at heightened risk of losing their lives. Sad but true, four out of every 10 transgender people face violence and sexual abuse before turning 18. Previous documents cited several instances where transgender individuals are tortured to death. Such as, Gauri, a 35-year-old transgender person from Kerala, was strangled to death in August 2017. Her body was found in bushes near Railway Goods Shed in Aluva.

Similarly, another transgender activist from Kerala named Sweet Maria was stabbed multiple times, and her neck was slit open. The barbaric assailants had sprinkled chili powder over her body and have tortured her till her last breath. Sonia, a 20-year-old transgender person, was brutally raped by two men and have emptied a bottle of acid on her face. The assaulters have abandoned her on the road in this condition to face an accident and die [39]. Unfortunately, physical and sexual abuse against transgender individuals is considered a petty offense. It is merely punished with an imprisonment period of less than 6 months to two years with a certain fine amount. However, sexual assaults/rape against women are punished with lifetime imprisonment whereas, against transgender, it is merely considered as an assault. The gender-neutral rape law is yet to be implemented profoundly [40] (Figure 7.2).

Under such a situation where the lives of transgender people are at stake, certain applications or devices need to be designed to detect the critical situation faced by the victim and aptly send a sensation to the near and dear ones for their rescue. They can be advised to dial codes like *91# for receiving emergency service from police control during crisis times. Single click free application to receive help during an emergency is also designed, such as 'Help me on mobile.' Some systems are used in India for the safety of women which transgender women can also use for their safety and security such as (a) Society Harnessing Equipment is a garment implanted with an electronic device which is inserted with an electric circuit radiating 388 KV, which will give a jerk to the assaulter and help finally help the victim escape. However, in case of multiple attacks, it can provide 80 back to back electric shocks; (b) ILA security has designed three alarms that can shock and confuse the attackers and protect the victim from the unsafe situation; (c) advanced electronics system for human safety is a device which is designed to track the current location of the victim using GPS; (d) VithU app is an emergency application designed for sending alerts in the form of links of current location

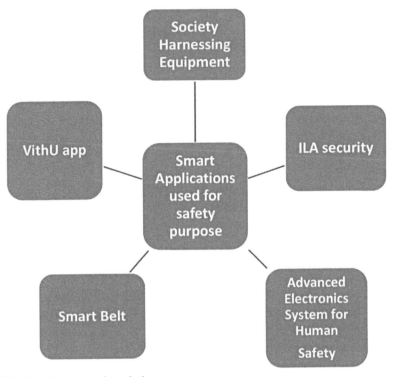

FIGURE 7.2   Smart security solutions.

to the nearest person in your contact list by pressing the power button twice consecutively; (e) smart belt is a portable system designed as a normal belt consisting of Arduino Board, screaming alarm and pressure sensors. The device gets activated automatically once the sensors receive pressure and cross the threshold. The screaming alarm will be activated and send sirens to near and dear ones asking for immediate help. But when a person is in trouble, they fail to press any button; thus, automated sensation could be of great help.

Figure 7.3 comprises a smartphone that is in sync with the smart band over Bluetooth low energy (BLE) and the control unit. A special application is designed, which acts as an interface to connect the smart band with the smartphone. The smart band unit comprises of pulse rate sensor, Dual technology motion sensor, temperature sensor, BLE, and power supply. The application, which is pre-installed in the smartphone, continuously monitors pulse rate, the motion of the body, and temperature with the help of the smart band. When the assaulter abuses the victim, the application directs the smartphone to send current coordinates and help messages to family members, nearest police station, along with the near and dear ones pre-decided by the user for immediate action. The GSM ability inbuilt in the smartphone sends the coordinates to the people near surroundings requesting public attention. The control unit will collect information regarding changing pulse rate and temperature through pulse rate sensor and body temperature sensor through RF Module. The pulse rate sensor measures the heartbeat, and the digital output of the heartbeat is detected with the help of a led that flashes for every heartbeat. The digital output of the heartbeat is sent to the microcontroller that calculates the Beats per minute rate. The data is tracked using the principle of light modulation of network satellites whose frequency ranges from 1.2 to 1.6 GHz. The motion sensor is considered one of the important parts of security.

It detects the victims' unusual motions by using multiple sensing techniques, which reduces the false triggers and verifies the correct ones. BLE is designed to enable low energy consumption and reduced power by getting connected through Bluetooth, which can be used for several days with a single shot of charge. Human body temperature can act as a major detector of the emergency faced by the victim. The temperature sensor used in the smart band monitors the victim's body temperature. It sends a signal for rescue when the body temperature rises abruptly while facing any perilous situation.

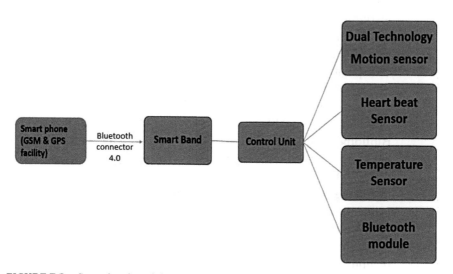

FIGURE 7.3 Smart band module.

7.4   RESULT

ICT can instill power and effectively affect change by creating new opportunities by expanding the flow of information and making communication more feasible and accessible. This has made people aware transgender people make better choices, raise their voices, vocal about their opinions, demand their rights, and control their own lives. The feasibility and efficacy of IoTs have optimized the power of technology. They have brought in e-health services and smart security solutions for safety purposes, which are the basic requirements for reducing the heightened risk of lives of transgender individuals. ICT has played a significant role in empowering transgender people socially, economically, and psychologically. This chapter has focused on the social and psychological empowerment of transgender people and the steps that could be taken for their safety.

- The use of new and innovative technology has empowered transgender people by broadening their thinking, establishing easy family communication, and escalating social awareness. Further, in the health sector, electronic health intervention such as paper based reporting system for antiretroviral therapy, Medicom and Paab modules, Smart Card for ART by NACO, OpenMRS, ARV medication, Mediware Datamate Info Solutions, Unisolv, iDART, Pharm, ASSIST, **AIDS-Drugs-Online.com,** HIV Vaccine Translational Research Laboratory, Telemedicine consultations, Blended learning in the form of Broadcasting health content related to HIV/AIDS through radio and TV helps deliver the better healthcare facilities towards them and improved monitoring of the status of HIV positive transgender patients and better policy framework for bringing HIV positive transgender patients into the loop of proper attention and care.
- The electronic-health systems such as Tele Psychiatry Services, Bibliotherapy, Tele-medicine Technology and Self-Help Programs based on Tele-Cognitive Behavior Therapy for reaching mentally disturbed transgender patients is a new healthcare process introduced to provide better mental healthcare to them as they are most prone to depression and anxiety disorder which can be treated with appropriate therapy by discussing their problems in a private online room which will be confined to only the caregiver and the receptor and will remain confidential for maintaining the comfort of transgender patients. This will boost their self-confidence and

self-esteem and make them feel valued. The greater motivation derived by them through these e-services, which would have been very difficult to access in the offline world, will motivate and inspire them, bringing greater wellness and positivity in their lives.

- The nature of the job victimizes them towards verbal abuses, physical violence, rapes, assaults, and other harassments throughout their lives, which puts them at heightened risk of losing their lives. Under such a situation where the lives of transgender people are at stake, certain applications or devices need to be designed so that it would detect the critical situation faced by the victim and aptly send a sensation to the near and dear ones for their rescue. Such applications are used by women in India and can also be used by transgender people for their safety and security. Society Harnessing Equipment, ILA Security, Advanced Electronics System, VithU, and Smart Belt can save numerous transgender lives.

7.5 CONCLUSION

India is a nation of vivid contradictions. On the one hand, it has turned out to be a knowledgeable economy in the global forum. On the other hand, it has several illustrations of gender inequality persisting for years. The marginalization of transgender people from the social, economic, and political mainstream has pushed them into extremes with limited opportunities for growth and development. However, the development and proliferation of information and communication technologies and the IoT have brought significant positive changes in transgender people who are standing in a disadvantageous situation in the country. ICT has opened the gates for the inflow of information without any distortion, which has significantly transformed their lives. It offers opportunities for direct and interactive communications even by those who lack skills and mobility, are uneducated, and have little self-confidence. With the rapid development in internet technology coverage, e-health services and e-security solutions through IoT devices have redesigned the healthcare systems to improve the quality of care for transgender patients who are generally ignored by healthcare professionals and help the victimized transgender people stuck in a perilous situation.

KEYWORDS

- **digital health**
- **electronic-health intervention**
- **healthcare settings**
- **HIV**
- **smart security solution**
- **tele-psychiatry**
- **transgender**

REFERENCES

1. Divan, V., Cortez, C., Smelyanskaya, M., & Keatley, J., (2016). Transgender social inclusion and equality: A pivotal path to development. *Journal of the International AIDS Society, 19,* 20803. https://doi.org/10.7448/IAS.19.3.20803.
2. *Blueprint for the Provision of Comprehensive Care for Trans People and Trans Communities in Asia and the Pacific,* (2015). UNDP in the Asia and the Pacific. UNDP. https://www.asia-pacific.undp.org/content/rbap/en/home/library/democratic_governance/hiv_aids/blueprint-for-the-provision-of-comprehensive-care-for-trans-peop.html (accessed on 10 July 2023).
3. Grossman, A. H., D'Augelli, A. R., Howell, T. J., & Hubbard, S., (2005). Parent' reactions to transgender youth' gender nonconforming expression and identity. *Journal of Gay & Lesbian Social Services, 18*(1), 3–16. https://doi.org/10.1300/J041v18n01_02.
4. Grant, J., Mottet, L., Tanis, J., Harrison, J., Herman, J., & Keisling, M., (2011). *Injustice at Every Turn: A Report of the National Transgender Discrimination Survey.* Washington, DC: National Center for Transgender Equality and National Gay and Lesbian Task Force. https://www.transequality.org/sites/default/files/docs/resources/NTDS_Report.pdf (accessed on 10 July 2023).
5. Attawell, K., (2012). *Education Sector Responses to Homophobic Bullying.* UNESCO, & Section of HIV and Health Education. https://unesdoc.unesco.org/ark:/48223/pf0000216493 (accessed on 10 July 2023).
6. Priyadarshini, S., & Swain, S. C., (2020a). Impact of adolescent school victimization on health of transgender. *Journal of Critical Reviews, 7*(14), 1464–1471. doi: 10.31838/jcr.07.14.331.
7. Suriyasarn, B., (2014). ILO Country Office for Thailand, C. and L. P. D. R., & Promoting Rights, D. and E. in the World of Work. (PRIDE) Project. *Gender Identity and Sexual Orientation in Thailand.* ILO. http://www.ilo.org/public/libdoc/ilo/2015/486318.pdf (accessed on 10 July 2023).
8. Perez, A., Correa, M. G., & Castaneda, C. W., (2013). *Raros y Oficios: Diversidad Sexual y Mundo Laboral.* Discriminacio´n y Exclusio´n. Escuela Nacional Sindical

& Corporacio´n Caribe Afirmativo. http://biblioteca.clacso.edu.ar/Colombia/ens/20140506064520/Raros_y_oficios.pdf (accessed on 10 July 2023).

9. Priyadarshini, S., & Swain, S. C., (2020). Life of transgender in ethical milieu: A study of selected transgenders of Bhubaneswar, India. *Academic Journal of Interdisciplinary Studies, 9*(4), 125. https://doi.org/10.36941/ajis-2020-0067.

10. Baral, S., Beyrer, C., & Poteat, T., (2011). *Human Rights, the Law, and HIV Among Transgender People*, 13. https://hivlawcommission.org/wp-content/uploads/2017/06/Human-Rights-the-Law-and-HIV-among-Transgender-People.pdf (accessed on 10 July 2023).

11. Camminga, B., (2018). "Gender refugees" in South Africa: The "common-sense" paradox. *Africa Spectrum, 53*(1), 89–112. https://doi.org/10.1177/000203971805300105.

12. Winter, S., (2012). *Lost in Transition: Transgender People, Rights and HIV Vulnerability in the Asia-Pacific Region.* New York, UNDP. https://www.undp.org/publications/lost-transition-transgender-people-rights-and-hiv-vulnerability-asia-pacific-region-0 (accessed on 10 July 2023).

13. Asia-Pacific Regional Dialogue, (2011). *Global Commission on HIV and the Law.* https://hivlawcommission.org/dialogues/asia-pacific/ (accessed on 10 July 2023).

14. *Trans Murder Monitoring,* (2015). TGEU https://tgeu.org/tmm-idahot-update-2015/ (accessed on 10 July 2023).

15. Poteat, T., German, D., & Kerrigan, D., (2013). Managing uncertainty: A grounded theory of stigma in transgender health care encounters. *Social Science & Medicine, 84,* 22–29. https://doi.org/10.1016/j.socscimed.2013.02.019.

16. Beattie, T. S. H., Bhattacharjee, P., Suresh, M., Isac, S., Ramesh, B. M., & Moses, S., (2012). Personal, interpersonal and structural challenges to accessing HIV testing, treatment and care services among female sex workers, men who have sex with men and transgenders in Karnataka state, South India. *Journal of Epidemiology and Community Health, 66*(Suppl 2), ii42–ii48. https://doi.org/10.1136/jech-2011-200475.

17. Keiswetter, S., & Brotemarkle, B., (2010). Culturally competent care for HIV-infected transgender persons in the inpatient hospital setting: The role of the clinical nurse leader. *Journal of the Association of Nurses in AIDS Care, 21*(3), 272–277. https://doi.org/10.1016/j.jana.2010.02.003.

18. Sanchez, N. F., Sanchez, J. P., & Danoff, A., (2009). Health care utilization, barriers to care, and hormone usage among male-to-female transgender persons in New York City. *American Journal of Public Health, 99*(4), 713–719. https://doi.org/10.2105/AJPH.2007.132035.

19. Sevelius, J. M., Carrico, A., & Johnson, M. O., (2010). Antiretroviral therapy adherence among transgender women living with HIV. *Journal of the Association of Nurses in AIDS Care, 21*(3), 256–264. https://doi.org/10.1016/j.jana.2010.01.005.

20. Chakrapani, V., Newman, P. A., Shunmugam, M., & Dubrow, R., (2011). Barriers to free anti-retroviral treatment access among Kothi-identified men who have sex with men and aravanis (transgender women) in Chennai, India. *AIDS Care, 23*(12), 1687–1694. https://doi.org/10.1080/09540121.2011.582076.

21. Shah, C. M., Sangoi, V. B., & Visharia, R. M., (2014). *Smart Security Solutions Based on Internet of Things (IoT),* 4. https://inpressco.com/wp-content/uploads/2014/09/Paper573401-3404.pdf (accessed on 10 July 2023).

22. Nikam, S., Patil, S., Powar, P., & Bendre, V. S., (2013). *GPS Based Soldier Tracking and Health Indication System, 2*(3), 7. https://www.ijareeie.com/upload/march/17_GPS%20 BASED%20SOLDIER.pdf (accessed on 10 July 2023).

23. Safer, J. D., Coleman, E., Feldman, J., Garofalo, R., Hembree, W., Radix, A., & Sevelius, J., (2016). Barriers to health care for transgender individuals. *Current Opinion in Endocrinology, Diabetes, and Obesity, 23*(2), 168–171. https://doi.org/10.1097/ MED.0000000000000227.

24. Baral, S. D., Poteat, T., Strömdahl, S., Wirtz, A. L., Guadamuz, T. E., & Beyrer, C., (2013). Worldwide burden of HIV in transgender women: A systematic review and meta-analysis. *The Lancet. Infectious Diseases, 13*(3), 214–222. https://doi.org/10.1016/ S1473-3099(12)70315-8.

25. Lombardi, E., (2010). Transgender health: A review and guidance for future research— Proceedings from the summer institute at the center for research on health and sexual orientation, university of Pittsburgh. *International Journal of Transgenderism, 12*(4), 211–229. https://doi.org/10.1080/15532739.2010.544232.

26. Sørensen, T., Rivett, U., & Fortuin, J., (2008). A review of ICT systems for HIV/AIDS and anti-retroviral treatment management in South Africa. *Journal of Telemedicine and Telecare, 14*(1), 37–41. https://doi.org/10.1258/jtt.2007.070502.

27. Brown, S. L., De Jager, D., Wood, R., & Rivett, U., (2006). *A Pharmacy Stock Control Management System to Effectively Monitor and Manage Patients on ART* (pp. 27–35). 4th IET Seminar on Appropriate Healthcare Technologies for Developing Countries. https://doi.org/10.1049/ic.2006.0657.

28. Fynn, R. W., De Jager, D., Chan, H. A., Anand, S., & Rivett, U., (2006). *Remote HIV/ AIDS Patient Monitoring Tool Using 3G/GPRS Packet-Switched Mobile Technology* (pp. 129–137). 4th IET Seminar on Appropriate Healthcare Technologies for Developing Countries. https://doi.org/10.1049/ic.2006.0670.

29. Boyce, P., (2014). Desirable rights: Same-sex sexual subjectivities, socio-economic transformations, global flows and boundaries – in India and beyond. *Culture, Health & Sexuality, 16*(10), 1201–1215. https://doi.org/10.1080/13691058.2014.944936.

30. Singh, Y., Aher, A., Shaikh, S., Mehta, S., Robertson, J., & Chakrapani, V., (2014). Gender transition services for hijras and other male-to-female transgender people in India: Availability and barriers to access and use. *International Journal of Transgenderism, 15*(1), 1–15. https://doi.org/10.1080/15532739.2014.890559.

31. Saraswathi, A., & Prakash, A. P., (2015). *To Analyze the Problems of Transgender in India/Study Using New Triangular Combined Block Fuzzy Cognitive Maps (TrCBFCM), 6*(3), 10.

32. Shaikh, S., Mburu, G., Arumugam, V., Mattipalli, N., Aher, A., Mehta, S., & Robertson, J., (2016). Empowering communities and strengthening systems to improve transgender health: Outcomes from the Pehchan program in India. *Journal of the International AIDS Society, 19*, 20809. https://doi.org/10.7448/IAS.19.3.20809.

33. *Prevention Gap Report*, (2016). UNAIDS. https://www.unaids.org/sites/default/files/ media_asset/2016-prevention-gap-report_en.pdf (accessed on 10 July 2023).

34. Chakrabarti, S., (2015). Usefulness of telepsychiatry: A critical evaluation of videoconferencing-based approaches. *World Journal of Psychiatry, 5*(3), 286. https:// doi.org/10.5498/wjp.v5.i3.286.

35. Thompson, L. H., Dutta, S., Bhattacharjee, P., Leung, S., Bhowmik, A., Prakash, R., Isac, S., & Lorway, R. R., (2019). Violence and mental health among gender-diverse

individuals enrolled in a human immunodeficiency virus program in Karnataka, South India. *Transgender Health*, *4*(1), 316–325. https://doi.org/10.1089/trgh.2018.0051.

36. Nemoto, T., Bödeker, B., & Iwamoto, M., (2011). Social support, exposure to violence and transphobia, and correlates of depression among male-to-female transgender women with a history of sex work. *American Journal of Public Health*, *101*(10), 1980–1988. https://doi.org/10.2105/AJPH.2010.197285.

37. Meyer, I. H., (1995). Minority stress and mental health in gay men. *Journal of Health and Social Behavior*, *36*(1), 38. https://doi.org/10.2307/2137286.

38. García-Lizana, F., & Muñoz-Mayorga, I., (2010). Telemedicine for depression: A systematic review. *Perspectives in Psychiatric Care*, *46*(2), 119–126. https://doi.org/10.1111/j.1744-6163.2010.00247.x.

39. Gopinath, V., (2017). *On Transgender Day of Remembrance, the Screams That India Ignored.* TheQuint. https://www.thequint.com/neon/gender/transgender-day-of-remembrance-tracking-violence-against-lgbt-community-in-india (accessed on 10 July 2023).

40. Chabria, R., & Tripathy, A., (2020). *Transgenders and Rape Law: Is Equal Protection of Law Still a Pipe Dream?* TheLeaflet. https://theleaflet.in/transgenders-and-rape-law-is-equal-protection-of-law-still-a-pipe-dream/ (accessed on 10 July 2023).

CHAPTER 8

Energy Aware Cross-Layer Routing Protocol for Body-to-Body Network in Healthcare

DEEPIKA NASIKA and KAVITHA ATHOTA

Department of Computer Science and Engineering, Jawaharlal Nehru Technological University, Hyderabad, Telangana, India

ABSTRACT

The field of body area networks (BAN) is becoming popular today as it provides ubiquitous health monitoring. Several BANed people will form a network of BANs known as Body-to-Body-Network (BBN). BBN provides cooperation among these BANed people. Thus, BBN improves the operational capacity of remote health checkup of patients. The energy of the coordinator nodes, i.e., base stations of each BAN may get depleted while collecting the information from the other coordinator nodes and while passing it to the nearby router. There is a chance of collision while two or more coordinator nodes try to send the data packets at same time. This chapter addresses the above-mentioned problems by implementing energy aware cross-layer routing protocol (ECRP). ECRP provides energy aware routing and prioritized service differentiation. The simulation was done on NS2 simulator. ECRP achieves an improvement in lifetime of the coordinator nodes and in throughput of the packets with high priority.

8.1 INTRODUCTION

A wireless body area network (WBAN) is formed by a group of nodes which can sense the important health parameters of a human being. The

Reconnoitering the Landscape of Edge Intelligence in Healthcare.
Suneeta Satpathy, Sachi Nandan Mohanty, and Sirisha Potluri (Eds.)

characteristics of these sensor nodes are less weight, low battery life, etc. These sensor nodes are implemented into the human body, or they can be worn on the body. Figure 8.1 depicts different kind of sensors were implanted into or worn by the human body. Those sensors include:

EEG (electroencephalogram) is used to detect electrical activity in human brain positioning and motion sensors – used to detect the body posture and movement of the human body. Insulin injection – used to detect the amount of insulin to be injected into the human body. ECG (electrocardiogram) is used to detect the electrical pulses that the heart generates during a cardiac cycle. Blood oxygen is used to detect the oxygen level in the human blood. Pressure sensor are used to measure the pressure that is being experienced in the foot during gait analysis. All these sensors along with a personal device which can be a mobile phone or PDA (Personal Digital Assistance) device form a body area network (BAN).

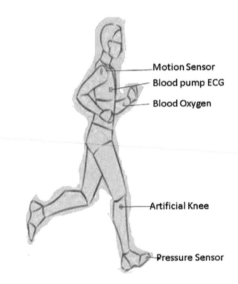

FIGURE 8.1   Wireless body area network.

BAN plays a key role in increasing the life span of human beings by providing remote health control of the patients. BAN is formed by a group of sensors and a coordinator node implanted into or worn by the human body. The coordinator node can be a mobile phone or Personal Assistance Device (PDA). These sensors collect values of the health parameters within the body of aged people and pass these readings to the coordinator node. The coordinator node passes these parameters to the nearby router which is within the network of the hospital. Thus, the patients' health will be monitored while they are being at home.

A group of people who are equipped with BAN in their body can form a network of BANs. The coordinator node of each BANed person will form a communication network with the coordinator nodes of the other BANed persons. This network is known as Body-to-Body Network (BBN). Figure 8.2 shows a group of BANs having sensor nodes and a coordinator node. The coordinator nodes form a network among themselves to form BBN.

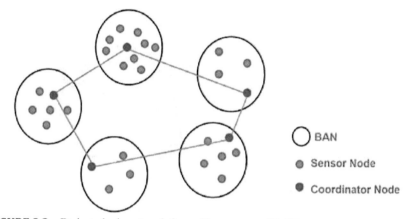

FIGURE 8.2 Body-to-body network formed by a group of BANs.

Body-to-Body networks have many advantages in real life scenarios like gaming, military, and medical fields. The following are the two example scenarios where BBN is used. First, in a cycle racing game, a number of cyclists will be competing for the cycle race in such a way that they all will go in the same direction towards the destination but with different speed. These persons are equipped with BANs so that their energy levels are being sensed and passed to an ambulance which is behind all these cyclists. Suppose the energy of a person who is far from the ambulance is getting depleted off, it takes time to get the information from this person to the ambulance. Instead, if that person's data can be passed to the intermediate persons who are nearer to the ambulance, his energy levels can be quickly reached to the ambulance, and he/she can be saved. Second, there are four patients who were equipped with BANs in or on their bodies. If the heart rate of a person with in BAN1 should be monitored by the remote doctor, that data should be forwarded with high priority. If BAN1 directly tries to forward data to the doctor, its energy will get depleted due to the long distance between them. The alternative solution for the above scenario would be careful forwarding of heartbeat data by the intermediate BANs such as BAN2 and BAN3. This mechanism helps in minimizing the energy consumption of the BAN1 to reach the destination. As shown in Figure 8.3 if every BAN tries to reach the base station, they will deplete the energy, alternatively if they form a multi-hop network then the network lifetime can be maximized.

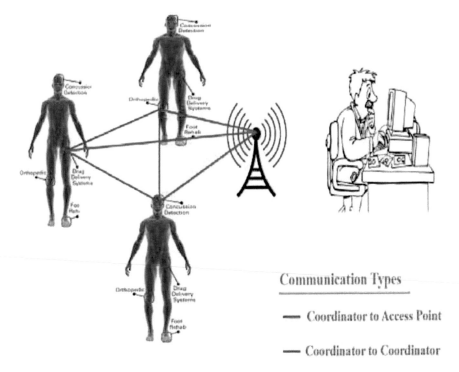

Communication Types

— Coordinator to Access Point

— Coordinator to Coordinator

FIGURE 8.3 A typical instance in patient monitoring system.

The major issues in the area of the BBN are: (i). The coordinator nodes energy may get depleted off because they are the ones who should collect the data from the sensor nodes and pass it to the nearer access point (AP). The solution to the above problem is to design a routing protocol which takes care of the residual energy (RE) in the coordinator nodes. (ii) As a number of coordinator nodes try to forward the data at same time to the AP, some of the data packets may be lost due to collisions. Here the data with high priority need to be communicated by using a cooperative scheduling mechanism to the data packets.

In Ref. [3] authors have offered a review of BAN presenting applications, communication protocols and standards being used in implementing the BAN. The two communication types observed in the BBN network are:

i. Coordinator to router; and
ii. Coordinator to coordinator.

In coordinator to router communication, there is a direct link between coordinator and the router. Suppose there is an abnormal reading of the heartbeat rate, it may take time to send that reading to the router via this direct link. On the other hand, in coordinator-to-coordinator communication, there are links between the coordinator nodes. The heartbeat rate can be reached to the intermediate coordinator node via the second communication type and then to the router via the first communication type. This gives assurance in faster delivery of data to the router and in saving energy of the coordinator node that initiated the communication, till the complete data is delivered.

The energy of the coordinator nodes of each BAN may get depleted due to the additional task of cooperating with the coordinator nodes of other BANs. There is a chance of getting collisions when two or more coordinator nodes try sending the data at the same time. Thus, BBN requires a proper routing algorithm to route the data packets for energy conservation and a proper scheduling scheme to provide service differentiation. This can be done by implementing a cross-layer protocol.

8.2 RELATED WORK

There are several algorithms proposed for communication within the BAN. In Ref. [4], authors discuss about cross-layer messaging interface between network layer and MAC layer. BackOff in the MAC layer is generated based on the remaining buffer space in the network layer.

Another cross-layer protocol by combining routing and scheduling is proposed in Ref. [5]. Reverse tree approach has been implemented in routing layer by using beacon messages. It consists of two phases namely Personal Coordinator Discovery and Reverse tree Route Configuration. 802.15.6 has been used as underlying MAC protocol to provide QoS differentiation. The data packets were grouped into different categories such as Emergency, Medical Data and Control Load. Prioritized Scheduling has been achieved by assigning different priorities to each category.

In Ref. [6], authors discussed about cross-layer opportunistic protocol. In this chapter, CSMA/CD with RTS/CTS mechanism is applied by changing the BackOff. BackOff is determined by considering RE of the node and received signal strength indicator (RSSI). RE metric is calculated by using Eqn. (1). RSSI metric is calculated by using Eqn. (2).

$$m_e = w_e \times (e_i \div e_r) \tag{1}$$

where; e_i is the initial energy; e_r is the RE; and w_e is the Tunable factor according to the priority given to m_o.

$$m_\Upsilon = w_e \times (\Upsilon_{rts} \div P_{prt}) \tag{2}$$

where; Υ_{rts} is the received signal strength value of the RTS packet at the relay node; and P_{prt} is the packet reception-power threshold.

Coming to the Body-to-Body Network, the communication network of coordinator nodes is similar to mobile ad hoc network (MANET). Several routing protocols such as ad hoc on-demand distance vector (AODV) routing, dynamic source routing (DSR) have been applied as the routing protocols for BBN.

In Ref. [7] authors discuss about energy aware routing protocol for inter BAN communication. There are three types of communication scenarios namely Coordinator-Coordinator communication, Coordinator-Node communication and Node-Node communication. The working of sensor node and the communication node consists of three phases:

1. **WBAN Initialization:** The coordinator node broadcasts a special packet known as DISCOVERY packet. It contains additional information such as RE and time to live (TTL).

2. **Neighborhood and Network Topology Setup:** This has similar kind of MANET topology setup. Optimized Link State Routing (OLSR) protocol is used with some modifications as routing protocol. The modifications are done in processing of topology control (TC) packet. Another modification is done in HELLO packets by including additional information such as RE of all the neighboring nodes. A special time period known as HelloP is given as time interval between two HELLO packets. This is determined by average mobility speed which is calculated by Eqn. (3). Thus, HelloP is calculated by using mobSpeed as mentioned in Eqn. (4).

$$mobSpeed = (highMobSpeed + lowMobSpeed) / 2 \tag{3}$$

where; *highMobSpeed* is the high mobility speed; and *lowMobSpeed* is the low mobility speed.

$$HelloP = coverage / mobSpeed \tag{4}$$

where; *coverage* is the transmission coverage radius of coordinator node.

3. **Smart Relaying:** RE threshold technique is used in which coordinator node periodically checks its RE. When its RE reaches LeaveThreshold, it broadcasts a LEAVE packet containing alternate route having coordinator node with high energy. If it reaches StopThreshold, it looks for the optimal route in case of energy consumption.

In Ref. [8] authors discuss about energy aware multi-point relay (MPR) node selection in OLSR protocol. Let us consider the node as X for which MPR set needs to be found. MPR set for the node X is calculated by considering the relative difference of highest energy and energy of all the other nodes in the neighborhood of node X. If the difference exceeds by a factor α, the node with highest energy is selected as an MPR node. Otherwise, the node with highest reachability in the neighborhood of node X is selected as MPR node. This node should have more energy than the difference of the highest energy and the factor α.

In Ref. [9] authors discuss about QoS differentiation using 802.11e as underlying MAC protocol. In this chapter, different priority levels are assigned with different traffic category identifications (TCId). These TCIds are mapped to four access categories (AC). Thus, Prioritized throughput has been achieved according to the priorities assigned to the data flows.

In Refs. [10] and [11], the authors have proposed systematic review on WBANs with respect to technologies, protocols, and standards.

In Ref. [12], author have proposed optimization models and game theory-based routing algorithms for BBN.

8.3 ENERGY-AWARE CROSS-LAYER ROUTING PROTOCOL

The above-mentioned routing and scheduling issues have been solved by implementing Energy-aware Cross-layer Routing Protocol (ECRP). The working of ECRP is explained below.

Let us consider c_1, c_2, c_3. c_i,..., c_N be the coordinator nodes of BAN$_1$, BAN$_2$, BAN$_3$, ..., BAN$_i$, ..., BAN$_n$ and e_1, e_2, e_3, ..., e_i, ..., e_n be the RE values of the corresponding nodes where $1 < i < N$. If one coordinator node falls in the circumference range of another coordinator node, then there will be a communication link between those two nodes. In this fashion, several communication links will be formed among c_1, c_2, c_3, ..., c_i. Let d_1, d_2, d_3, ...,

d_j are data flows on those communication links where $1 < j < n$ and i need not be equal to j. This newly formed communication network among the coordinator nodes of all the BANs is known as body-to-body network (BBN). BBN can be represented as a graph with nodes acting as vertices and data flows acting as edges as shown in Figure 8.4.

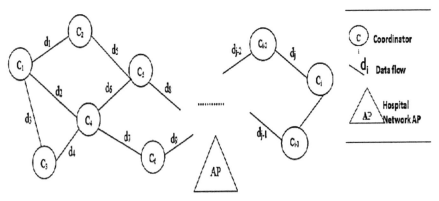

FIGURE 8.4   A typical body to body network architecture.

Let us consider c_1, c_2, c_3, ..., c_i get different types of data from the sensor nodes such as temperature, heartbeat, blood sugar level, position parameter, etc.... This data is transmitted among the nodes through the data flows d_1, d_2, d_3, ..., d_j. Assume d_1 has temperature data, d_4 has heartbeat reading, d_5 has blood sugar level reading and so on. d_4 needs to reach the AP prior to the other data flows. Prioritization can be achieved by assigning 8 different priority levels to the data flows according to 802.11e. These are mapped into four AC which are differentiated by parameters such as AIFS, CW_{min}, CW_{max}, and BackOff Exponent (PF). These parameters are assigned such that data with highest priority get lower BackOff than other data. Thus, the throughput for data flow with highest priority data is more.

If the energy of any coordinator node which is carrying data with high priority to AP is drained out in the middle of the data transmission, the QoS differentiation explained above will have no impact on the throughput. So, a proper energy aware routing algorithm needs to be implemented in the network layer. This is done by selecting MPR nodes based on the RE of the coordinator nodes. Now data with high priority can reach AP with the help of nodes having more RE.

Energy-aware MPR selection is explained in the following algorithm:

1. **Energy-Aware OLSR Algorithm:** Let us consider 1-hop neighbors set 'N' and 2-hop neighbors set 'N2' of the node whose MPR nodes need to be computed.

  i.   Start with an MPR set made of all members of N with N_willingness equal to WILL_ALWAYS.

  ii. Calculate D(y), where y is a member of N, for all nodes in N.

  iii. Add to the MPR set those nodes in N, which are the *only* nodes to provide reachability to a node in N2. For example, if Node_b in N2 can be reached only through a symmetric link to Node_a in N, then add Node_a to the MPR set. Remove the nodes from N2 which are now covered by a node in the MPR set.

  iv. Until all nodes in N2 are covered by nodes in the MPR set, the following Steps (a), (b), and (c) are repeated:

     a. For each node y in N1, calculate the reachability R(y).

     b. For each node y in N1, calculate the residual energy E(y). Let y_h denotes the node with the highest RE whose reachability more than 0, i.e., $R(y_h) > 0$.

     c. If $E(y_h)–E(y) \geq \alpha$ for each node y in N1, add the node y_h to the MPR set, where α is a parameter. Otherwise select a node with the highest R(y) from nodes whose residual energy E(y) is bigger than $(E(y_h) - \alpha)$ in N1. If there are multiple nodes with highest reachability, select one with largest D(y) from those nodes. Then add selected nodes to the MPR set and remove the nodes from N2 which are covered by the selected node.

        The above algorithm is illustrated on the sample topology given in Figure 8.5 to calculate the MPR nodes.

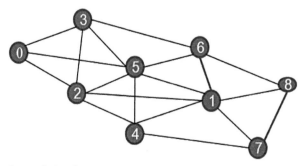

FIGURE 8.5 A sample topology.

2. **MPR nodes for Node_4:** N: 1 5 2 7   N2: 0 3 6 8

    i.   1 5 2 7 (Considering Willingness of all nodes is same)

    ii. Calculating degree of each node in N:

        1-hop neighbors of Node_1: 5 4 **6** 2 7 **8** => D(1): 2

        1-hop neighbors of Node_5: **0** 1 4 **6** 2 **3** => D(5): 3

        1-hop neighbors of Node_2: **0** 1 5 4 **3** => D(2): 2

        1-hop neighbors of Node_7: 1 4 **8** => D(7): 1

    iii. Node_0 can be reached through Node_5, Node_2

        Node_3 can be reached through Node_5, Node_2

        Node_6 can be reached through Node_1, Node_5

    iv. N2: 0 3 6 8:

        Iteration 1:

        a.   Calculating Reachability of nodes in N:

            R(1): 2 R(5): 3 R(2): 2 R(7):1

            Calculating Energy of nodes in N:

            E(1): 9.1 E(5): 9.2 E(2): 9.7 E(7): 9.1

        b. $E(2) > E(all\ nodes\ in\ N)\ \&\ \&\ R(2) > 0$

            $y_h = 2$

        c.   If $\alpha = 0.5$, E(2) – E(all nodes in N) $\geq \alpha$

            MPR Set: 2 => N2: 6 8

        Iteration 2:

        d.   Calculating Reachability of nodes in N:

            R(1): 2 R(5): 1 R(2): 0 R(7):1

            Calculating Energy of nodes in N:

            E(1): 9.1 E(5): 9.2 E(7): 9.0

        e. $E(1) > E(all\ nodes\ in\ N)\ \&\ \&\ R(1) > 0$

            $y_h = 1$

f. If $\alpha=0.5$, $E(1) - E(all\ nodes\ in\ N)\ not \geq\ \alpha$

E(all nodes in N) > (E(1) – α) &&

R(1) > R(all nodes in N)

=>MPR Set: 2

The details of prioritized scheduling have been discussed in subsection.

8.3.1 MAC

QoS has been implemented using 802.11e in enhanced distributed channel access (EDCA) mode. EDCA is contention-based mode. Around eight priority levels have been identified among the data flows with distinct TCId. These priority levels have been mapped to following four AC.

- VO (voice flow);
- VI (video flow);
- BE (best effort services); and
- BK (background traffic).

These ACs have been defined based on the following parameters. Those parameters are:

- Arbitration IFS (AIFS);
- CWmin;
- CWmax;
- Back off exponent (PF).

The conditions to categorize the data flows as different ACs are:

- AIFS(AC1) < AIFS(AC2) => Source node in a flow with AC1 decrements its backoff timer in prior to the source node in a flow with AC2.
- CWmin(AC1) < CWmin(AC2) => In average, Source node in a flow with AC1 has a lower backoff than source node in a flow with AC2.
- CWmax(AC1) < CWmax(AC2) => Source node in a flow with AC1 extracts probabilistically a lower backoff value due to its lower CWmax.
- PF(AC1) < PF(AC2) => Once a collision occurs, Source node in a flow with AC1 has probabilistically higher chance to extract a lower backoff value, thus it may retransmit first.

8.4 SIMULATION AND ANALYSIS

Simulation and performance analysis of ECRP is carried over ns2 [13]. The simulation has been done with 50 nodes network topology. The nodes were placed in random positions. Each node is given with 50J initial energy. Simulation was done for 5 scenarios. In each scenario, 30 out of 50 nodes were chosen randomly. Around 15 nodes were chosen as source nodes and other 15 nodes as destination nodes. Around 15 data flows were initiated between these source and destination nodes. Four ACs have been defined as priority_0, priority_1, priority_2 and priority_3. Each data flow is assigned with different ACs among the above-mentioned ACs. The simulation design explained above has been shown in Figure 8.6.

8.4.1 SIMULATION PARAMETERS

The simulation parameters are presented in Table 8.1. Simulation has been done using ns2 simulator and it is run for 200 sec. The trace file contents have been processed to get the parameters namely throughput and the number of active nodes by the end of the simulation. The results have been stored in a file which is given to a plotting tool known as gnuplot. The results of ECRP are shown with the label CrossLayerOLSR. The result graphs are discussed in the following section.

TABLE 8.1 Simulation Parameters

Parameter	Value
Number of WBANs	50
Transmission rate	1 Mbps
Network topology	Ad-hoc
Initial energy	50 J
Simulation time	200 s
Number of data flows	15
Number of access categories	4

8.5 RESULTS DISCUSSION

All the nodes in the network start the data flow at the beginning of the simulation time. The simulation was done for 5 scenarios. Each scenario picks up different source and destination nodes randomly for each data flow. The simulation time is 200 s. Around 15 data flows have been initiated

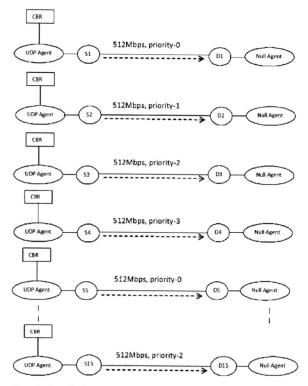

FIGURE 8.6   Simulation design of ECRP.

for different source and destination nodes. Different priorities have been assigned to those data flows.

1. **Energy Analysis:** The number of nodes which are still alive till the end of the simulation have been counted with original OLSR by applying 802.11 as underlying MAC protocol as well as with ECRP for 5 different random scenarios. Figure 8.7 shows the graph drawn by taking the scenario number as X-axis and the number of active nodes as Y-axis. ECRP is giving better results at different values of α, in case of active nodes compared to the original OLSR.

2. **Overall Throughput Analysis:** Overall throughput has been calculated for all the data flows in each scenario. Figure 8.8 shows the graph drawn by taking the scenario number as X-axis and the overall throughput as Y-axis. ECRP is giving better throughput results compared to the original OLSR.

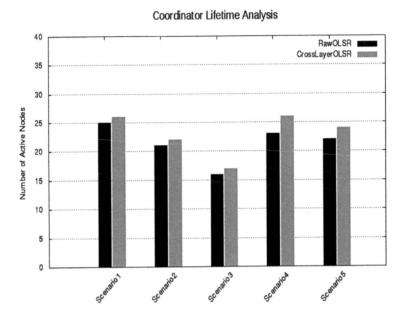

FIGURE 8.7 Performance analysis between OLSR and ECRP in terms of coordinator lifetime.

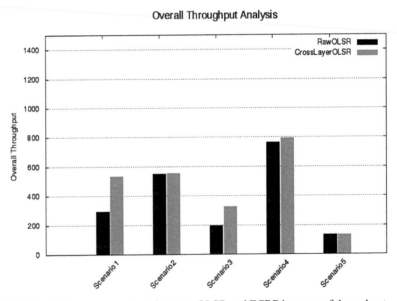

FIGURE 8.8 Performance analysis between OLSR and ECRP in terms of throughput.

3. Throughput Evaluation for Prioritized Flows: Four kinds of AC (priorities) have been assigned to the data flows by assigning priority 0 to four data flows, priority 1 to four data flows, priority 2 to four data flows and priority 3 to three data flows. The average throughput for all the data flows in each access category has been calculated. Figure 8.9 shows the graph drawn by taking the priority number as X-axis and the throughput for each priority as Y-axis. The data flows with high priority are giving better throughput compared to the data flows with low priority. This problem is known as starvation.

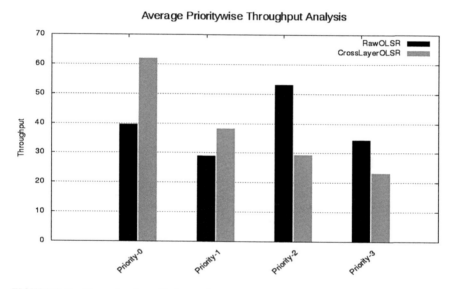

FIGURE 8.9 Throughput results for each access category.

8.6 CONCLUSION AND FUTURE WORK

Body-to-Body network (BBN) is a network formed by a collection of individual BANs. The coordinator nodes of BANs should coordinate with each other for proper data transfer. Energy aware cross-layer routing protocol (ECRP) implements both routing and MAC layer protocols. Energy aware OLSR is used for routing and 802.11e is used for MAC. ECRP is giving better energy results and throughput compared to the original OLSR. Data flows with high priority have achieved better throughput compared to the data flows with low priority Thus the data of the patients with more serious diseases will be given high priority and that data will be reached as fast as possible. But the data flows with low priority are giving low throughput values as they suffer from starvation and taking measures for avoidance of starvation can be addressed in future.

KEYWORDS

- body area network
- body-to-body network
- coordinator
- energy aware cross-layer routing protocol
- energy-aware routing
- service differentiation
- starvation

REFERENCES

1. Jing, C. W., Mark, L., Zhao, W., Eng, G. L., Ka Lok, M., & Yi, H., (2015). *Wireless Body Area Network and its Applications.* International SoC Design Conference (ISOCC).
2. Amira, M., Jocelyne, E., & Ahmed, M., (2015). *Future Body-to-Body Networks for Ubiquitous Healthcare: A Survey, Taxonomy and Challenges.* Future Information and Communication Technologies for Ubiquitous HealthCare (Ubi-HealthTech), 2nd International Symposium.
3. Carlos, A. T., Jesús, H. O., Osamah, I. K., Diego, F. S., & Theyazn, H. H. A., (2021). Wearable wireless body area networks for medical applications. *Computational and Mathematical Methods in Medicine, 2021*, 9. Article ID 5574376. https://doi.org/10.1155/2021/5574376.
4. Anirban, B., & Mostafa, A. B., (2008). BioComm – a cross-layer medium access control (MAC) and routing protocol co-design for biomedical sensor networks. *International Journal of Parallel, Emergent and Distributed Systems.*
5. Saadi, B., Hadda, B. E., & Lamia, C. F., (2013). A cross-layer based data dissemination algorithm for IEEE 802.15.6 WBANS. *International Conference on Smart Communications in Network Technologies (SaCoNeT).*
6. Umer, F. A., Azlan, A., & Nor, H. H., (2014). A cross-layer opportunistic MAC/routing protocol to improve reliability in WBAN. *The 20th Asia-Pacific Conference on Communication (APCC2014).*
7. Audace, M., Saadi, B., & Lamia, C. F., (2015). Energy aware routing protocol for inter WBANs cooperative communication. *International Symposium on Networks, Computers and Communications (ISNCC).*

8. Wardi, K. H., Yoshinobu, H., & Shin-Ya, K., (2011). Residual energy-based OLSR in mobile ad hoc networks. *International Conference on Multimedia Technology*.

9. Ramakristanaiah, C., Chenna, R. P., & Praveen, S. R., (2016). Evaluation of starvation problem under saturated loads in IEEE 802.11e. *International Conference on Emerging Technological Trends (ICETT)*.

10. Carlos, A. T., Jesús, H. O., Osamah, I. K., Diego, F. S., & Theyazn, H. H. A., (2021). Wearable wireless body area networks for medical applications. *Computational and Mathematical Methods in Medicine, 2021*, 9. Article ID 5574376. https://doi.org/10.1155/2021/5574376.

11. Meharouech, A., Elias, J., & Mehaoua, A., (2019). Moving towards body-to-body sensor networks for ubiquitous applications: A survey. *J. Sens. Actuator Netw., 8*, 27. https://doi.org/10.3390/jsan8020027.

12. Amira, M. A., (2016). *Wireless Body-to-Body Sensor Networks: Optimization Models and Algorithms*. Networking and Internet Architecture [cs.NI]. Université Sorbonne Paris Cité.

13. Teerawat, I., & Ekram, H., (2012). *Introduction to Network Simulator NS2* (2nd edn.).

CHAPTER 9

Edge Intelligence – A Smart Healthcare Scenario in Ambient-Assisted Living

BIBHU KALYAN MISHRA[1] and S. K. YADAV[2]

[1]Sri Sri University, Cuttack, Odisha, India

[2]Shri JJT University, Vidya Nagari, Jhunjhunu, Rajasthan, India

ABSTRACT

The expanding population creates a lot of challenges for people at all stages of life, including older people and their careers, which has a negative impact on the healthcare industry. Many efforts have been made all around the world to serve the aging population with artificial intelligence (AI), with the goal of posing an ecosystem that is social and ethical. In this study, we focus on a close assisted Living situation in which a sensible home environment is provided to assist elders with their reception, enacting reliable machine-driven advanced choices through the use of IoT sensors, good healthcare equipment, and a terminal workstation. The key is to use comparisons between computing and principal requirement sources to your benefit. Using AI to make advanced machine-driven decisions.

9.1 INTRODUCTION

One of the most serious issues confronting the aid industry is the aging population, which may result in an ever-increasing rise in the costs of intervention, diagnosis, and covers. Artificial neuron techniques have recently drawn attention to AAL topics such as "aging well" and "domiciliary hospitalization." The latter, in particular, deals with the situation in which a person is

Reconnoitering the Landscape of Edge Intelligence in Healthcare.
Suneeta Satpathy, Sachi Nandan Mohanty, and Sirisha Potluri (Eds.)
© 2024 Apple Academic Press, Inc. Co-published with CRC Press (Taylor & Francis)

considered or treated as if he or she is hospitalized even when they are not. In this situation, computing artificial intelligence (AI) algorithms and methods will play a critical role in the near future. The advancement of recent AI techniques, which assist older adults in addressing the changes of aging and providing assistance, represents one of the most advanced information and communication technology (ICT) areas.

Because of the increasing accessibility of online materials and other cutting-edge technologies such as IoT, it is now possible to move the revolution and trail of interference, designation, and care to the patient's home by authorizing and utilizing aid facilities, people, and machinery solely in cases of urgency or specialized experience. Edge computing (EC) approaches are rising promise and a promising resolution that pushes computing jobs and services from the network core to the network edge due to a variety of challenging difficulties, such as machine quality and added latency in CC. EC, a cutting-edge technology, has recently outperformed the traditional way in terms of efficiency and evenly distributing resources, such as electricity and battery life of internet of things (IoT) appliances.

Meanwhile, because AI is required for processing large amounts of data and extracting the essence, there is a strong need to combine EC and AI, which will meet the demand for edge intelligence (EI). Furthermore, huge information has now transcended the mega-scale dimension shift of information supply. We're then confronted with a pressing need to push AI's boundaries to the network edge, in order to fully realize the potential of sting vast data.

As a result, the chapter has three objectives: (i) to introduce a novel EI architecture; (ii) to employ a variety of reticular AI approaches in a footing computing solution; and (iii) to provide a unique full-edge platform, known as eLifeCare, that is enhanced by the In Edge computation of AI-based methodologies to undertake reliable decision-making activities in a|during a|in AN exceedingly|in a very high quality state of affairs like AAL hospitalization.

The eLifeCare platform is introduced, taking into account all of the requirements arising from various AI disciplines. Section 9.2 discusses the application scenarios that are specifically designed for our methodology, such as AAL assistance. Finally, Section 9.3 examines and concludes the proposed framework.

- **Background and Previous Research:** Here, we'll go over the fundamentals of EI and AI-based reasoning tasks, as well as some recent work, in order to demonstrate the architecture of our proposed platform.

9.1.1 EDGE INTELLIGENCE (EI)

Also, the ability to perform & cost are the factors so is privacy.

Essentially, the physical proximity of the computers ensures numerous advantages over traditional cloud computing (CC) technology, including efficiency and information measurement on demand services [37]. EC, on the one hand, believes in coordinating a multifunction of cooperative EC and supplying to method information in the vicinity. EI does not imply that AI technology is perfect inferred at sting, but it does add a cloud edge mechanism via information transfer. As seen in Figure 9.1. Aside from data centers, AI and IoT create a lot of and a lot of information. It will transform information into a wealth of useful data and practical industrial management groups that will benefit people in a variety of ways [26].

Sixth Level – On remote edge computer in detail
Fifth Level- Artificial intelligence & edge computing in detail
Fourth level- Training on detail about cloud & edge computing correlation
Third level- On remote computer inference testing
Second level- Edge computing inference testing
First level- Cloud & edge computing correlation inference testing
OVERALL TRAINING ON CLOUD & EDGE COMPUTING

FIGURE 9.1   6 levels of Artificial intelligence & edge computing.

Regarding EI scenarios in the context of AAL, [14] proposed an agent-based system that works in a SHE state of affairs and is responsible for managing the various options and capabilities of a situation-aware environment, ensuring appropriate contextualized and customized support to the user's actions, adaptivity to the user's standing and desires, and changes over time, as well as automatic management of the environment. While focusing on the care domain, [19] proposed a Telemedicine Platform for the treatment, care, and early intervention of patients with a secure transition from the hospital to the home dimension (also known as proximity medicine) through the use of advanced sensors for observing and administering patient home-based therapies, as well as data analytics.

It is planned to employ the concept of in Ref. [27]. Instead, one of the most advanced data & Communication Technology (ICT) sectors is [22] anticipated association design in IoT principally u-healthcare observance with them to meet the modifications of aging and care help. Because of the increasing accessibility of IoT and communication, the care protocol now has the option of shifting a revolution trail of interference, designation, and care to the patient's home by relegating the use of care facilities, personnel, and machinery to only emergency or specialized experience cases.

A rising paradigm and a potential resolution are associated due to various challenging difficulties such as process quality and a lot of delay in emerging technology. In IoT industrialization, it recently surpassed the old way, within the given time frame, Furthermore, huge data has recently experienced a 360° transformation in knowledge supply. We have a propensity to therefore be confronted with an imperative to view AI accomplishing the actual work and to fully utilize the power of enormous data.

As a result, the chapter's goals are threefold: (i) to present a completely unique EI architecture; (ii) to use many reticular AI techniques that will be involved in a foothold Computing solution; and (iii) to present a completely unique full-edge platform, referred to as eLifeCare, that is enhanced by the In-Edge computation of AI-based techniques to perform reliable decision-making activities.

In this section, we'll go over all of the fundamentals and most recent advancements in EI and AI-based reasoning tasks that will be useful in presenting the architecture of our proposed platform.

9.1.1.1 EDGE INTELLIGENCE (EI)

It is anticipated that a three-layer patient-driven aid architecture will be developed for knowledge collection on a periodic basis, its processing, and transmission, providing end-users with insights into the usefulness of fog devices and gateways. ECC-based intelligent health technology is capable of displaying users' physical health using psychological feature computing and enacting optimal resource allotment total edge technology in accordance with each individual's body problem rate [7].

Recently, an AI-driven EC method was proposed as a dynamic solution to change the time period in Ref. [35]. On the other hand, improvements AI mechanism of laptop Vision and informal Interfaces are implemented on gadgets in Ref. [25] to improve sensible manufacturing processes. Alternatively, AI for Edge Technology could be a research path that focuses on offering a more robust solution to the affected development challenges in developing technology such as EC in modern AI. EC makes use of AI [18].

Our research usually falls under the latter category of EI. Furthermore, our contribution is situated in a situation where the convergence of multiple AI-technologies enables the United States of America to modify advanced decision-making activities resulting from a multi-strategic abstract thought approach. In fact, the definition of EI does not exclude machine learning (ML) or deep learning (DL) models [36].

Following techniques are vital:

- ML/DL (training & inferring) models;
- Information illustration (KR) and linguistics internet Technologies for IoT;
- Reasoning over unsure, partial, and conflicting data.

To this finish, we are able to reach trustable and explicable results, in so much that associate AI distributed at the sting of a multi-IoT network, like in an exceedingly sensible home atmosphere (SHE), would justify its choices in an exceedingly reliable and clear approach.

9.1.1.2   INFORMATION ILLUSTRATION WITH LINGUISTICS IN IOT

In linguistics, IoT SWOT analysis links developing ICT challenges to the linguistics internet and IoT. On the one hand, the Linguistics Internet Initiative [3] proposes to allow computer code agents to share, reprocess, and combine data on the market over the internet. On the other hand, the IoT vision promotes the pervasive computing paradigm on a global scale, which intends to embed intelligence into everyday things and physical locations by implying an enormous range of heterogeneous micro-devices, each transmitting a small amount of data [31].

As shown in Figure 9.2, the purpose of SWoT is to embed semantically created and easily available data into the physical environment by allowing the storing and retrieval of annotations from small sensible objects [28]. As a result, SWoT settings have an active provision of workstations. The SWoT vision has a significant impact on human-computer interaction models, with the goal of lowering the amount of user effort and focusing required to get the most out of computing systems. Exaggerated deliberation of ubiquitous wise technology is required in IT. SWoT could improve milliliter categorization tasks by combining edge characterizations of data [29]. During this process, a milliliter categorization disadvantage is frequently encountered.

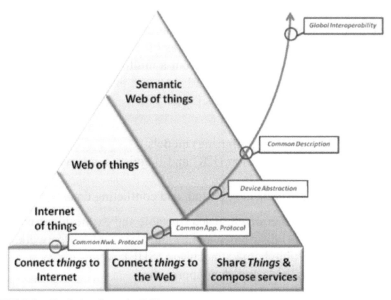

FIGURE 9.2   Evolution from the IoT.

Source: Reprinted from Ref. [15]. Copyright 2020 authors. https://creativecommons.org/licenses/by/4.0/

9.1.2   EXPLAINABLE AND RELIABLE DECISION-MAKING WITH ARGUMENTATION

In AI, Abstract Argumentation could be a terribly easy however conjointly terribly powerful formalism to reason over conflicting data. It studies the satisfactoriness of arguments primarily based strictly on their relationships and abstracted from their content. Associate in nursing argument could be a set of assumptions (i.e., info from that conclusions will be drawn), along with a conclusion which will be obtained by one or additional reasoning steps. Given a tangle to unravel (making call, reasoning with unsure info, classifying associate in nursing object), arguments area unit totally different from proofs in this they're defeasible, that is, a sort of non-monotonic reasoning within which the validity of their conclusions will be controversial by alternative arguments within the lightweight of latest proof. Then, argumentation is that the method by those arguments and counterarguments area unit created and handled. Handling arguments might involve scrutiny arguments, evaluating them in some respects, and judgment a constellation of arguments and counterarguments to think about whether or not any of them area unit secured consistent with some scrupulous criterion [4].

Basically, Abstract Argumentation, introduced by Dung [12], could be a graph-based formalism to reason over conflicting data while not considering the inner structure of the arguments however solely on their relations of attack, denoting the conflicts between the arguments, and a linguistics for evaluating them, i.e., assessing to what extent every argument is suitable.

Building applicable argumentation formalism will cause far more concern than expected. Attention should be paid to avoid the chance of violating some natural rationality postulates [5] within the overall instantiate-based argumentation.

9.2   EXPRIVIA'S ARTIFICIAL INTELLIGENCE (AI) ON EMERGING TECHNOLOGY EDGE COMPUTING (EC)

Here we firstly showcase a normal edge technology system architecture that exploits several AI techniques to optimize healthcare in a SHE autonomous setting, and then we focus on eLifeCare, that is our platform in which AI on Edge is actually performed.

9.2.1   AI ON EDGE ARCHITECTURE FOR HEALTHCARE IN AAL

Here Focus is placed on planning and developing edge nodes, with associated end-nodes for numerous patient observance applications. During this complicated state of affairs, we have a tendency to modify an oversized scale of heterogeneous devices as edge nodes in associate degree IoT surroundings, which, at totally different|completely different} levels of abstractions and different roles, communicate and convey totally different styles of information:

1. End-nodes/device layer:
    • Simple, complicated sensor;
    • Mobile, Wearable, Embedded devices;
    • Actuators.

2. Edge nodes/edge layer:
    • ·   Gateway, Sink devices;
    • ·   Fog, Decider nodes.

3. Cloud datacenter/cloud layer.

In associate degree aid state of affairs, end-nodes will be distinguished in a very additional taxonomy, as shown in Figure 9.3.

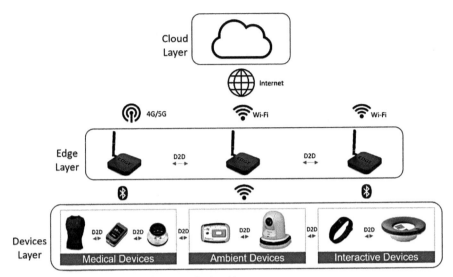

FIGURE 9.3   AI on edge architecture for healthcare.

Source: Reprinted from Ref. [15]. Copyright 2020 authors. https://creativecommons.org/li-censes/by/4.0/

Focusing on AI, we have a tendency to envision a EC network capable of performing not solely knowledge analysis, classification, regression, and/or agglomeration via ML/DL on-line coaching and reasoning, however conjointly a wider vary of AI techniques, adding a context-awareness and explainability/reliability of results. During this vision, ML/DL models area unit deployed in a very hybrid mode which mixes the suburbanized training/inferring mode with a centralized revised/refined mode.

As shown in Figure 9.4, the sting servers could train the ML/DL technology suburbanized one another centrally located is additionally referred to as cloud edge into technology thanks in concerned roles. Because the hub of the ML/DL design is placed as shut as doable to end-nodes and edge nodes, there's associate degree improvement of performances concerning the coaching loss, convergence, privacy, communication value, latency, and energy potency.

The structure of such a posh heterogeneous network of edge nodes could have a pyramidic topology, as in Figure 9.4. During this configuration, the nodes at the higher-level area unit supposed to own a distinct role since at the next level of "abstraction" of the heterogeneous network, and may, therefore, have totally different tasks from the end-nodes, not excluding that they'll embrace associate degree exclusive partial data over the complete network. Therefore, they will act as straightforward collectors of knowledge explanation from teams of sensors, or from aggregators of such info, or they will build additional process steps on the sting network. A key issue during this complicated state of affairs is that of the honesty and responsibility of knowledge gathered by teams of heterogeneous sensors that can:

- Notice conflicting info at intervals an end-nodes and/or edge nodes;
- Cluster info at totally different levels of abstraction;
- Perform partial process at the sting layer.

In explicit, a foothold Intelligence task may well be performed either with partial ML/DL model coaching or with specific reasoning and reasoning tasks on the info collected through linguistics descriptions and metaphysics dictionaries. A definite degree of uncertainty or inconsistency is probably going to arise from all the partial touch of processed knowledge by any style of device within the heterogeneous network. Therefore, a key downside regards to gauge the responsibility of the partial results from the complete network. Moreover, such data could also be conflicting, yielding the system unable to require autonomous trust-able choices.

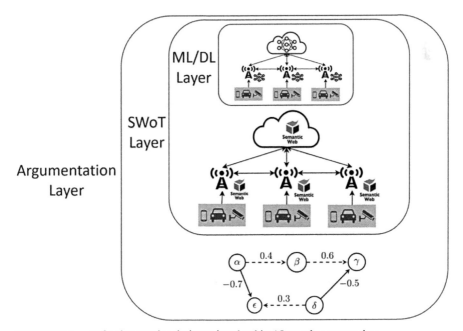

FIGURE 9.4 AI fundamental techniques involved in AI on edge processing.

Source: Reprinted from Ref. [15]. Copyright 2020 authors. https://creativecommons.org/licenses/by/4.0/

A procedure model of argumentation, like the BWAF, may solve 2 sorts of inconsistencies between conflicting information:

i.   In a "horizontal" manner, it will resolve the conflicts created by the end-nodes that transmit similar however conflicting information;

ii. In a "vertical" manner, it will solve issues of conflicting data between the data (possibly aggregated) sent by the lower levels of the pyramiddle towards the upper levels, during which associate inconsistency is found between partly disjointed data between the end-nodes and edge-nodes.

The automatic building of associate argumentation framework just like the BWAF and its resulting analysis through eristical linguistics for the choice of acceptable arguments could be an excellent resolution during this context. Specifically, endowing the data coming back from end-nodes and edge nodes with linguistics annotations permits a machine-understandable illustration of data that may be exploited to mechanically build the BWAF, which may provide an illustration of conflicting and/or supporting arguments of the whole network. Specially, the non-standard abstract thought technique of linguistics matchmaking between pairs of arguments is utilized to outline a weighted notion of relation between arguments (i.e., attack or support; Figure 9.5).

FIGURE 9.5   The eLifeCare platform dashboard.

From the result obtained it'll thus be potential to be sure of the honesty and reliableness of the data detected and processed at the sting, in an exceedingly heterogeneous and complicated multi-IoT network, which may be crucial once a fancy call is mechanically taken.

9.2.2 THE ELIFECARE PLATFORM

- Supervising from any place;
- Medicinal consultation over phone;
- Medicative product procurance monitoring;
- News and recording;
- Individual patients' file in system.

The E-Lifecare platform has specific mobile applications to be used by the patient that is as follows:

- Care can be given at the house of patient;
- Measuring the main criteria;
- Video conferencing system for consultation;
- Demographic location of patient;
- Medicative product procurance requests.

If the cloud-edge-device coordination of AI/ML models with SWoT annotation and higher cognitive process and argumentation autonomously decides to make a modification at intervals the patient's treatment, the platform starts teleconsulting or video consulting session with the specialists that unit following the patient to speak the treatment variation and send a confirmation request. As briefly delineate in Figure 9.6, the eLifeCare platform exploits AI on the sting level to perform utterly completely different varieties of reasoning degree take advanced autonomous decisions at different layers of the edge network.

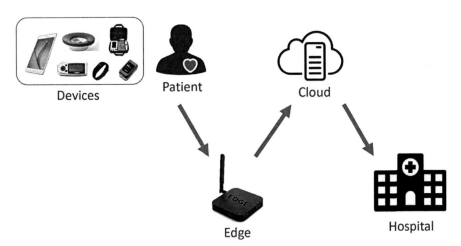

FIGURE 9.6   Healthcare scenario in AAL.

This is helpful in recognizing the severity, timeliness, and appropriateness of intervention among the factors determining the clinical outcome. Moreover, the platform acts as an alert system, such as early warning scores (EWS), which help in identifying specific phases of illness and provide appropriate care.

9.3 CONCLUSION AND FUTURE WORK

EC technology, while still in its infancy, has piqued the interest of many scientists and organizations, prompting them to become concerned about discovering and using it. The purpose of this research is to provide possible analytical opportunities for AI nervy. In particular, we have a proclivity to connect EC with AI. I believe that the use of different AI technologies will enable change complex decision-making processes resulting from a multi-strategic logical thinking approach. In fact, I believe that EC is the next generation of technology for optimizing overall performance, not just for ML models, but also for other logical thinking and reasoning tasks, such as linguistics, the IoT, and argumentation.

KEYWORDS

- **argumentation**
- **artificial house environment**
- **decision support systems**
- **edge ultra-intelligence**
- **explainable AI**
- **public healthcare system**
- **semantic web and things**
- **smart edge computing**
- **ultra-model thinking ability**

REFERENCES

1. Baroni, P., Gabbay, D., Giacomin, M., & Van, D. T. L., (2018). *Handbook of Formal Argumentation* (Vol. 1). College Publications.
2. Bench-Capon, T. J. M., Doutre, S., & Dunne, P. E., (2002). Value-based argumentation frame- works. In: *Artificial Intelligence* (pp. 444–453).

3. Berners-Lee, T., Hendler, J., Lassila, O., et al., (2001). *The Semantic Web, 284*(5), 28–37. Scientific American.

4. Besnard, P., & Hunter, A., (2008). *Elements of Argumentation*. The MIT Press.

5. Caminada, M., & Amgoud, L., (2007). On the evaluation of argumentation formalisms. *Artificial Intelligence, 171*(5, 6), 286–310.

6. Cayrol, C., & Lagasquie-Schiex, M., (2005). On the acceptability of arguments in bipolar argumentation frameworks. In: *European Conference on Symbolic and Quantitative Approaches to Reasoning and Uncertainty, ECSQARU: Lecture Notes in Computer Science* (Vol. 3571, pp. 378–389). Springer.

7. Chen, M., Li, W., Hao, Y., Qian, Y., & Humar, I., (2018). Edge cognitive computing based smart healthcare system. *Future Generation Computer Systems, 86*, 403–411.

8. Chen, X., Pu, L., Gao, L., Wu, W., & Wu, D., (2017). Exploiting massive D2D collaboration for energy-efficient mobile edge computing. *IEEE Wireless Communications, 24*(4), 64–71.

9. Colucci, S., Di Noia, T., Pinto, A., Ruta, M., Ragone, A., & Tinelli, E., (2007). A nonmonotonic approach to semantic matchmaking and request refinement in e-marketplaces. *International Journal of Electronic Commerce, 12*(2), 127–154.

10. Coste-Marquis, S., Konieczny, S., Marquis, P., & Ouali, M. A., (2012). Selecting extensions in weighted argumentation frameworks. In: *Computational Models of Argument – Proceedings of COMMA* (pp. 342–349).

11. Deng, S., Zhao, H., Yin, J., Dustdar, S., & Zomaya, A. Y., (2019). *Edge Intelligence: The Confluence of Edge Computing and Artificial Intelligence.* arXiv preprint arXiv:1909.00560.

12. Dung, P. M., (1995). On the acceptability of arguments and its fundamental role in non-monotonic reasoning, logic programming and n-person games. *Artificial Intelligence, 77*(2), 321–357.

13. Dunne, P. E., Hunter, A., McBurney, P., Parsons, S., & Wooldridge, M., (2011). Weighted argument systems: Basic definitions, algorithms, and complexity results. *Artificial Intelligence, 175*(2), 457–486.

14. Ferilli, S., De Carolis, B., Pazienza, A., Esposito, F., & Redavid, D., (2015). An agent architecture for adaptive supervision and control of smart environments. In: *PECCS 2015 – Proceedings of the 5th International Conference on Pervasive and Embedded Computing and Communication Systems* (pp. 160–167).

15. Jara, A. J., Olivieri, A. C., Bocchi, Y., Jung, M., Kastner, W., & Skarmeta, A. F., (2014). Semantic web of things: An analysis of the application semantics for the IoT moving towards the IoT convergence. *International Journal of Web and Grid Services, 10*(2, 3), 244–272.

16. Kumari, A., Tanwar, S., Tyagi, S., & Kumar, N., (2018). Fog computing for healthcare 4.0 environment: Opportunities and challenges. *Computers & Electrical Engineering, 72*, 1–13.

17. Lippi, M., Mamei, M., Mariani, S., & Zambonelli, F., (2018). An argumentation-based perspective over the social IoT. *IEEE Internet of Things Journal, 5*(4), 2537–2547.

18. Lov'en, L., Leppanen, T., Peltonen, E., Partala, J., Harjula, E., Porambage, P., Ylianttila, M., & Riekki, J., (2019). *Edgeai: A Vision for Distributed, Edge-Native Artificial Intelligence in Future 6G Networks* (pp. 1–2). The 1st 6G Wireless Summit.

19. Mallardi, G., Mariani, A. M., Altomare, E., Maruccia, Y., Vitulano, F., & Bellifemine, F., (2017). Telemedicine solutions and services: A new challenge that supports active

participation of patients. In: *I-CiTies 2017 (3rd CINI Annual Conference on ICT for Smart Cities & Communities).*

20. Miraz, M. H., Ali, M., Excell, P. S., & Picking, R., (2015). A review on internet of things (IoT), internet of everything (IoE) and internet of nano things (IoNT). In: *2015 Internet Technologies and Applications (ITA)* (pp. 219–224). IEEE.

21. Modgil, S., (2009). Reasoning about preferences in argumentation frameworks. *Artificial Intelligence, 173*(9), 901–934.

22. Nandyala, C. S., & Kim, H. K., (2016). From cloud to fog and IoT-based real-time u-healthcare monitoring for smart homes and hospitals. *International Journal of Smart Home, 10*(2), 187–196.

23. Pazienza, A., Ferilli, S., & Esposito, F., (2017). Constructing and evaluating bipolar weighted argumentation frameworks for online debating systems. In: *Proceedings of the 1st Workshop on Advances in Argumentation in Artificial Intelligence Co-located with XVI International Conference of the Italian Association for Artificial Intelligence, AI³@ AI*IA 2017* (pp. 111–125).

24. Pazienza, A., Ferilli, S., & Esposito, F., (2017). On the gradual acceptability of arguments in bipolar weighted argumentation frameworks with degrees of trust. In: *Foundations of Intelligent Systems – 23rd International Symposium, ISMIS 2017, Proceedings* (pp. 195–204).

25. Pazienza, A., Macchiarulo, N., Vitulano, F., Fiorentini, A., Cammisa, M., Rigutini, L., Di Iorio, E., Globo, A., & Trevisi, A., (2019). A novel integrated industrial approach with cobots in the age of industry 4.0 through conversational interaction and computer vision. In: *Proceedings of the Sixth Italian Conference on Computational Linguistics (CLiC-it 2019).*

26. Pazienza, A., Polimeno, G., Vitulano, F., & Maruccia, Y., (2019). Towards a digital future: An innovative semantic IoT integrated platform for industry 4.0, healthcare, and territorial control. In: *2019 IEEE International Conference on Systems, Man and Cybernetics (SMC)* (pp. 587–592).

27. Rahmani, A. M., Gia, T. N., Negash, B., Anzanpour, A., Azimi, I., Jiang, M., Lil-Jeberg, P., (2018). Exploiting smart e-health gateways at the edge of healthcare internet- of-things: A fog computing approach. *Future Generation Computer Systems, 78*, 641–658.

28. Ruta, M., Scioscia, F., & Di Sciascio, E., (2012). Enabling the semantic web of things: Frame- work and architecture. In: *2012 IEEE Sixth International Conference on Semantic Computing* (pp. 345–347). IEEE.

29. Ruta, M., Scioscia, F., Loseto, G., Pinto, A., & Di Sciascio, E., (2019). *Machine Learning in the Internet of Things: A Semantic-Enhanced Approach* (pp. 1–22). Semantic Web (Preprint).

30. Ruta, M., Scioscia, F., Pinto, A., Gramegna, F., Ieva, S., Loseto, G., & Di Sciascio, E., (2019). Coap-based collaborative sensor networks in the semantic web of things. *Journal of Ambient Intelligence and Humanized Computing, 10*(7), 2545–2562.

31. Satyanarayanan, M., et al., (2001). Pervasive computing: Vision and challenges. *IEEE Personal Communications, 8*(4), 10–17.

32. Scioscia, F., Ruta, M., Loseto, G., Gramegna, F., Ieva, S., Pinto, A., & Di Sciascio, E., (2014). A mobile matchmaker for the ubiquitous semantic web. *International Journal on Semantic Web and Information Systems (IJSWIS), 10*(4), 77–100.

33. Scioscia, F., Ruta, M., Loseto, G., Gramegna, F., Ieva, S., Pinto, A., & Di Sciascio, E., (2018). Mini-me matchmaker and reasoner for the semantic web of things. In:

Innovations, Developments, and Applications of Semantic Web and Information Systems (pp. 262–294). IGI Global.

34. Simari, G. R., & Rahwan, I., (2009). *Argumentation in Artificial Intelligence*. Springer.
35. Sodhro, A. H., Pirbhulal, S., & De Albuquerque, V. H. C., (2019). Artificial intelligence driven mechanism for edge computing based industrial applications. *IEEE Transactions on Industrial Informatics*.
36. Wang, X., Han, Y., Wang, C., Zhao, Q., Chen, X., & Chen, M., (2019). *In-edge AI: Intelligentizing Mobile Edge Computing, Caching and Communication by Federated Learning*. IEEE Network.
37. Zhou, Z., Chen, X., Li, E., Zeng, L., Luo, K., & Zhang, J., (2019). Edge intelligence: Paving the last mile of artificial intelligence with edge computing. Proceedings of the IEEE, 107(8), 1738–1762.

PART III
Research Challenges and Opportunities in Edge Computing

CHAPTER 10

Edge Intelligence to Smart Management and Control of Epidemic

PREETHI NANJUNDAN,[1] JOSSY P. GEORGE,[1] and C. KARPAGAM[2]

[1]Department of Data Science, Christ University, Lavasa, Pune, Maharashtra, India

[2]Department of Computer Science with Data Analytics, Dr. N.G.P. Arts and Science College, Tamil Nadu, India

ABSTRACT

The effects of COVID-19 vary from person to person. A pandemic is devastating economically and socially. Thousands of enterprises face the possibility of collapse. More than half of the world's 3.3 billion workers may lose their livelihoods if the current crisis continues. The world's healthcare services are facing an unprecedented situation due to the recent outbreak of a novel coronavirus (COVID-19). Community and government health are adversely affected by the COVID-19 pandemic. COVID-19 has continued to spread, and mortalities have risen steadily. The spread of this disease can therefore be controlled utilizing nonpharmacological methods, such as quarantine, isolation, and public health education. Recent breakthroughs in deep learning (DL) have led to an explosion in applications and services relating to artificial intelligence (AI). The rapid advancements in mobile computing and AI have enabled zillions of Bytes of data to be generated at the network edge from thousands of mobile devices and internet of things (IoT) devices connected to the Internet. As a result of the success of IoT and AI technologies, it is of utmost importance that we expand the AI frontiers to the network edge in order for big data to be fully tapped. Edge computing (EC) can help overcome this trend because it allows computation-intensive

Reconnoitering the Landscape of Edge Intelligence in Healthcare.
Suneeta Satpathy, Sachi Nandan Mohanty, and Sirisha Potluri (Eds.)
© 2024 Apple Academic Press, Inc. Co-published with CRC Press (Taylor & Francis)

AI applications to run on edge hardware. The topic of discussion in this chapter is edge intelligence (EI) technology's application in limiting virus spread during pandemics.

10.1   INTRODUCTION

Existential threats are threatening many companies. The economic downturn may lead to nearly half of the world's 3.3 billion workers losing their jobs. Because of the lack of social protection, poor healthcare, and a lack of access to assets, informal economy workers are particularly vulnerable [1].

A global health emergency was also declared by the WHO Emergency Committee on January 21, 2020, due to the increase in COVID-19 cases reported from overseas countries. In addition to socioeconomic phenomena and numerous global phenomena such as commodity prices, remittances, trade, and tourism, the pandemic also caused significant job losses and significantly lower wages. The advancement of technology has led to significant changes in many aspects of our lives, including gaining access to better information, data, and medical resources through telemedicine [2]. The chapter describes how smart technologies assist us in preventing infectious diseases and protecting people's privacy through the rapid development of intelligence.

10.1.1   WHAT DOES EDGE INTELLIGENCE (EI) MEAN?

The vision of edge computing (EC) is to collect, store, and process data closer to the point of use and analyze it to improve response times and save bandwidth. The primary function of EC is to enable applications to run in proximity to data sources such as internet of things (IoT) devices, endpoints, or edge servers.

EC is based on the philosophy that computing should be done close to data sources. EC will therefore have a similar impact to cloud computing (CC), as we have observed with CC [3].

A combination of machine learning (ML) algorithms and artificial intelligence (AI) is edge intelligence (Edge AI); it is based on ML algorithms deployed at the device where data is generated. Every person and organization can benefit from AI wherever they are with EI [3].

Smart, connected, computational, and controlling is the essence of intelligent EC. Fundamentally, Intelligent Edge is a solution that offers analytics capabilities previously only available in-house or in clouds [4].

Intelligent edge has three components [4]:

1. **Connect:** When people and devices exchange data over networks, new sources and quantities of data are established.

2. **Compute:** Processing of this data can allow access to applications and provide deep insights into connected things, devices, and the surrounding environment.

3. **Control:** Based on these computed insights, actions can be taken, devices and things at the edge may be controlled, or other types of controls for businesses and enterprises may be prompted [4].

10.1.2   EDGE INTELLIGENCE (EI): WHY IT IS IMPORTANT?

Cloud-based centers currently handle the vast majority of AI processes, as these processes require extensive computing power. Downsides include the possibility of rapid service slowdowns or interruptions due to connectivity issues. By integrating AI into EC devices, edge AI eliminates these issues. Users benefit from saving time by aggregating data and serving users without contacting other locations physically. Edge AI benefits include [5]:

1. Bringing real-time data processing capabilities to the edge is Edge AI's major advantage, as it allows high-performance computing capability to be applied to sensors and IoT devices. ML and deep learning (DL) algorithms are able to run directly on the field device using AI EC [5].

   CC processes data in seconds. Alternatively, data can be processed at the edge in milliseconds or less. An autonomous vehicle that performs data processing at the edge can make decisions faster than one that processes data in the cloud. Data processing in near real-time is critical because these decisions affect human lives [5].

2. The bandwidth should be reduced. Big data can consume lots of bandwidth when it is sent back and forth from devices to the cloud. An EC solution would be the easiest way to resolve this problem [4].

3. Cost-effective. Access to bandwidth can be costly, even if it is available. Incorporating IoT into any business strategy requires efficiency.

4. Threats should be identified and reduced. Data is more vulnerable to attacks and breaches when it is transferred across campus, state, country, and ocean. Using edge processing to reduce security vulnerabilities is a good idea [4].
5. Duplicate work should be avoided. Using all data will probably result in a lot of duplicate hardware in terms of memory, storage, networking, and software. When this duplication is not necessary, the increase in capital expenditures and operating expenses are unnecessary [4].
6. Increase reliability. Data can be corrupted on its own even without the nefarious actions of hackers. Retrying, dropping, and missing connections will be a problem for edge-to-datacenter communications. Cell phones may break up or drop calls even today [4].
7. Keep compliance up to date. Data transfer is governed by laws and corporate policies. Companies in certain countries are prohibited from transferring personal information about their citizens outside the borders of those countries [4].

10.1.3 *CLOUD COMPUTING (CC) VERSUS EDGE COMPUTING (EC)*

Extreme latency operations are regarded as ideal for EC. Due to this, medium-sized companies with limited financial resources can benefit from EC. Projects and organizations involving large amounts of data storage are more suitable for CC [6].

Programming can be done on several different platforms using various runtimes in EC. CC, on the other hand, is better equipped for actual programming since they are designed for a single target platform and use a single programming language [6].

Security plans for EC must include advanced authentication methods and be proactive in addressing attacks. Security plans for CC are less stringent.

10.1.3.1 *COMPUTE IN THE CLOUD: CHALLENGES*

AI and DL have had a profound effect on many aspects of people's lives, particularly in the fields of computer vision (CV) and natural language processing (NLP) [3].

Due to the inefficiency and latency of CC service architecture, most people and organizations cannot access AI. Many intelligent services are unavailable to answer a broader range of applications, including intelligent factories, smart cities, biometrics, medical imaging, etc. [3].

Using CC enabled organizations to train large-scale models quickly because the hardware was highly scalable and low cost. Although the cloud is well suited to model training, it may be difficult for inference – the use of AI to provide a prediction in response to a user's query – in the cloud.

There are several challenges associated with inference in the cloud:

- Several AI use cases require real-time responses, which cloud-based inference may not be able to provide. Because the request must be transferred from an edge device to the cloud, then the response must also be transferred back to the edge device.
- No matter whether the real-time response is not needed, cloud-based inference has a high degree of latency that can negatively affect the user experience.
- The edge device cannot perform cloud inference if it is not connected to the Internet or encounters connectivity problems. A device may not be capable of transferring as much data in a reasonable amount of time, even if it has an Internet connection [5].

Many companies have begun to implement EC. The solution, however, is not limited to EC. Vendors and organizations facing computing challenges should continue to consider CC as a viable solution. Sometimes EC is used to provide a more comprehensive solution. A decision to delegate all data to the edge is also not recommended. The IoT and EC are then combined to make public cloud providers more competitive [6].

In the EC vs. CC debate, they are neither either-or nor direct contenders. As a team, they provide your business with a broader range of computing options. The first step in evaluating which hybrid solution will work best for your organization is identifying its needs and comparing them with its costs [6].

10.2 INNOVATION RESULTS FROM COMPUTATIONAL INTELLIGENCE

Coronavirus pandemics have caused unprecedented economic crises and lifestyle changes that haven't been experienced before. This has caused the authorities to implement global movement restrictions in order to stop the spread of disease. Global researchers have applied computational intelligence methods across a wide range of fields with great success. Computing intelligence methods are important in dealing with coronavirus epidemics [7].

CI Agnostic computing is a branch of AI that examines the use of versatile components in ever-changing and intricate situations to make shrewd decisions. As part of CI, all aspects of AI are covered, as well as real-world applications being improved and advanced. The field of cognitive science is developing, and it focuses on identifying a variety of ideal models including "ambient intelligence," "artificial life," "artificial endocrine networks," "social reasoning," and "artificial hormone networks." A crucial role for CI is the development of insight frameworks such as games and cognitive developmental systems. Research into deep convolutional neural networks, in particular, has boomed over the past couple of years.

In many medical areas, such as diagnosis, treatment, and prediction, the application of computational intelligence is opening up new opportunities. Computing intelligence, such as the handling of patient information, does not exempt administrative management of the patient. COVID-19 can take several hours or days to be screened using polymerase chain reaction (PCR). To provide alternatives for the diagnosis and treatment of COVID-19, computational intelligence methods should be applied to screening processes [7].

10.2.1 CONSTRUCTION OF EDGE COMPUTING (EC) PROCESSES

Essentially, EC is about pushing data, applications, and compute power to the extremes, allowing fragments of data to be stored on distributed networks of servers. Using EC, any internet client that uses commercial internet application services can access the internet. Small and medium-sized businesses can now take advantage of the technology because of the cost reduction in large-scale implementations.

Computing at the edge of the network is enabled by these technologies:

1. **Mobile Edge Computing (EC):** Multi-access EC, or mobile EC, refers to strategies for placing computing and storage resources within radio access networks (RANs) in order to improve network efficiency and provide content to users.

2. **Fog Computing (FC):** CC, in this context, is the extension of the cloud to the edge of a network, with data, computation, storage, and applications situated at points that are convenient and logical between the cloud and its origin. This type of placement is sometimes referred to as "out in the fog" [8].

3. **Cloudlets:** Mobile-enhanced, small-scale cloud data centers are located at the edges of an organization's network and form part of three tiers: Mobile devices, Cloudlets, and Cloud services. Through Cloudlets, mobile devices can take advantage of more powerful computing resources and lower latencies, allowing them to run resource-intensive and interactive mobile applications in close proximity [8].

4. **Microdata Centers:** Despite being smaller than traditional data centers, these systems provide all the elements of a data center. The benefits of micro-data centers are estimated to be greatest for small and medium-sized businesses without their own data centers since larger corporations will be able to utilize their resources and therefore won't need such a solution [8].

10.2.2   A DIFFERENT LEVEL OF EDGE INTELLIGENCE (EI)

EI emphasizes the inference phase (the execution of the AI model) and assumes that training of the model takes place in cloud data centers, as training consumes a lot of resources [3].

Regardless, EI's full scope and features allow it to fully exploit the data and resources available across a hierarchy of end devices, edge nodes, and cloud data centers to optimize the overall performance of both training and inferencing deep neural networks (DNNs). EI has no "best level" as the optimal configuration varies by application and is determined by a variety of factors such as latency, privacy, energy efficiency, resource costs, and bandwidth costs [3].

- An AI model is trained and inferred entirely on the cloud using cloud-based intelligence.
- Inference performed on the device includes cloud-based AI model training, while inference takes place locally on the device. This inference does not use offloaded data.
- Designed to train and infer AI models on-device, All On-Device incorporates both training and inference seamlessly into the device.

Offloading task execution to the edge has a variety of benefits including reducing data transmission latency, increasing data privacy, and reducing bandwidth costs. The problem is that this comes at the cost of increased energy consumption and latency. For many AI applications on-device, on-device Inference has proven to be a powerful approach that is optimally balanced for many use cases [3].

10.3   CONFRONTING COVID-19 WITH A NEW APPROACH

The growth of EC is due to the great availability of computational resources, mobile devices, sensors, and actuators that are widespread and now number over 7 billion interfaces with the network. Computing can be done at the edge of the network and away from data centers in this way, so it can be used close to people and data sources. EC and EI are the smart exploitation of AI and cognitive technologies that leverage distributed data and IoT devices with EC technologies and AI.

10.3.1   SCOOP ON MOBILE LOCATION DATA

Human movement is a significant factor in the spread of viruses across space. Viruses are spread by direct contact with infectious sources as well as inhalation of viruses released by sneezing or coughing. Viruses that can resist and survive hostile conditions and then become infectious under particular circumstances have a direct association with the host. The most common non-living substances that carry infection are door handles, table chairs, keyboard mice, etc. An indirect way of spreading disease is by consuming infected food or water items [10].

A Disease can be prevented by a detection, identification, and tracking system that can detect, identify, and track outbreaks in real-time or near real-time. The location of users via their mobile devices is collected in certain studies and correlated with sites where diseases have been identified. After receiving a report of an infected user, the system alerts those in the user's immediate vicinity when the disease is incubating. Analytics of big data construct basic pre-processing statistical learning operations that can be used to identify infections based on the optimal inferences [10].

A virtual private server based on EC receives GPS data about different individuals and the contagious sites they are associated with. This module anonymizes the search log data of infected subjects. With Location Comparison Module, you can recognize towns/areas nearby based on the GPS data from Log Search Module. As part of the Pandemic Spread Detection Module, a report containing the Location Comparison Module results will be delivered to verify whether there is a local or global spread. Once the Regional/Global Pandemic Spread Detection Module decides to send an alert, the Regional/Global Pandemic Alert Module issues it.

Using GPS and a cell phone allows you to track your location. Cell phone location information is collected from the base station before being stored in the database. Location recognition data (bus, cineplex, etc.) can be augmented by correlation to add links to other users whose locations have concurred (bus, cineplex, etc.). Time and distance, as well as crossing paths for an adequate amount of time with proximity, determine coordinates. Being on a bus and riding around in an enclosed area for 15 minutes might trigger a proximity correlation, rather than waiting at a bus stop.

Input and output data dimensions should be smaller than transitional data dimensions for EC. As a result of the difficulties in storing and processing large amounts of data, real-time processing, and protecting privacy [10], EC has been developed as a tool for backtracking and finding suspects using location information.

10.3.2   ASSESSMENT OF ILLNESSES SUCH AS COUGH

Research at the University of Massachusetts (UMass), Amherst, has developed a portable surveillance device that can track influenza-like illnesses (ILIs) and flu trends through the analysis of coughing sounds and crowd sizes in a real-time environment, such as a hospital waiting room. They say FluSense, an edge-computing platform that could be used in hospitals or larger public areas, opens up the potential for broader health surveillance tools to be used in forecasting not only seasonal flu outbreaks but also other infectious respiratory outbreaks such as the COVID-19 pandemic or SARS [11].

Public health responses directly informed by such models can help to save lives during flu epidemics. These data sources may also be used to decide when flu vaccine campaigns, travel restrictions, and medical supplies should be allocated. Researchers concluded that their study shows the potential of using EC to provide important epidemiological data about influenza trends by capturing coughs and population counts anonymously in a noisy environment [11].

10.3.3   MEASUREMENT OF SOCIAL DISTANCE AND MASK DETECTION

An AI framework is proposed in this chapter, based on EC and citizen-centric services, which can be used to follow and track individuals who avoid safety policies, such as mask detection and social distancing. Further, the framework offers guidelines for how to implement the framework in industrial setups, governance, and contact tracking. There is a selection of AI models and performance analysis for benchmark analysis as well as accuracy assessment for a large-scale societal setup using EC technology [12].

Edge IoT devices are used in industrial settings and public areas to track people's movements using surveillance camera video feeds. The architecture proposed incorporates EC environments on the cloud in conjunction with existing cameras and IoT devices. Based on EC, the framework can detect face masks in specific environments (workshops, hospitals, industrial settings). The benefits of EC include being able to attain localized insights, near-real-time insight, and reduce your overall costs [12].

Edge cameras perform local feed collection and feed processing using DL models deployed on the edge. At the edge environment, the sequence of inferencing occurs with the implementation of the people detection and mask detection modules, the image segmentation modules, and the social distancing module. Edge devices may be used for local inference, as well as real-time inference on-camera devices. As the new technology does not have a transmission delay, and it allows a faster debugging of errors than the previous method, DL models should be evaluated to ensure that they offer more effectiveness in the problem domain while remaining computationally inexpensive [12].

10.3.4 ROVERS FOR COVID-19 OUTBREAK

AI A fundamental advantage of CC and EC is the speed and efficiency with which they can process large amounts of data. The big data analytics and algorithms deployed across edge and cloud services can be used to analyze the data. Computing devices on the edge and drones with processing power combined can reduce the necessary bandwidth requirement, resulting in higher throughput, scalability, and latency. As the COVID-19 outbreak spread throughout large crowds, intelligent drones could provide the ability to identify people of interest. As an alternative, the problem of power and computing can be resolved by implementing EC devices on drones, which will allow data to be offloaded for pre-processing and action to be taken.

Through the seamless deployment of algorithms and the transfer of data between the edge and the cloud, EC and IoT applications facilitate analytics and ML. The presence of drones in public places poses serious problems because they can damage buildings, property, people, and other infrastructure. A DL method is also proposed by the researchers to identify illegal drones in real-time in a region of interest [13].

The use of drones and devices allows us to locate people who are stuck in such a situation. Due to their limited resources, drones can carry only a limited amount of weight and lightweight batteries. Multiple drones may also be needed for certain applications, and they have to work together. Additionally, some limitations in the use of drones and multiple drowns can be overcome by combining additional resources (edge devices). AI and EC devices such as robots and drones can counter early warning systems for disasters and social control. Implementing EC devices also makes it possible to filter large and noisy data at the edge [13].

10.4   THE EDGE OF HEALTHCARE INTELLIGENCE

Mobile EC architectures provide lower latency, greater coverage, and higher reliability to users when compared to cloud-based models, particularly in smart healthcare. There are high data transmission costs associated with mobile cloud architectures and their coverage area is limited.

It is possible to process healthcare sensor data collaboratively and efficiently by using multiple edge devices and local servers with EC. Through the application of EI, we can build smart healthcare frameworks that have human-like intelligence and even cognitive intelligence. In addition to training edge intelligent architectures at the edge level, cloud processing can also be used to perform computationally intensive applications, or distributed processing can also be done between edge and fog nodes [14].

The most common, edge based IoT healthcare frameworks use remote monitoring systems to implement diagnostic, sensitive, and preventive healthcare systems through the use of smart sensors. Taking advantage of IoT technology advancements, intelligent solutions are now possible that make use of software platforms and system architectures. Healthcare is addressed on a number of levels, including chronic illness monitoring, monitoring and controlling epidemics, providing elderly and pediatric care, as well as managing health and fitness.

In order to achieve edge/fog computing, an architecture with multiple levels is necessary, the three basic levels are:

- Data is sent from IoT body sensors at the edge node level. A number of low-level devices, including smartwatches, mobile phones, tablets, and embedded devices, as well as gateways, perform low-level processing [14].

- Those fog nodes that collect data from IoT field sensors and edge devices fall under this level. To store and process data locally, servers, and PCs are used [14].
- CC level, where all the data is collected and stored. Various algorithms and data analyze are applied here, including high-level processing [14].

EC maximizes the efficiency of local data processing by combining edge devices and servers, while EI integrates AI and cognitive intelligence into edge architectures based on human behavior. CC, FC, and EC are all examples of IoT-enabled intelligent EC, and they may also be incorporated into IoT-enabled intelligent EC. IoT has enabled the internet of everything (IoE) through the development and advancement of devices. EI is crucial to processing so much information, as cloud data centers are distributed worldwide [14].

10.5   THE CHALLENGE OF EDGE INTELLIGENCE (EI)

10.5.1   EFFICIENCIES IN POWER AND ENERGY

A variety of different AI advancements, such as neural networks, show dramatic promise for solving a variety of different problems. Unfortunately, these solutions usually require considerable computing time and memory. As a result, most of today's typical applications use powerful GPUs that consume a lot of power to run these neural networks. The advantage of embedded processors and DSPs is their low-power consumption and fixed-point capabilities. For the deployment of CNN models on mobile devices, an embedded processor is required. When using fixed-point operations, algorithms should maintain accuracy without sacrificing speed. By enhancing the structure of neural networks and making them more resource-efficient [15], neural networks' underlying operations can be enhanced not only in terms of their efficiency but also in terms of their efficiency.

10.5.2   ACHIEVE OUTSTANDING PERFORMANCE

The linear algebra operations involved in machine learning (ML) algorithms are extensive, as are vector and matrix data processing operations. The traditional Von Neumann architecture is not suited for safety-critical applications, such as self-driving cars and unmanned aerial vehicles (UAVs), and therefore specialized processing and parallel architectures are needed. So, EI presents a very clear opportunity for the development of customized and specialized hardware that can support ML applications [15].

10.5.3   A LIMITED NUMBER OF RESOURCES

The memory available to EI devices for storing and accessing data is smaller and has less computing power compared to traditional computers. When describing the architecture of a neural network or ML algorithm as well as its weight values, a number of parameters are usually required. Recently, neural network architectures have accessed enormous amounts of memory while classifying data. ML algorithms need to be deployed on a device with limited hardware resources with a minimum number of memory accesses and with data kept local to avoid costly reads and writes to external memory systems [15].

10.5.4   ISSUES RELATED TO PRIVACY AND SECURITY

To Edge, computing resources must be provided by heterogeneous edge devices and edge servers for EI to be realized. The data and computation tasks cached locally in this manner could be sent to an unfamiliar device for further processing. A data leak may occur if users' private information is included in the data, e.g., photos and tokens, which might lead to malicious attacks and data leaks. Unless the data is encrypted, malicious users could easily obtain private information [16].

10.5.5   DATA WITH HETEROGENEITY

Several types of architectures, sensors, and companies deploy sensors at the network edge, which makes Edge AI function in a heterogeneous environment by integrating heterogeneous devices at the network edge. Because of this, the data at the edge of the network, as well as the preprocessing techniques, may significantly differ from application to application. Algorithms for ML must learn how to combine data with different features including images, sounds, and texts that can be provided by these devices. DL techniques such as multi-modal DL can be used to extract features from heterogeneous data [17].

10.6   EDGE INTERACTIVE IN THE FUTURE

In recent years, DL has grown rapidly, leading to numerous AI applications and services ranging from video surveillance to recommendation systems to personal assistants. Researchers studying EI are still in their infancy, and there is considerable interest from the computer and AI communities toward a devoted market for exchanging up-to-date advances in EI. Despite the proliferation of EI (Event Intelligence), a centralized CI (cloud intelligence) will still be useful in the future.

The growth of EC is attributed to a number of factors and advantages, such as the expansion of markets, the expansion of applications, and the growing demands on computation power and data. Since dependable, adaptable, and contextual data play an increasingly crucial role in our daily lives, many tasks are now carried out locally on the device, resulting in better performance, the better response time (within milliseconds), lower latency, enhanced energy efficiency, increased security, and reduction of costs by eliminating the need for data centers [18].

EC provides real-time results for a wide range of time-sensitive needs, which is perhaps its biggest advantage. Data collected by sensors can usually be analyzed, communicated, and transmitted immediately without sending the data to a cloud center. A key requirement for edge devices is scalability so that decision-making can be accelerated locally. Information that can be trusted and delivered immediately builds confidence, engages customers, and, in many cases, saves lives [18].

A Network with embedded pervasive intelligence (such as CC with EI embedded in nodes and smarter and smarter terminals) would be able to leverage the accomplishments made in developing distributed ledger technologies.

The world is filled with innovative companies supporting AI at the edge, such as Amazon, Google, Apple, BMW, Volkswagen, Tesla, Airbus, Fraunhofer, Vodafone, Deutsche Telekom, Ericsson, and Harting. As a result, some of these institutions, like the European Edge Computing Consortium (EECC), have formed trade associations to inform and convince manufacturers and manufacturers' associations about EC's benefits [18].

10.7   CONCLUSION

Despite COVID-19's misery and destruction, its fight has also shown what we can achieve with a coordinated effort. The collaborative and open nature of AI research and development across borders demonstrates what the future might hold for such progress [19]. EI has a number of benefits such as reducing latency, increasing efficiency, and preserving privacy [20]. With more effective implementation, these advantages will be even more apparent.

KEYWORDS

- **artificial intelligence**
- **computational intelligence**
- **edge computing**
- **edge COVID-19**
- **edge intelligence**
- **internet of things**
- **smart healthcare**

REFERENCES

1. https://extranet.who.int/goarn/content/impact-covid-19-peoples-livelihoods-their-health-and-our-food-systems-0 (accessed on 10 July 2023).
2. Jin, Z., Zubair, A., Saima, K. K., Yusuf, M., Osama, A. A., & Mohamed, S. M., (2021). The role of technology in COVID-19 pandemic management and its financial impact. *Complexity, 2021*, 12, Article ID 4860704. https://doi.org/10.1155/2021/4860704.
3. https://viso.ai/edge-ai/edge-intelligence-deep-learning-with-edge-computing/#:~:text=Edge%20Intelligence%20or%20Edge%20AI,every%20organization%20at%20any%20place (accessed on 10 July 2023).
4. https://www.hpe.com/us/en/insights/articles/the-intelligent-edge-what-it-is-what-its-not-and-why-its-useful-1711.html (accessed on 10 July 2023).
5. https://www.run.ai/guides/machine-learning-operations/edge-ai (accessed on 10 July 2023).
6. https://phoenixnap.com/blog/edge-computing-vs-cloud-computing (accessed on 10 July 2023).
7. Isa, A., & Ndahi, B. P., (2021). The power of computational intelligence methods in the containment of COVID-19 pandemic from detection to recovery. In: *Current Perspectives on Viral Disease Outbreaks – Epidemiology, Detection and Control*. London, United Kingdom: IntechOpen, [Online]. Available: https://www.intechopen.com/chapters/77453 doi: 10.5772/intechopen.98931 (accessed on 10 July 2023).
8. https://www.srijan.net/resources/blog/what-is-edge-computing-industry-use-cases (accessed on 10 July 2023).

9. https://www.comsoc.org/publications/journals/ieee-tgcn/cfp/edge-intelligence-sustainable-smart-environments (accessed on 10 July 2023).

10. Hemant, G., Muhammad, A., Prosanta, G., Sharnil, P., & Shubhankar, M., (2021). ReCognizing SUspect and PredictiNg ThE SpRead of contagion based on mobile phone LoCation DaTa (COUNTERACT): A system of identifying COVID-19 infectious and hazardous sites, detecting disease outbreaks based on the internet of things, edge computing, and artificial intelligence. *Sustainable Cities and Society*. doi: 10.1016/j.scs.2021.102798.

11. https://www.genengnews.com/news/ai-and-edge-computing-combine-in-portable-platform-for-flu-and-potentially-coronavirus-forecasting/ (accessed on 10 July 2023).

12. Sengupta, K., & Praveen, R. S., (2022). HRNET: AI-on-edge for mask detection and social distancing calculation. *SN Computer Science, 3*(2), 157. doi: 10.1007/s42979-022-01023-1.

13. Joshi, A., Dey, N., & Santosh, K. C., (2020). Intelligent systems and methods to combat COVID-19. *Springer Briefs in Applied Sciences and Technology*. doi: 10.1007/978-981-15-6572-4.

14. Syed, U. A., & Shamim, H. M., (2021). Edge intelligence and internet of things in healthcare: A survey. *IEEE Access*. doi: 10.1109/access.2020.3045115.

15. Plastiras, G., Terzi, M., Kyrkou, C., & Theocharides, T., (2018). *[IEEE 2018 IEEE 29th International Conference on Application-specific Systems, Architectures and Processors (ASAP) - Milano, Italy (2018.7.10-2018.7.12)] 2018 IEEE 29th International Conference on Application-specific Systems, Architectures and Processors (ASAP) – Edge Intelligence: Challenges and Opportunities of Near-Sensor Machine Learning Applications, 1–7.* doi: 10.1109/ASAP.2018.8445118.

16. Plastiras, G., Terzi, M., Kyrkou, C., & Theocharides, T., (2018). Edge intelligence: Challenges and opportunities of near-sensor machine learning applications. In: *2018 IEEE 29th International Conference on Application-specific Systems, Architectures and Processors (ASAP), 2018* (pp. 1–7). doi: 10.1109/ASAP.2018.8445118.

17. Javier, M., Kay, B., Cuéllar, M. P., & Diego, P. M., (2021). Edge intelligence: Concepts, architectures, applications and future directions. *ACM Trans. Embed. Comput. Syst.* https://doi.org/10.1145/3486674.

18. https://www.analyticsinsight.net/future-ai-edge-intelligence/ (accessed on 10 July 2023).

19. https://www.weforum.org/agenda/2020/06/this-is-how-ai-can-help-us-fight-covid-19/ (accessed on 10 July 2023).

20. Shah, S., Tariq, Z., Lee, J., & Lee, Y., (2021). Event-driven deep learning for edge intelligence (EDL-EI). *Sensors, 21*, 6023. 10.3390/s21186023.

CHAPTER 11

Visual Image Reconstruction Using fMRI Analysis

ANAGHA ZACHARIAH, SANDEEP KUMAR SATAPATHY, and
SHRUTI MISHRA

Vellore Institute of Technology, Chennai, Tamil Nadu, India

ABSTRACT

Decoding and analysis of visual perception from neural patterns is a challenging research topic in neuroscience. However, the advances in deep neural networks (DNNs) and fMRI have introduced new openings to untangle this challenge. The deep neural network extracts high-level features from visual cortical responses and generates images similar to the presented stimuli in fMRI experiments. In order to effectively utilize the information provided and for reliable reconstruction, recent research focuses more on generative adversarial networks (GAN). Encoder presents the semantic features from given fMRI images and corresponding natural images to GAN to perform reconstruction. However, deep learning (DL) methods for Reconstructing visual objects are as yet in the beginning stage, while the chance of the strategies is enormous. Consequently, to work on the exhibition of such methodologies, it is essential to concentrate on the research and uses of the methodologies through writing surveys. Therefore, this chapter audits profound learning-based strategies in the 2D remaking of visual images.

11.1 INTRODUCTION

While mind-reading is a long-standing subject in sci-fi, it is only a few years that the world came to know about the potential of machine learning (ML)-based analysis of fMRI and its applications. Functional magnetic

Reconnoitering the Landscape of Edge Intelligence in Healthcare.
Suneeta Satpathy, Sachi Nandan Mohanty, and Sirisha Potluri (Eds.)
© 2024 Apple Academic Press, Inc. Co-published with CRC Press (Taylor & Francis)

resonance imaging (fMRI) estimates brain activity by identifying changes related to blood flow [1]. fMRI utilizes the blood-oxygen-level-dependent (BOLD) contrast [1] to map neural movement in the human brain by imaging the adjustment of bloodstream identified with energy use by brain cells. Although there are few models to encode and decode brain signals, the methods are restricted to low-level reproduction quality [2, 3] by skipping visual features of numerous progressive levels. Few methods have used deep neural networks (DNNs) for reconstruction for the last decade. However, most failed to use various leveled data for reproduction [4, 5]. Moreover, reconstructing actual and constructed pictures is challenging [6]. With the help of recent advancements in DNN, it is possible to analyze, and study leveled data [7]. DNN tries to imitate the neural representations of our brain. Because of this similarity, the patterns measured by the fMRI can be decoded with the help of DNN in multiple layers [8]. This provides a new opportunity for researchers to learn more about the brain and its neural patterns.

In visual image reconstruction, the stimuli are selected from a dataset of natural images. The goal of reconstruction is to learn a mapping from an fMRI pattern to a digital image. However, the major challenge in reconstruction is maintaining the quality and features of the actual image as a constructed image. The reconstructed image should have lower-level and higher-level details. However, there are also no standard evaluation techniques to measure the quality of reconstructed images. Recently, a few research studies have utilized generative adversarial networks (GANs) for facial and natural images reconstruction [4, 9, 10]. In GAN, we train two models: a generative model G, which tries to catch information from fMRI, and a discriminative model D, which tries to estimate the probability that an image is natural. The generator will increase the probability that the created image is natural. The ultimate goal of the generator is to fool the discriminator. Although the above investigations made a few advances, the current strategies still lack accuracy while giving figures similar to visual stimuli. High-quality reconstruction of images from fMRI is extensive work. Here, we review various methods to deal with visual perceptual content from the human brain by deep learning (DL) methods, which can reconstruct what we see during perception. We further investigated the generalizability of reproduction models to fake images. To research the impacts of various algorithms' impacts in reproduction, we studied various GAN models. Finally, to comprehend the impact of the model on reconstruction quality, we analyzed the reconstruction results of various models.

11.2   FUNCTIONAL MAGNETIC RESONANCE IMAGINING

An fMRI is used to track the brain's activities through scanning. It is not harmful to patients and uses similar technology like MRI. MRI is performed using Magnetic fields and Radio-Waves for generating the image of a brain. fMRI is different from MRI in creating the image. fMRI produces the image which also shows the blood flow whereas MRI output is completely based on organs or tissues. MRI can easily detect the parts of the brain using a magnetic field that aligns the protons relative to the magnetic field and radio waves realign the protons. Then the system receives a signal once the protons get back into their original position and the radio waves generate the image after emission. The reason behind the discovery of fMRI is while performing an MRI, it focuses more on oxygen-poor blood, but brain activity depends more on oxygen-rich blood than oxygen-poor blood when speaking, listening, and reading. fMRI mainly focuses on blood flow to detect the stimulated parts of the brain while performing an activity. Brain energy is completely based on glucose even though it is not stored in it. When having to perform an action the blood flows into the body for transporting glucose to the active parts in the brain so oxygen-rich blood is higher in that area which outclasses the MRI. For example, when you are speaking, the oxygen-rich blood that flows to the brain which is designated for speaking. While performing an fMRI scan a patient must do a task to increase the oxygen rich blood in the brain. fMRI scan is useful for doctors to check the mental condition of the people to perform surgery and to know the feeling, thinking capability of depressed people. These scans are used in Interrogation to detect lies which are the pieces of evidence to judge them. The image generated by the fMRI scan is high resolution which shows the stimulation of the brain parts while performing the action or activity.

11.3   DATA SETS

This section sums up public datasets for image reconstruction from fMRI with the help of DL methods. Each sample of these datasets has fMRI patterns and a corresponding image. Properties of dataset are summarized in Table 11.1.

11.3.1   VIM-1

Vim dataset is introduced in Kay et al. [11]. The dataset contains various natural images and corresponding fMRI data. The image set contains photographs of food, buildings, indoor and outdoor scenes, animals, and manmade objects. All the images were changed to grayscale and reduced the dimensions to 500 × 500 pixels. Two subjects participated in this experiment. The images are presented as three trials. In all trials all photographs were presented. Each image presented for 1s and gray background presented for 3s. In order to increase signal to noise ratio each photograph was flashed on-off-on-off-on where in one state the actual image is flashed while in off state the gray background is flashed. Seeliger et al. [4], Kay et al. [11] and Qiao et al. [12] was using vim-1 dataset for visual image reconstruction. In Order to correct the head positioning the authors performed coregistration. Voxel specific response time is computed and deconvolved. For all voxels, an amplitude value is estimated, and identification process runs. The experiment also collects retinotopic mapping data from subjects in different scan sessions. This data is used to assign voxels to visual areas.

11.3.2   FACES

VanRullen and Reddy [14] introduced Faces dataset. The dataset includes the data collected from experiment including three subjects. The testing is done in eight scan sessions. Each face has presented for 1s and 6s blank interval. The training image set was drawn randomly from CelebA dataset with equal number of male and female faces. The dataset is preprocessed using SPM12 software. Slice time correction and co-registration is performed in each data in the dataset. In Ref. [14], the authors are not doing any kind of normalization or preprocessing.

11.3.3   GENERIC OBJECT DECODING DATASET

Kamitani Lab had been released Generic Object Decoding dataset, contains fMRI recordings and corresponding 500 × 500-pixel images. The images are selected from ImageNet, and the recordings were collected from five subjects. The selected images from ImageNet dataset contained 200 image categories. For all images with any one dimension greater than 100 pixel the image is cropped to center. The experiment conducted as two separate sessions: training and testing. The training session had 24 runs and testing session had 35 runs. In Ref. [8], the data got preprocessed using SPM15 (Table 11.2).

TABLE 11.1 Characteristics of Datasets

Datasets	Number of Subjects	Image Stimuli Train/Test	ROIs
Vim-1	2	1750/120	V1, V2, V3, V4, LO
Deep image reconstruction:	3	1200/50	V1, V2, V3
	3	0/40	V1, V2, V3, V4, LOC, FFA, PPA
• Natural images	3	0/10	V1, V2, V3, V4, LOC, FFA, PP
• Artificial shapes			
• Alphabetical letters			
Generic object decoding	5	1200/50	V1, V2, V3, V4, LOC, FFA, PPA
BRAINS	3	290/70	V1, V2
Faces	4	88/20	N/A
vanGerven10	1	90/10	V1, V2, V3
Miyawaki08	1	1320/80	V1
DS105	6	3465/693	N/A

TABLE 11.2 Pre-Processing Methods of Surveyed Works

Method	Preprocessing Methods	Tools
CNN based method	• Manual co-registration • Motion correction • Slice time correction	SPM
Deep image reconstruction	• 3D motion correction • Co-registration • Normalization and despiking of voxel amplitudes • Averaging and shifting	SPM
Brains	• Slice time correction. • Functional volume reconstruction • Construction and shaping of design matrix of GLM • Voxel isolation	• SPM8 • Freesurfer
Vim-1	• Co-registration • Reconstruction of functional brain volume • Slice time correction • Estimation of voxel amplitude • Assignment of voxels to visual area	NA

TABLE 11.2 *(Continued)*

Method	Preprocessing Methods	Tools
Generic object decoding	• 3D motion correction • Co-registration • Normalization and despiking of voxel amplitudes • Averaging and shifting	SPM5
Miyawaki08	• Co-registration • Slice time correction • 3D motion correction • Transformation of retinopy data to Talairach coordinates • Delineation of visual cortical borders • Normalization and despiking of voxel amplitudes • Averaging and shifting	• SPM2 • Brain Voyager 2000
Faces	• Co-registration • Slice time correction • Construction and shaping of design matrix of GLM	SPM12

11.3.4 DEEP IMAGE RECONSTRUCTION DATASET

Deep image reconstruction dataset [9, 10] contains data from three subjects. The dataset is available in OpenNeuro. The dataset contains natural images and artificially generated letters, and geometric shapes. The artificially generated dataset has 40 images. The natural images are similar to Horikawa Kamitani [8] which are collected from ImageNet dataset. The dimensions of images are reduced to 500×500. The shapes have 5 shapes with 8 colors. The shapes are similar to Miyawaki et al. [2]. The letters consist of 10 alphabets.

11.3.5 MIYAWAKI08

In the visual image dataset [2], the fMRI patterns of two subjects are recorded while presenting 10×10-pixel images. The experiment is carried out in two sessions. In the first session, which is known as a random image session, a random image is shown for 6s. In the second session, known as the figure image session, an image of alphabets or letters or shapes is shown for the 12s period. The images used during the initial session are used to train the model. The images in the second session used for testing.

11.3.6   VANGERVEN10

Qiao et al., [12] used 69 datasets containing 28 × 28-pixel images and corresponding fMRI recordings. The experiment was carried with the help of 1 subject, and the participant was provided with a 100 gray-scale images of 6 and 9 letters. 90 fMRI-image pairs were used for training and 10 images for testing.

11.3.7   BRAINS

BRAINS dataset contains 360 grayscale images of six written characters. The dataset was published in Van der Maaten et al., [20] and had a size of 56 × 56. The images were visible to three subjects for 1s and repeated two times.

11.4   DEEP LEARNING (DL)-BASED APPROACHES FOR IMAGE RECONSTRUCTION

Traditional visual image reconstruction methods use linear mapping to map fMRI brain signals and image features. The main focus of this method was to extract low-level features [15, 19]. In the last decade, DL made considerable advancements in computer vision (CV) research. It helped to improve the accuracy of various tasks. Due to the multi-layer architecture, which allows them to learn mappings from brain fMRI signals to raw images, they were shown to be very powerful than traditional techniques. Inspired by the success of DL, many frameworks used DL for image reconstruction for various reasons. The first reason is the similarity between DNNs and human visual processing systems. Second is DL's capacity to learn underlying data distribution and synthesize high-quality images. Finally, DNN also helps to work on pre-trained models. This section classifies DL-based learning-based image reconstruction tasks as generative and non-generative methods. We also analyze their architectures, datasets, and training techniques.

11.4.1   NON-GENERATIVE METHODS

11.4.1.1   CONVOLUTIONAL NEURAL NETWORK (CNN)

While compared to simple neural networks in terms of structural information, CNN provides better feature extraction methods with the help of
convolutional layers [16]. Lower layers of CNN try to extract low-level
visual details, while higher layers of CNN study high-level details [9, 22]
uses DNN, which utilizes VGG-19 for feature extraction. The DNN has 16
convolutional layers and multiple connected layers. Recent studies show
that the layers of DNN correlate with brain activity [23]. So, it's possible to
create a mapping between fMRI signals and DNN. So, for this mapping, the
authors implemented a decoder. The decoder in the model tries to map fMRI
and DNN patterns. With the help of the strategy mentioned in Ref. [13],
decoder is trained for reconstruction purposes. By reducing the difference
between decoded features and image features, we can do optimization.

11.4.1.2   DETERMINISTIC ENCODER-DECODER MODELS

In most image-to-image translation techniques, the authors prefer to use the
encoder-decoder model or sequence-to-sequence models [24]. The encoder
in encoder-decoder architecture converts the input to latent representations.
The decoder in encoder–decoder tries to output from latent representation.
The model will try to reduce the reconstruction error. The encoder-decoder
model mentioned in Beliy et al., [15] has an encoder to map input features
to latent space and a decoder to learn fMRI mappings. The training dataset
contains more than 50,000 images and corresponding fMRI samples.
The authors achieved better accuracy by using vim-1 and Generic Object
decoding datasets. The training has been done in two steps. In the first step,
they created a mapping from image to fMRI activity utilizing weights of
pretrained AlexNet's first convolutional layers weights. During the second
step, the decoder is trained on the training data and has distinguished between
real and fake images. The authors of Gaziv et al., [16] improve this method
by considering perceptual similarity loss. They collected features from
original and constructed pictures and calculated loss by comparing features.

11.4.2   GENERATIVE METHODS

In generative models, the data is created from some probability distribution.
We can classify generative methods as implicit and explicit based on the

probability distribution. Implicit methods state a sampling process instead of defining data distribution to get samples from the probability distribution (Tables 11.3 and 11.4).

TABLE 11.3   Advantages and Disadvantages of Surveyed Works

Method	Advantages	Disadvantages
GAN-BVRM	• Modular approach • Preserves the naturalness and fidelity • Reconstructed images have size of 128×128	• Non-uniform categories between Gallant and ImageNet effects performance. • Low efficiency of search-based approach
CNN-based method	• Prior information of semantics is not needed • Works well with natural images.	• Low efficiency on videos and colorful images.
DNN+DGN	• Naturalness • Renders semantically meaningful details during re construction	• Not optimal for the images which does not contain object in the center • General reconstruction performance is low because of the limited object categories identifiable by DNN
TIGAN	• Considers temporal information during reconstruction • Pairwise ranking loss to find strongly associated stimuli and fMRI data	• Small dataset • Increased memory consumption because of three sub-networks • Less utilization of whole brain structural information.
Hybrid Bayesian network	• Considers low-level and high-level semantic information. • Fully automated multi-model decoding.	• Biasing towards highly probable categories cause in correct predictions.
DCGAN	• End-to-end training not required • Prevents noisy images	• Not possible to reconstruct handwritten characters or comic scenes • Mode collapse

TABLE 11.3   *(Continued)*

Method	Advantages	Disadvantages
D-Vae/Gan	• Realistic reconstruction • Optimization is stable • Avoids mode collapse	• Small dataset
Encoder-decoder based method	• Supports unsupervised training of unlabeled images and fMRI data • Supports training on fMRI data which does not have corresponding image Improved performance • High generalization power	• Edges in the reconstructed image are not correctly aligned with corresponding image • Blurred images
GAN based method	• Voxel denoising strategy • Generates probability distribution from voxels	• Small dataset • Overfitting • Poor generalization

TABLE 11.4   Comparative Tables of Surveyed Works

Loss Function	End-to-End Training	Pre-Training	Code Availability
• KL • Adv	No	• Model is pre trained using external data from ImageNet.	No
• MSE • Adv	No	• Generator and Denoiser are pretrained on CIFAR-10.	Yes
• Adv • MSE • MAE	No Yes	• Model is pre trained using ImageNet. • Pre-trained AlexNet based encoder.	No Yes
• MSE	No	• Pretrained DGN • Pretrained VGG-1 using ImageNet dataset	Yes
• MSE • Adv	Yes	Comparator pre trained using ImageNet dataset	Yes
• MSE • Adv	No	• Pre-trained on CelebA	Yes
• MSE • MAE • Cos	No	• Pre-trained on AlexNet based encoder.	No
• MSE	No	• Generator pre trained on ImageNet.	Partially

TABLE 11.4 *(Continued)*

Loss Function	End-to-End Training	Pre-Training	Code Availability
• Adv	No	NA	Partially
• MAE			
• MSE	No	• Pretrained generator	No
• MAE		• Comparator based on AlexNet	

In explicit methods, the probability density function is well defined. That probability distribution function can be used to train the model.

11.4.2.1 GENERATIVE ADVERSARIAL NETWORK (GAN)

GANs are very well known for their natural-looking image generation capacity [25]. Basic GAN networks have a generator and a discriminator. The generator has to generate images similar to training images from random noise. The generator has to fool the discriminator with its natural-like image reconstruction capability. Generators' ability will keep increasing until the discriminator cannot distinguish between real and fake. One of the main advantages of GAN is, it does not require strong assumptions about the output probability distribution. Seeliger et al., [4] suggest a deep convolutional generative adversarial network (DCGAN) [26] based architecture to reconstruct visual images. The generator consists of linear and deconvolutional layers, where each layer followed by ReLu activation-functions and batch normalization layers. The output of generator is normalized between −1 and 1 with tanh function. The discriminator network has convolutional layers followed by ELU activations and batch normalization. Before the output of generator given to descrimator handicap gaussian noise is added to those images. The method outperforms basic GAN methods by stacking deconvolutional layers and convolutional layers. The framework works on grayscale images. The framework also has a comparator network to compute feature loss. The framework is trained on ImageNet [27] and Microsoft COCO [28] datasets (Figure 11.1).

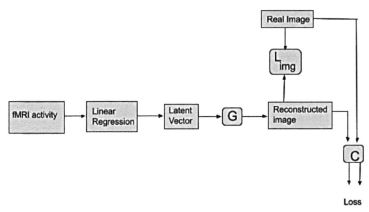

FIGURE 11.1   Architecture of DCGAN by Seeliger et al. (2008).

Source: Reprinted with permission from Ref. [4]. Copyright © 2018 Elsevier Inc.

The method proposed in Huang et al. [29] introduces an end-to-end image reconstruction model. The model uses a GAN based model called similarity conditions generative adversarial network (SC-GAN). The model is able to extract high level semantic features. The semantic features are given to GAN as conditions. The SC-GAN framework consists of four submodules. Image feature extractor, generator, brain feature extractor and discriminator. The image feature extractor encodes the images to latent image features. The brain feature extractor encodes visual responses into latent brain features. The authors used a cosine similarity function to find the similarity between image and brain features. The brain features are the input to generator network and discriminator network. In order to update parameters of generator and discriminator C-GAN uses similarity loss function and a C-GAN loss function. The similarity loss function tries to optimize the parameters of brain and image feature extractor. The main objective is to get latent brain features from the response patterns of stimuli.

Mozafari et al. [24] introduced BigBiGAN. BigBiGAN is a bidirectional network with an encoder, generator, and a discriminator. Encoder map the data to latent vectors. These latent vectors are given to generator and the generator generates data from these latent vectors. The generator of BigBiGAN have 120D latent space. It captures almost all object properties including pose and category of object. The authors used a linear encoder to map the BigBiGAN representation to its brain representation using linear regression. The mapping process is performed with the help of a general linear regression model (GLM). For test images we derive the brain representations first. The already computed mapping is inverted to predict latent vectors from brain representations.

Fang et al., [19] used two decoders with GAN for fMRI image reconstruction. The purpose of decoders is to get sematis and shape related information from fMRI recordings. The generator, which is a CNN network architecture, uses these features as a condition for image generation. The method also uses data augmentation to improve the quality of constructed images. The architecture of the framework is depicted in Figure 11.2.

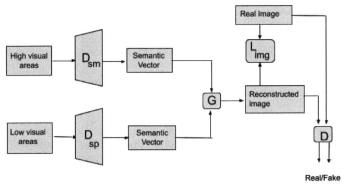

FIGURE 11.2 Architecture of method proposed by Fang et al. (2020). [19]

The method proposed in Shen et al., [9] maps the fMRI signals of the subject to output without performing feature extraction. This chapter introduces a framework that contains three convolutional neural networks: a comparator, a generator and discriminator. The generator performs mapping. It maps the fMRI data to the reconstructed image. The discriminator identifies which image is fake and which one is real. The comparator network, pretrained on the ImageNet used to evaluate the model by calculating perceptual loss. The loss function can be seen as a weighted sum of the adversarial loss and loss in image space and perceptual loss.

In order to introduce more flexibility in reconstruction [17], used energy-based conditional GAN (EBGAN). The method introduces a denoising autoencoder to compress noisy fMRI representations in high dimensions to low dimensions. The low dimensional representations are used as conditions in GAN for reconstruction. The method uses a deep autoencoder instead of a binary classifier as a discriminator. The method is stable, and the quality of reconstructions is dependent on the denoising autoencoder (Figure 11.3).

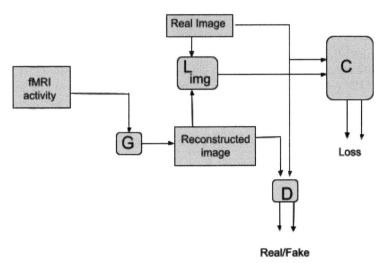

FIGURE 11.3   Architecture of method proposed by Shen et al. (2019). [9].

In order to improve the naturalness of images, the authors of [24] introduced BigBiGAN. The framework can capture high-level details of fMRI data in BigBiGAN's latent space and generate high-level semantic information. The method has a pre-trained encoder to generate a latent space vector. During training with the help of a linear regression model, a linear mapping is created between latent vectors and fMRI images. During testing, the mapping is inverted to find latent vectors from fMRI. The limited dataset is one of the major problems while dealing with medical data. In order to come up with a solution to this problem [12], come up with a framework titled GAN-based Bayesian visual reconstruction model (GAN-BVRM). The method is the combination of Bayesianc learning and GAN. An encoder that constructs fMRI activity from the image corresponds to a conditional distribution p(v given x). The decoder can be seen as a conditional distribution p(x given v) which reconstructs an image from fMRI activity. We must reconstruct an image with a maximum p(x given v). GAN-BVRM has four subnetworks: a classifier, encoder, conditional generator, and evaluator. Classifier helps to classify the objects into different categories. A conditional generator is used to create images according to categories. The generated images were given to the encoder. The encoder will generate the fMRI pattern of the image. The reconstruction quality is measured by an evaluation network using mean squared error (MSE). The GAN maximizes evaluation network scores by updating input noises (Figure 11.4).

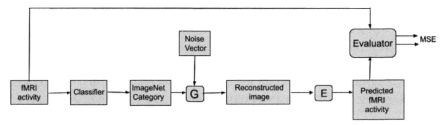

FIGURE 11.4   Architecture of GAN-BVRM.

11.4.2.2   VAE-GENERATIVE ADVERSARIAL NETWORK (GAN)

Kingma et al., [30] proposed variational autoencoder (VAE). Variational encoders have an encoder and a decoder. VAE encodes distribution over latent space instead of encoding latent vector. Larsen et al., [31] created a hybrid model incorporating VAE and GAN. The hybrid framework is known as VAE-GAN. In VAE-GAN, the latent features are produced by VAE. In VAE GAN, the generator from GAN network is merged with VAE decoder. The output of the VAE-GAN model has naturalness and stability. The usage of GAN ensures the naturalness of images. The VAE based optimization helps to increase the stability of reconstruction. With improved stability, we can avoid mode collapse [32, 33]. Ren et al. [32] proposed dual-variational autoencoder/generative adversarial network (D-VAE/GAN) for reconstructing images from fMRI recordings. The network has two VAE encoders and an adversarial decoder. The two encoders are visual encoders and cognitive encoders. The training of the framework is done in three steps. The visual encoder learns a mapping from given images to latent representations in the first step. The generator uses these latent representations to predict images. Discriminator tries to distinguish between given image and predicted images. In the second step cognitive encoder learns to map fMRI data to latent cognitive features. The generator tries to generate images from latent cognitive features. However, the discriminator tries to discriminate images produced in the first step with reconstructions from latent cognitive features. This strategy ensures that the cognitive encoder generates features similar to the visual encoder. The third step generator and discriminator are tuned of fMRI data to improve the reconstruction quality and accuracy. In this step, the discriminator will distinguish between reconstructed and real images. During testing, the visual encoder will not be there in the picture. VanRullen et al., [14] used VAE-GAN to reconstruct faces. The method uses a trained VAE-GAN encoder. The model learns a linear mapping between fMRI patterns and latent space in the training stage. In testing, the fMRI data is converted to VAE latent codes with the help of inverse mapping. The latent space contains features and descriptions of each facial image as linear combinations. If points are nearer in latent space, the corresponding facial image is similar. This increases the accuracy and naturalness of facial reconstruction. The method can also predict a gender by looking at the images.

11.5   EVALUATIONS

11.5.1   EVALUATION TECHNIQUES

Evaluation of reconstructed images can be performed with human assistance or image-metric based. Different models and their evaluation methods are displayed in Figure 11.5.

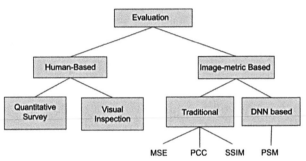

FIGURE 11.5   Evaluation methods.

11.5.1.1   HUMAN-BASED EVALUATION

The simplest method to evaluate the quality of reconstruction is to use human resources. The human-based evaluation is conducted through visual inspection. The human-based evaluation can be classified into quantitative surveys and simple visual inspection. In a quantitative study, the subject is given a set of candidate images. The candidate images contain the reconstructed image and some random images. Then the candidate is asked to select the image with maximum similarity to the actual image. These studies can be performed with the help of human subjects or using Amazon Mechanical Turk [4, 16]. The reconstructed images of different models will be displayed to conduct a visual comparison. The human subjects can compare the reconstructed images in terms of sharpness, colors, shapes, low-level features, and high-level features. Human evaluation techniques are time-consuming.

Another limitation with human-based methods is the emotional and physical environment of subjects. In addition, the human decision-making process is highly affected by external conditions. So, there can be a chance of error during evaluation (Figures 11.6 and 11.7).

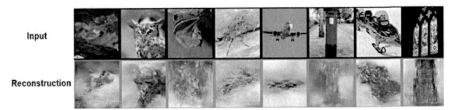

FIGURE 11.6   Reconstruction of natural images by Shen et al. (2019a). [9]

Source: Adapted from Ref. [9]

FIGURE 11.7   Reconstruction of natural images by Gaziv et al. (2020). [16]

Source: Adapted from Ref. [16]

11.5.1.2   IMAGE METRIC-BASED EVALUATION

Another option to evaluate the reconstructed images is using image metric-based techniques. The method shows better precision and accuracy than human judgments. The image-based methods are unbiased and don't affect any external factors. Different image evaluation methods are available to analyze the images at various degrees. The methods can fall into two categories. In the first category, conventional methods are used to capture low-level features and patterns. The second category contains methods that extract high-level information. The traditional measurements like MSE, structural similarity index, pixelwise variations can assess the quality. MSE measures the square of the distance between the observed value and predicted value. It is one of the traditional and straightforward methods to assess the quality of images. MSE is easy to implement and calculate. The method considers each image pixel equally important. The Pearson correlation coefficient (PCC) measures how many images are correlated. If the correlated value higher than 7, we can say that the two images are highly correlated. If the correlation coefficient is 0, the two images are not correlated. Structural similarity index (SSIM) captures the structural information from given images. SSIM measures the similarity of nearest pixels of actual and reconstructed pictures. The structural similarity index measures (SSIM) contrast, structure, and luminance for the given two images. In perceptual similarity metric (PSM), which is a high-level similarity capturing mechanism, instead of calculating image space distance, we are using DNNs to find the distance between image features.

11.5.2 IMAGE COMPARISON

To evaluate the Reconstruction, we must compare the reconstructed images to other images. The comparison can be one-to-one, n-way comparison, or pairwise comparison. In one-to-one comparison, the image constructed by the model is evaluated against the ground truth. For evaluation, we can use any metric like MSE or PCC, we have only a single pair of reconstructed-original images in a one-to-one comparison. For better interpretation, pairwise, and n-way comparison methods can be used. The pairwise comparison involves a reconstructed image and two images. One image is the ground truth and a random non-relevant image. If the reconstruction quality is good, the evaluation score gained after comparing reconstructed image with ground truth should be higher than the score of the generated image with a random non relevant image. In n way comparison method, the reconstructed image is compared with a candidate image set. The candidate image set contains n random images, including ground truth. Beliy et al., [15] uses 2, 5, and 10 as the values of n, and the accuracy is calculated using PCC. Beliy et al., [15] used 50-way identification (Table 11.5).

TABLE 11.5   Comparison of Evaluation Methods

Quantitative Survey	Visual Inspection	Traditional	PSM
Yes	Yes	No	No
Yes	Yes	Pairwise PCC	No
Yes	Yes	Pairwise SSIM	No
		Pairwise PCC	
No	Yes	2,5,10-way PCC	No
Yes	Yes	No	2,5,10-way PSM

TABLE 11.5 *(Continued)*

Quantitative Survey	Visual Inspection	Traditional	PSM
No	Yes	SSIM	Alexnet
		PCC	
No	Yes	Pairwise PCC	No
No	Yes	Pairwise PCC	Inception-V3
		Pix-Comp (2-way PCC)	
No	Yes	Pairwise PCC	Inception-V3
		Pix-Comp (2-way PCC)	

11.6 LIMITATIONS

We believe that there are still several limitations in visual image reconstruction methods. The sample size of the dataset, which contains the fMRI data and images, is small due to the difficulty of data collection. Most of the algorithms work well with large-scale datasets only. The algorithm's performance depends on the quality and quantity of datasets. So, lack of availability of good quality dataset is an important issue. To solve this issue, we can use an artificially generated dataset, or we can use transfer learning algorithms. The recent advancements in fMRI research show that we can utilize CNN for feature extraction and the DCNN-GAN for reconstructing realistic fMRI images. Another limitation is the memory constraint. The involvement of multiple sub-networks in the model increases the memory burden. So, we have to reduce the size by model compression. Furthermore, the methods mentioned in the chapter are not adequately using structural information of the brain. When we consider all data in the brain, we may end up with noise. But there can be significant and relevant areas to our task apart from the area of consideration. This limits the accuracy of our model. Another problem is mode collapse. In mode collapse, the discriminator fools the generator by learning only a limited set of data perfectly. This causes better results in already known data. But for new data, the performance accuracy will be less.

11.7 FUTURE WORK

We reviewed the current literature on applying DL in visual image reconstruction during this study. Recent studies support the idea that there is a strong correspondence between the neural representation of visual perception and mental imagery (reconstructing imagined letters). Furthermore, the results provide new evidence that the geometry of the objects is preserved during imagination and visual imagery. We are planning to reconstruct imagined objects to simulate human brain activities realistically in the future. We plan to develop a GAN-based method for reconstructing imagined objects from fMRI data. The proposed framework will take fMRI patterns are input and generate corresponding images. This can be utilized for content based BCI development. The current BCI system does not provide a mechanism to decode imagined shapes. This is very much useful for people who are suffering from severe paralysis. Our proposed mind-reading system will help users directly communicate their intention without any involvement of the motor periphery.

11.8 SUMMARY AND CONCLUSION

In this chapter, we review different image reconstruction methods to reconstruct visual images using DL applied on fMRI data. We can separate the reconstruction strategies into two broad categories: Non generative and Generative methods. Generative models use GAN or VAE-GAN to reconstruct images, while non-generative models include convolutional neural networks and encoder decoder methods. The reconstructed images can be evaluated using image metrics or by human evaluation. The ultimate aim of DL methods in visual image reconstruction is to reconstruct images preserving the naturalness and features of the actual image. But based on the purpose of reconstruction, sometimes we may have to tradeoff between fidelity and naturalness of reconstruction. While compared to non-generative methods, generative methods produce images that preserve naturalness. But to produce attractive output, generative models require extensive training and a large amount of training data. Moreover, even though generative models care for image quality, they do not guarantee object category. Therefore, when reconstruction focuses more on fidelity than naturalness, non-generative models will be a good choice. Non-generative models can also maintain low-level features of the actual image in the constructed image, but generated image quality is not impressive. We compared various generative and non-generative algorithms and their evaluation techniques. We hope this study will help future research in visual image reconstruction and related areas.

KEYWORDS

- **convolutional neural networks**
- **deep learning**
- **functional magnetic resonance imaging**
- **generative adversarial networks**
- **image reconstruction**
- **non-generative models**
- **visual perception**

REFERENCES

1. Huettel, S. A., Song, A. W., & McCarthy, G., (2009). *Functional Magnetic Resonance Imaging* (2nd edn.), Massachusetts: Sinauer, ISBN 978-0-87893- 286-3.
2. Miyawaki, Y., Uchida, H., Yamashita, O., Sato, M. A., Morito, Y., Tanabe, H. C., et al., (2008). Visual image reconstruction from human brain activity using a combination of multiscale local image decoders. *Neuron, 60*(5), 915–929. doi: 10.1016/j. neuron.2008.11.004.
3. Wen, H., Shi, J., Zhang, Y., Lu, K., Cao, J., & Liu, Z., (2017). Neural Encoding and Decoding with Deep Learning for Dynamic Natural Vision. Cereb Cortex. 2018 Dec 1;28(12), 4136–4160. doi: 10.1093/cercor/bhx268. PMID: 29059288; PMCID: PMC6215471..
4. Seeliger, K., Guc¸lu, U., Ambrogioni, L., Gucluturk, Y., & Van, G. M. A. J., (2018). Generative adversarial networks for reconstructing natural images from brain activity. *Neuroimage, 181*, 775–785. doi: 10.1016/j.neuroimage.2018.07.043.
5. Han, K., Wen, H., Shi, J., Lu, K., Zhang, Y., & Liu, Z., (2017). *Variational Autoencoder: An Unsupervised Model for Modeling and Decoding fMRI Activity in Visual Cortex.* Preprint. Available from: https://doi.org/10.1101/ 214247.
6. Thirion, B., Duchesnay, E., Hubbard, E., Dubois, J., Poline, J. B., Lebihan, D., et al., (2006). Inverse retinotopy: Inferring the visual content of images from brain activation patterns. *Neuroimage, 33*, 1104–1116. doi: 10.1016/j.neuroimage.2006.06.062.
7. Yamins, D. L., & DiCarlo, J. J., (2016). Using goal-driven deep learning models to understand sensory cortex. *Nat. Neurosci., 19*, 356–365. https://doi.org/10.1038/ nn.4244 PMID: 269065.
8. Horikawa, T., & Kamitani, Y., (2017). Generic decoding of seen and imagined objects using hierarchical visual features. *Nature Communications, 8*(1), 15037. doi: 10.1038/ ncomms15037. Number: 1 Publisher: Nature Publishing Group.
9. Shen, G., Dwivedi, K., Majima, K., Horikawa, T., & Kamitani, Y., (2019a). End-to-end deep image reconstruction from human brain activity. *Frontiers in Computational Neuroscience, 13*. doi: 10.3389/fncom.2019.00021. Publisher: Frontiers.

10. Shen, G., Horikawa, T., Majima, K., & Kamitani, Y., (2019b). Deep image reconstruction from human brain activity. *PLOS Computational Biology, 15*(1), e1006633. doi: 10.1371/journal.pcbi.1006633. Public Library of Science.

11. Kay, K. N., Naselaris, T., Prenger, R. J., & Gallant, J. L., (2008). Identifying natural images from human brain activity. *Nature, 452*(7185), 352–355. doi: 10.1038/nature06713.

12. Qiao, K., Chen, J., Wang, L., Zhang, C., Tong, L., & Yan, B., (2020). BigGAN-based Bayesian reconstruction of natural images from human brain activity. *Neuroscience, 444*, 92–105. doi: 10.1016/ j.neuroscience.2020.07.040.

13. Qiao, K., Zhang, C., Wang, L., Chen, J., Zeng, L., Tong, L., et al., (2018). Accurate reconstruction of image stimuli from human functional magnetic resonance imaging based on the decoding model with capsule network architecture. *Frontiers in Neuroinformatics, 12*, 62. doi: 10.3389/fninf.2018.00062.

14. VanRullen, R., & Reddy, L., (2019). Reconstructing faces from fMRI patterns using deep generative neural networks. *Communications Biology, 2*(1), 1–10. doi: 10.1038/s42003-019-0438-y. Nature Publishing Group.

15. Beliy, R., Gaziv, G., Hoogi, A., Strappini, F., Golan, T., & Irani, M., (2019). From voxels to pixels and back: Self-supervision in natural-image reconstruction from fMRI. In: Wallach, H., Larochelle, H., Beygelzimer, A., Alche-Buc, F. D., Fox, E., & Garnett, R., (eds.), *Advances in Neural Information Processing Systems* (Vol. 32, pp. 6517–6527). Curran Associates, Inc.

16. Gaziv, G., Beliy, R., Granot, N., Hoogi, A., Strappini, F., Golan, T., et al., (2020). Self-supervised natural image reconstruction and rich semantic classification from brain activity. *Neuroscience.* doi: 10.1101/2020.09.06.284794.

17. St-Yves, G., & Naselaris, T., (2018). Generative adversarial networks conditioned on brain activity reconstruct seen images. In: *2018 IEEE International Conference on Systems, Man, and Cybernetics (SMC)* (pp. 1054–1061). doi: 10.1109/SMC.2018.00187. ISSN: 2577-1655.

18. Zhang, R., Isola, P., Efros, A. A., Shechtman, E., & Wang, O., (2018). The unreasonable effectiveness of deep features as a perceptual metric. In: *2018 IEEE/CVF Conference on Computer Vision and Pattern Recognition* (pp. 586–595). Salt Lake City, UT: IEEE. doi: 10.1109/CVPR.2018.00068.

19. Fang, T., Qi, Y., & Pan, G., (2020). Reconstructing perceptive images from brain activity by shape semantic GAN. *Advances in Neural Information Processing Systems, 33.*

20. Van der Maaten, (2009). *A New Benchmark Dataset for Handwritten Character Recognition.* Tilburg University, Tilburg, The Netherlands.

21. Corel Corporation, (1994). *Corel Stock Photo Library.* ISBN: 9780969660552 Place: Ottawa OCLC: 872594087.

22. Mahendran, A., & Vedaldi, A., (2015). Understanding deep image representations by inverting them. In: *2015 IEEE Conference on Computer Vision and Pattern Recognition (CVPR)* (pp. 5188–5196). doi: 10.1109/ CVPR.2015.7299155. ISSN: 1063–6919.

23. Eickenberg, M., Gramfort, A., Varoquaux, G., & Thirion, B., (2017). Seeing it all: Convolutional network layers map the function of the human visual system. *Neuroimage, 152*, 184–194. doi: 10.1016/j.neuroimage.2016.10.001.

24. Mozafari, M., Reddy, L., & VanRullen, R., (2020). Reconstructing natural scenes from fMRI patterns using BigBiGAN. In: *2020 International Joint Conference on*

Neural Networks (IJCNN) (pp. 1–8). Glasgow, United Kingdom: IEEE. doi: 10.1109/ IJCNN48605.2020.9206960.

25. Goodfellow, I. J., Pouget-Abadie, J., Mirza, M., Xu, B., Warde-Farley, D., Ozair, S., et al., (2014). Generative adversarial nets. In: *Proceedings of the 27*[th] *International Conference on Neural Information Processing Systems; NIPS'14* (Vol. 2, pp. 2672– 2680). Cambridge, MA, USA: MIT Press.

26. Radford, A., Metz, L., & Chintala, S., (2016). *Unsupervised Representation Learning with Deep Convolutional Generative Adversarial Networks.* In arXiv:1511.06434 [cs]. ArXiv: 1511.06434.

27. Chrabaszcz, P., Loshchilov, I., & Hutter, F., (2017). *A Downsampled Variant of ImageNet as an Alternative to the CIFAR Datasets.* arXiv:1707.08819 [cs] ArXiv: 1707.08819.

28. Lin, T. Y., Maire, M., Belongie, S., Hays, J., Perona, P., Ramanan, D., et al., (2014). Microsoft COCO: Common objects in context. In: Fleet, D., Pajdla, T., Schiele, B., & Tuytelaars, T., (eds.), *Computer Vision – ECCV 2014; Lecture Notes in Computer Science* (pp. 740–755). Cham: Springer International Publishing. doi: 10.1007/978-3- 319-10602-1 48.

29. Huang, S., Sun, L., Yousefnezhad, M., Wang, M., & Zhang, D., (2021). Temporal information guided generative adversarial networks for stimuli image reconstruction from human brain activities. *IEEE Transactions on Cognitive and Developmental Systems.* 10.1109/TCDS.2021.3098743.

30. Kingma, D. P., & Welling, M., (2014). *Auto-Encoding Variational Bayes.* arXiv:1312.6114 [cs,stat] ArXiv: 1312.6114.

31. Larsen, A. B. L., Sønderby, S. K., Larochelle, H., & Winther, O., (2016). Autoencoding be-yond pixels using a learned similarity metric. In: *International Conference on Machine Learning (PMLR)* (pp. 1558–1566). ISSN: 1938–7228.

32. Ren, Z., Li, J., Xue, X., Li, X., Yang, F., Jiao, Z., et al., (2021). Reconstructing seen image from brain activity by visually-guided cognitive representation and adversarial learning. *Neuroimage* doi: 10.1016/j. neuroimage.2020.117602.

33. Xu, K., Du, C., Li, C., Zhu, J., & Zhang, B., (2021). Learning implicit generative models by teaching density estimators. In: Hutter, F., Kersting, K., Lijffijt, J., & Valera, I., (eds.), *Machine Learning and Knowledge Discovery in Databases: Lecture Notes in Computer Science* (pp. 239–255). Cham: Springer International Publishing. doi: 10.1007/978-3-030-67661-215.

34. Bandettini, P. A., (2012). Twenty years of functional MRI: The science and the stories. *Neuroimage, 62*(2), 575–588. doi: 10.1016/j.neuroimage.2012.04.026.

35. Chen, L. C., Papandreou, G., Kokkinos, I., Murphy, K., & Yuille, A. L., (2015). Semantic image segmentation with deep convolutional nets and fully connected CRFs. In: Bengio, Y., & LeCun, Y., (eds.), *3*[rd] *International Conference on Learning Representations; ICLR 2015.* San Diego, CA, USA, Conference Track Proceedings.

36. Chen, M., Han, J., Hu, X., Jiang, X., Guo, L., & Liu, T., (2014). Survey of encoding and decoding of visual stimulus via FMRI: An image analysis perspective. *Brain Imaging and Behavior, 8,* 7–23. doi: 10.1007/s11682-013-9238-z.

37. Cho, K., Van, M. B., Gulcehre, C., Bahdanau, D., Bougares, F., Schwenk, H., et al., (2014). Learning phrase representations using RNN encoder–decoder for statistical machine translation. In: *Proceedings of the 2014 Conference on Empirical Methods in Natural Language Processing (EMNLP)* (pp. 1724–1734). Doha, Qatar: Association for Computational Linguistics. doi: 10.3115/v1/D14-1179.

38. Deng, J., Dong, W., Socher, R., Li, L. J., Li, K., & Fei-Fei, L., (2009). ImageNet:A large-scale hierarchical image database. In: *2009 IEEE Conference on Computer Vision and Pattern Recognition* (pp. 248–255). doi: 10.1109/CVPR.2009.5206848. ISSN: 1063-6919.

39. Donahue, J., & Simonyan, K., (2019). Large scale adversarial representation learning. In: Wallach, H., Larochelle, H., Beygelzimer, A., Alche-Buc, F. D., Fox, E., & Garnett, R., (eds.), *Advances in Neural Information Processing Systems* (Vol. 32). Curran Associates, Inc.

40. Dosovitskiy, A., & Brox, T., (2016). *Inverting Visual Representations with Convolutional Networks,* 4829–4837.

41. Du, C., Changying, D., Lijie, H., & Huiguang, H., (2018). Reconstructing perceived images from human brain activities with Bayesian deep Multiview learning. *IEEE Transactions on Neural Networks and Learning Systems,* 1–14. 10.1109/ TNNLS.2018.2882456.

42. Fujiwara, Y., Miyawaki, Y., & Kamitani, Y., (2013). Modular encoding and decoding models derived from Bayesian canonical correlation analysis. *Neural Computation, 25*(4), 979–1005. doi: 10.1162/NECOa 00423.

43. Gucluturk, Y., Guclu, U., Seeliger, K., Bosch, S., Van, L. R., & Van, G. M. A., (2017). Reconstructing perceived faces from brain activations with deep adversarial neural decoding. *Advances in Neural Information Processing Systems, 30,* 4246–4257.

44. Haxby, J. V., Gobbini, M. I., Furey, M. L., Ishai, A., Schouten, J. L., & Pietrini, P., (2001). Distributed and overlapping representations of faces and objects in ventral temporal cortex. *Science, 293*(5539), 2425–2430. doi: 10.1126/science.1063736. Publisher: American Association for the Advancement of Science Section: Research Article.

45. Hinton, G., Vinyals, O., & Dean, J., (2015). *Distilling the Knowledge in a Neural Network.* arXiv:1503.02531 [cs, stat] ArXiv: 1503.02531.

46. Isola, P., Zhu, J. Y., Zhou, T., & Efros, A. A., (2017). *Image-to-Image Translation with Conditional Adversarial Networks,* 1125–1134.

47. Jakub, L., & Vladimir, B., (2019). *GANs in Action (Manning).* https://www.oreilly.com/ library/view/gans-in-action/9781617295560/.

48. Kamitani, Y., & Tong, F., (2005). Decoding the visual and subjective contents of the human brain. *Nature Neuroscience, 8*(5), 679–685. doi: 10.1038/nn1444.

49. Kamnitsas, K., Ledig, C., Newcombe, V. F. J., Simpson, J. P., Kane, A. D., Menon, D. K., et al., (2017). Efficient multi-scale 3D CNN with fully connected CRF for accurate brain lesion seg-mentation. *Medical Image Analysis, 36,* 61–78. doi: 10.1016/j. media.2016.10.004.

50. Kriegeskorte, N., (2015). Deep neural networks: A new framework for modeling biological vision and brain information processing. *Annual Review of Vision Science, 1,* 417–446. doi: 10.1146/annurev-vision-082114-035447.

51. Krizhevsky, A., (2009). *Learning Multiple Layers of Features from Tiny Images.* Tech. Rep.

52. Krizhevsky, A., Sutskever, I., & Hinton, G. E., (2012). ImageNet classification with deep convolutional neural networks. *Advances in Neural Information Processing Systems, 25,* 1097–1105.

53. LeCun, Y., Boser, B., Denker, J. S., Henderson, D., Howard, R. E., Hubbard, W., et al., (1989). Backpropagation applied to handwritten zip code recognition. *Neural Computation, 1*(4), 541–551. doi: 10.1162/neco.1989.1.4.541. Publisher: MIT Press.

54. Liu, Z., Luo, P., Wang, X., & Tang, X., (2015). Deep learning face attributes in the wild. In: *2015 IEEE International Conference on Computer Vision (ICCV)* (pp. 3730–3738). doi: 10.1109/ICCV.2015.425. ISSN:2380-7504.

55. Logothetis, N. K., & Sheinberg, D. L., (1996). Visual object recognition. *Annual Review of Neuroscience, 19*(1), 577–621. doi: 10.1146/annurev.ne.19.030196.003045. e-print: https://doi.org/10.1146/annurev.ne.19.030196.003045.

56. Martin, D., Fowlkes, C., Tal, D., & Malik, J., (2001). A database of human segmented natural images and its application to evaluating segmentation algorithms and measuring ecological statistics. In: *Proceedings Eighth IEEE International Conference on Computer Vision: ICCV 2001* (Vol. 2, pp. 416–423). doi: 10.1109/ICCV.2001.937655.

57. Minaee, S., Boykov, Y. Y., Porikli, F., Plaza, A. J., Kehtarnavaz, N., & Terzopoulos, D., (2021). Image segmentation using deep learning: A survey. *IEEE Transactions on Pattern Analysis and Machine Intelligence*, 1. doi: 10.1109/TPAMI.2021.3059968. Conference Name: IEEE Transactions on Pattern Analysis and Machine Intelligence.

58. Naselaris, T., Kay, K. N., Nishimoto, S., & Gallant, J. L., (2011). Encoding and decoding in fMRI. *Neuroimage, 56*(2), 400–410. doi: 10.1016/j.neuroimage.2010.07.073.

59. Naselaris, T., Prenger, R. J., Kay, K. N., Oliver, M., & Gallant, J. L., (2009). Bayesian reconstruction of natural images from human brain activity. *Neuron, 63*(6), 902–915. doi: 10.1016/j.neuron.2009.09.006.

60. Nestor, A., Lee, A. C. H., Plaut, D. C., & Behrmann, M., (2020). The face of image reconstruction: Progress, pitfalls, prospects. *Trends in Cognitive Sciences, 24*, 747–759. doi: 10.1016/j.tics.2020.06.006. Publisher: Elsevier.

61. Ogawa, S., Lee, T. M., Kay, A. R., & Tank, D. W., (1990). Brain magnetic resonance imaging with contrast dependent on blood oxygenation. *Proceedings of the National Academy of Sciences of the United States of America, 87*(24), 9868–9872.

62. Pinto, N., Doukhan, D., DiCarlo, J. J., & Cox, D. D., (2009). A high-throughput screening approach to discovering good forms of biologically inspired visual representation. *PLOS Computational Biology, 5*, e1000579. doi: 10.1371/journal.pcbi.1000579.

63. Poldrack, R. A., & Farah, M. J., (2015). Progress and challenges in probing the human brain. *Nature, 526*(7573), 371–379. doi: 10.1038/nature15692. Publisher: Nature Publishing Group.

64. Quiroga, R. Q., Reddy, L., Kreiman, G., Koch, C., & Fried, I., (2005). Invariant visual representation by single neurons in the human brain. *Nature, 435*(7045), 1102–1107. doi: 10.1038/nature03687. Publisher: Nature Publishing Group.

65. Rakhimberdina, Z., Liu, X., & Murata, T., (2020). Population graph-based multi-model ensemble method for diagnosing autism spectrum disorder. *Sensors, 20*(21), 6001. doi: 10.3390/s20216001. Publisher: Multidisciplinary Digital Publishing Institute.

66. Roelfsema, P. R., Denys, D., & Klink, P. C., (2018). Mind reading and writing: The future of neurotechnology. *Trends in Cognitive Sciences, 22*, 598–610. doi: 10.1016/j. tics.2018.04.001. Number.

67. Rolls, E. T., (2012). Invariant visual object and face recognition: Neural and computational bases, and a model, VisNet. *Frontiers in Computational Neuroscience, 6*. doi: 10.3389/fncom.2012.00035. Publisher: Frontiers.

68. Ronneberger, O., Fischer, P., & Brox, T., (2015). U-Net: Convolutional networks for biomedical image segmentation. In: Navab, N., Hornegger, J., Wells, W. M., & Frangi, A. F., (eds.), *Medical Image Computing and Computer-Assisted Intervention – MICCAI*

2015: Lecture Notes in Computer Science (pp. 234–241). Cham: Springer International Publishing doi: 10.1007/978-3-319-24574-4.

69. Salimans, T., Goodfellow, I., Zaremba, W., Cheung, V., Radford, A., & Chen, X., (2016). Improved techniques for training GANs. In: *Advances in Neural Information Processing Systems (NIPS)* (pp. 2234–2242).

70. Schoenmakers, S., Barth, M., Heskes, T., & Van, G. M., (2013). Linear reconstruction of perceive images from human brain activity. *Neuroimage, 83*, 951–961. doi: 10.1016/j. neuroimage.2013.07.043.

71. Schomaker, L., Vuurpijl, L., & Schomaker, L., (2000). *Forensic Writer Identification: A Benchmark Data Set and a Comparison of Two Systems.* NICI (NIjmegen Institute of Cognitive Information), Katholieke Universiteit Nijmegen. Type: Other.

72. Schrimpf, M., Kubilius, J., Hong, H., Majaj, N. J., Rajalingham, R., Issa, E. B., et al., (2018). *Brain-Score: Which Artificial Neural Network for Object Recognition is Most Brain-Like?* bioRxiv, 407007. doi: 10. 1101/407007. Publisher: Cold Spring Harbor Laboratory Section: New Results.

73. Simonyan, K., & Zisserman, A., (2015). *Very Deep Convolutional Networks for Large-Scale Image Recognition.* arXiv:1409.1556 [cs] ArXiv: 1409.1556.

74. Szegedy, C., Vanhoucke, V., Ioffe, S., Shlens, J., & Wojna, Z., (2016). Rethinking the inception architecture for computer vision. In: *2016 IEEE Conference on Computer Vision and Pattern Recognition (CVPR)* (pp. 2818–2826). Las Vegas, NV, USA: IEEE. doi: 10.1109/CVPR.2016.308.

75. Van, G. M. A. J., De Lange, F. P., & Heskes, T., (2010). Neural decoding with hierarchical generative models. *Neural Computation, 22*(12), 3127–3142. doi: 10.1162/NECO a 00047. Publisher: MIT Press.

76. Wang, Z., Bovik, A., Sheikh, H., & Simoncelli, E., (2004). Image quality assessment: From error visibility to structural similarity. *IEEE Transactions on Image Processing, 13*, 600–612. doi: 10.1109/TIP.2003. 819861.

77. Zhang, K., Zuo, W., Chen, Y., Meng, D., & Zhang, L., (2017). Beyond a gaussian denoiser: Residual learning of deep CNN for image denoising. *IEEE Transactions on Image Processing* (Vol. 26, pp. 3142–3155). doi: 10.1109/TIP.2017.2662206. Conference Name: IEEE Transactions on Image Processing.

78. Zhang, X., Yao, L., Wang, X., Monaghan, J. J. M., Mcalpine, D., & Zhang, Y., (2020). A survey on deep learning-based non-invasive brain signals: Recent advances and new frontiers. *Journal of Neural Engineering.* doi: 10.1088/1741-2552/abc902.

79. Zhao, J. J., Mathieu, M., & LeCun, Y., (2017). *Energy-Based Generative Adversarial Networks.* Paper presented at 5th International Conference on Learning Representations, ICLR 2017, Toulon, France.

80. Ziqi, R., Jie, L., Xuetong, X., Xin, L., Fan, Y., Zhicheng, J., & Xinbo, G., (2021). Reconstructing seen image from brain activity by visually-guided cognitive representation and adversarial learning, *Neuroimage, 228*, 117602, ISSN 1053-8119. https://doi.org/10.1016/j.neuroimage.2020.117602.

CHAPTER 12

New Research Challenges and Applications in Artificial Intelligence on Edge Computing

SASWATI CHATTERJEE,[1] SHIRIN SHARON MASIH,[1] and
SUNEETA SATPATHY[2]

[1]*Sunstone Eduversity, Kolkata Campus, Kolkata, West Bengal, India*

[2]*Center for AI & ML, SOA University, Bhubaneswar, Odisha*

ABSTRACT

Patients and family members have the necessity of efficient and complex healthcare in an intelligent structure customized as per their requirements of individual healthcare, as per the changing advancement of technologies and the rapidly changing lives of humans. Computation of Edge, within connection to 5G and piercing-edge internet of smart things (IoST) alertness, automatically enables requirements of exact-situation of intelligence result of healthcare that has come up to consumable electricity requirements about latency a significant decline in health. Many researchers have discovered that study on intelligence healthcare systems focuses on architecture computation, security, authentication, and the types of attentiveness and devices utilized in edge computation activity. They are not reliant on the (IoST) programs installed for piercing edge computation structures for their healthcare. The first and most important purpose of this study is to look at the current and changing edge computation structure as well as intelligent healthcare instruments.

Moreover, the identification and forecasting of demands and supply under challenging situations of different implicating scenarios have taken

Reconnoitering the Landscape of Edge Intelligence in Healthcare.
Suneeta Satpathy, Sachi Nandan Mohanty, and Sirisha Potluri (Eds.)
© 2024 Apple Academic Press, Inc. Co-published with CRC Press (Taylor & Francis)

measures. As per the forecast, edge structure has been used to pierce edges in deep learning (DL) tools to achieve stipulated health data details and outcomes with the tracks and records for identifying significant severe signals. These detailed studies have also proven that thorough observation and the cutting edge of artificial intelligence (AI) based on fake details tools usage for intelligence in piercing edge tools. Apart from its different use and many advantages, piercing-edge tools give a significant computational complexity and challenge insecurities and knowledge. Potential researchers have suggested that pierced edge computer technology be developed for healthcare progress in order to provide individuals with more quality and balance in their lives. This study will also give a clear idea of how the (IoST) method of solving edge problems with the help of medical healthcare therapy has recently been applied.

12.1   INTRODUCTION

Modern cities have an innovative concept based on various electronic devices and people for the rapid and efficient flow of information from one location to another. For new devices, the quality of service (QoS) provided by. Cloudlet and local cloud, closely complementary computing technologies, is poor. Excessive network traffic slows transmission times, resulting in expensive data transmission costs [2]. Cloudlet-based systems, despite having lower latency than MCC, fail to provide critical mobility for devices due to limited WIFI availability [1].

Many studies have examined cloud-based versus edge-based computing performance, concluding that all edge-based computing can meet current latency [3, 4], mobility [5–7], and energy efficiency [10] requirements. Modern cities have innovative intelligence, co-related, and cost-effective technologies that connect various aspects of the city, such as resource transportation, waste management, human health, and crisis management. These are perilous ways posed by enormous urban development, which has resulted in rapid population growth and issues such as rising costs, insecticide, and pesticide use, poor health management, crime, and environmental iterative and incremental development. Modern cities have played such an essential role due to advanced administration. Modern towns have played a significant role in improving citizens' way of living and healthcare conditions. It is also worth noting that, as cities have grown in size because of population, it has been complicated to meet the requirements of every citizen, particularly their health. Citizens' health has become a serious concern since pandemics. Because of a considerable population and black marketing of oxygen cylinders, there was a massive shortage of oxygen cylinders, and beds in hospitals were not readily available.

Moreover, it was more challenging to deal with the pandemic, and people were not aware of the medicines and how to save themselves. As well as more and more increase in death rate has caused people to fear more, management has become difficult. In modern cities, management was easier as people were aware of the new technologies, new constructions of hospitals were done, and management was comparatively easier. Smart cities are also characterized as information systems based on the internet of smart things (IoST) that have attempted to connect various parts of cities such as hospitals, houses, offices, and so on. According to a United Nations report, metropolitan regions are home to 68% of the global population. The healthcare industry has faced significant challenges as a result of a large number of patients and the limited number of hospital beds. The advancement of intelligent multisensory objects, intelligent systems (AI), computer science (ML), and learning techniques can be felt like a revolution in healthcare, and related medical terminology is garnering special attention from diverse communities. People with chronic illnesses can be cared for in their own homes by using environmental sensors put throughout their dwellings. It can be shared, allowing patients to receive proper medical treatment.

Multiple areas are allied in the structure are "attached" because they share accurate patient information on time. Excluding the healthcare studies, there are a significant number of surveys dedicated only to mobile edge computing (EC) applications [10–19].

12.2 LITERATURE REVIEW

1. **Privacy and Security:** These are essential to maintain privacy because any single part of a machine can endanger human life. For example, an insulin pump in an IoST glucose regulating device may be controlled by a machine that can be hacked within 50 feet, which can cause harm. The other parts of the machine consist of the gateway, nodes, sensor, Fog, and Cloud, which are completely protected and covered when delivering a safe IoST healthcare machine. T ensures safety at different levels and high-level security in literature.

2. **Edge Computing (EC):** This explains the astonishing eyes opening technology that helps us calculate the data eaten at the extremity linkage of the data in the form of downstream or upstream. Downstream will appear from the cloud services, whereas upstream data will come from IoST organized services. The edge has now been declared as the integrating grid system Figure 12.1 which is located along the way along with the server and cloud ability. As per different research, in the present day's scenario, fog computation can be replaced by edge computation, but both have advantages and disadvantages. Fog computation has extra marks on the side of the structure, whereas edge computation has mainly been noted on the sides, which are effective. Hence, it has been acknowledged that EC, when compared with cloud computing (CC), both had a significant impact on our community. This is the two-way process of edge and cloud computation. EC is a center of attention that makes the computers attached to the causes that bring data close. The CC paradigms have various advantages in contrast to the conventionality of edge and cloud service.

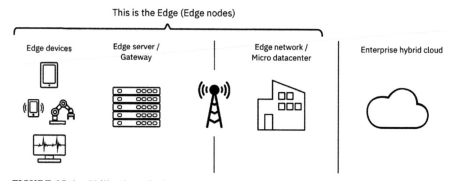

FIGURE 12.1   Utilization of edge nodes.

Image credit: https://www.ibm.com/cloud/architecture/architectures/edge-computing/

System architecture computation of fog and edge-this explains the whole diagram of IoST-healthcare. It shows how the elements can be in a sequential way or may be scattered over the layers, which can be used in hospitals. The sensors present in the materials of a patient's health monitor private variables that can be monitored with different variables. There can be an addition on the date, time, temperature, etc. (Figure 12.2). The various situations that have arisen help identify different designs and create inferences from different positions. The typical design allows for CAT scans. Magnetic images can be attached to other medical instruments in use for the transformation of information into machines. There are additional classifications of system architecture:

i.   **Medical Sensors with Actuators Network:** Few machines have powers to transmit capabilities, sensing, and perspective of biomedical signals that can be taken up from the body or surroundings. These are done with the help of protocols like Bluetooth, Wi-Fi, and networks of intelligence healthcare.

ii. **Gateways:** After the sensor, the medical actuators with medical sensors, the scattered geographical healthcare gateways have layers designed to develop fog. All the gateways act as a connecting point among the local networks. Because of their low cost and ease of use, these are popular options. In circumstances where photos can be explored [27] whereas research employs a graphics processing unit (GPU). Telos Mote [26], and Intel Edison [28] are also popular nodes, especially in applications involving ambient sensing.

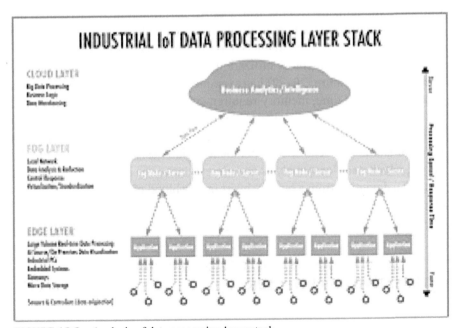

FIGURE 12.2   Analysis of data processing layer stack.

Image credit: https://www.winsystems.com/cloud-fog-and-edge-computing-whats-the-difference/

12.3 METHODOLOGY

The collection of data-The current methodology is built on a qualitative research method, which is pertinent to the study and is emphasized periodically. This has been maintained by the researcher in an interpretive manner. This promotes a more holistic approach to the studied phenomena rather than a quantitative one. In addition, because the current study is descriptive, the qualitative approach will allow the researcher to analyze and synthesize a considerable amount of relevant literature.

Data Analysis by psychological measures – IoT-based healthcare systems that focus on physiological health data to access and identify critical health problems have recently been proposed in a number of research projects. A wireless body sensor network is used in the study to track people's mobility and heart rates while they are inside their homes. Patients' families and healthcare professionals can receive health alerts on their smartphones thanks to the edge layer. The calculation of sudden changes in sensor data aids in the early detection of falls or serious health issues. Another IoT-based revolutionary healthcare system was presented for monitoring patients' vital signs at home utilizing ECG sensor data. To perform system interaction, the proposed method used a television interface. Cost differences include high memory consumption (due to encryption block size and key length), sensor energy consumption, memory utilization, and computation difficulty, to name a few. Recent literature [20–22] has examined many security models in terms of key generation time, memory requirements, bandwidth requirements, and encryption/decryption time, due to the necessity of maintaining client data in healthcare applications. Sensors capture data about a patient's present physical status and send it to a personal digital assistant (PDA) or mobile phone, which does local analysis and alerts relatives or emergency services if a fall or a deviation from a healthy heart rate or blood pressure (BP) is discovered [23–25]. Edge mining, which reduces the number of packets delivered to the cloud or cloud nodes, can save a significant amount of money.

12.4 HEALTHCARE SYSTEM EDGE COMPUTING (EC) ALTERNATIVES-ARCHITECTURE

An EC solution's generic architecture includes a user device, sensor, or IoT device, a smartphone with computing capabilities, and an edge, fog, or CC node. Computer resources are frequently shared between the fog node and the user device. The interaction of the architecture between the edge and the cloud is critical. The advantages of the cloud are realized in terms of long-term data, whereas the edge is focused on immediate action. This interplay [32, 33] between the overall architecture and the most popular types of devices complicates load balancing and routing on edge and cloud servers. A recently proposed architecture includes considerations for an IoT layer in addition to a fog and cloud layer, which is a common setup.

12.4.1 PROTOCOLS USED FOR COMMUNICATION

A cloud layer is commonly used in a fog or edge healthcare system, which is a common configuration in the literature. This IoT layer is in charge of all medical sensors.

To connect between a device and a fog node, short-range communication protocols like IEEE 802.15.1 or 802.15.4 are employed. A sensor node is typically connected to additional computing devices or cloud services via a wireless 802.11 connection. Protocol 36 makes use of a sensor node, mobile computing devices, and a cloud service. It's used in a lot of applications [34, 35].

12.4.2 OPERATIONS ON INFORMATION

Existing health-related EC studies aimed at identifying certain key performance indicators (KPIs) that are crucial to illness development. In healthcare, response speed, energy efficiency, and bandwidth cost are all important considerations. The majority of publications are concerned with improving the KPIs related to a single piece of the EC architecture, such as the edge device or fog node in a given system. The purpose of this section is to provide you with a thorough grasp of the finest data operations strategies for a healthcare EC environment. The terms "retrieval," "encryption," "categorization," "authentication," "data reduction," and "prediction" are used interchangeably.

12.5 DEMANDS FOR FUTURE RESEARCH-DATA RELATED TO PATIENT

While edge-enabled socialized healthcare equipment enhances the patient quality of life and provides revenue opportunities for healthcare providers and 5G network operators, there are serious worries about patient data privacy, which will only grow as the technology becomes more widely adopted. Existing HIPAA laws aren't yet well-developed enough to apply to edge-enabled technologies [37, 38].

Because various parties, such as research groups and insurance companies, consider patient data to be a valuable asset, any data breach will result in legal consequences for both the health provider and the network operator. To make matters even more complicated, these regulations and restrictions on patient data preservation differ by country and region. Privacy protocols for patient information now focus on securing personal information that is linked to an identifiable individual, and can become personal in nature, any data breach will result in legal implications for both the health practitioner and the patient because the information is such a valuable asset [39, 40].

Patient permission-based authorization is also required when patients obtain and own their own medical data through IoT devices. A blockchain-based MEC framework describes one such technique that is resistant to unauthorized access and single points of failure. Given the foregoing, advanced privacy and anonymization structures are required for large-scale healthcare systems. The efficiency of the computation is jeopardized by computationally complex cryptography algorithms.

12.6   EDGE-AI OPPORTUNITIES, CHALLENGES, AND APPLICATIONS

In smart cities, Edge-AI can be used for a variety of connected healthcare applications. The architecture of EC should be addressed so that processing can occur at gateways (edge nodes) or devices (end-nodes). It will help reduce needless processing latency and data traffic, which is required for crucial analysis and patient monitoring applications. The focus is on creating and implementing edge nodes for a variety of patient monitoring applications. In a hospital setting, however, the end nodes can be separated further. Interactive devices, for example, include wearables, voice recognition devices, and smartphones, and can refer to any fixed or mobile component that permits interaction between the user's environment and the human user. Connected healthcare is an area of digital health that is fast growing. It takes into account socio-technical frameworks. This approach may successfully interact with the environment, various adjacent intelligent devices, and smart city stakeholders to provide accessible and cheap healthcare. Voice pathology identification is implemented for the dazzling city in the case study of a healthcare monitoring system employing two different sorts of signals. Edge-AI-based connected healthcare systems include a three-tier design that connects devices to the Internet and allows alarms to be forwarded to the cloud. After processing, the signals are evaluated as pathologic or anticipated, and a confidence score is assigned. The results are communicated to healthcare specialists in order to assist them in making the best decision possible. After evaluating the data, it was observed that the proposed technique accurately predicts VPD (vaccine-preventable disease).

12.7   CONCLUSION

The Internet can help with consumer health, clinical care, healthcare financial and administrative transactions, public health, professional education, and biomedical research. Although the networking capabilities necessary to serve these applications are not unique, they do reflect certain elements of the healthcare setting. The Internet has the potential to increase the quality and efficiency of communications between parties in each of the committee's areas. Care practitioners already utilize the Internet to search the professional literature for information on specific diseases or to examine evidence-based practice guidelines for addressing a specific disorder in the clinical care area, for example. Continued study, development, and deployment of Internet applications will allow for greater care, as ongoing projects demonstrate, access to providers on a more regular basis in the National Academies of Sciences, Engineering, and Medicine. Internet Prescriptions, Networking Health, 2000. A considerable number of Internet-based health-related inquiries require reassurance concerning the service quality. The fact that the system is continually interactive and responsive necessitates QoS. During video monitoring conversations with patients or other care professionals, for example, persistent high connectivity (about 384 kbps for simple interactions and 768 kbps for higher quality video) is required. Medical students who wish to practice a surgical method utilizing multimedia simulations stored on distant servers, and groups of surgeons from across the country who want to collaborate all have something in common.

12.8   DETAILED ANALYSIS AND FUTURE SCOPE

Installation of smart healthcare systems is necessary for this era of current technologies. To meet the needs of individual patients and to provide support to healthcare practitioners to deliver more accurate diagnoses and treatment Opportunities for treatment [41]. With the use of sensors, 5G, and AI-EC, it's now possible to give superior healthcare real-time solutions promoting privacy, meeting latency requirements, lowering costs, and lowering energy use [42]. For diagnosis, detection, tracking, monitoring, resource allocation, and control, smart and connected healthcare have been employed in a number of nations. It's also been utilized for resource allocation, monitoring, tracking, and control. After reviewing various research papers, it has been determined that Smart Cities play an important part in the country's economic progress.

Not only that, but they also contribute significantly to the citizens' well-being. They also assist citizens in improving their abilities to use technology to create sustainable services. Computational approaches have been highlighted as playing a significant part in the development of smart cities. The reason for this is that these methods are the building blocks of decision-making, assisting in the formulation of policies and the provision of the best services to citizens.

This problem can be solved by combining artificial intelligence (AI) with strong edge computation to handle large amounts of complex data and computation edge services that are crucial for professional analysis [43]. EdgeIoT services have been highlighted as having potential to provide professionals, caregivers, and patients with a cutting-edge experience and physicians from any location and at any time without restriction interruption.

It's also been discovered that the solution is Edge's contribution [43] AI outperforms the cloud. It's been a while discovered that earlier research did not primarily focus on Authentication, fog, and CC architecture security, sensor types, and gadgets that can be used efficiently are all factors to consider, in the context of EC frameworks [44].

As a result, it has been forced to concentrate on IoT and edge applications in healthcare, AI is being used. Implementation is one of the most difficult tasks. Such systems by transforming cities into smart cities in need of detention research and financing through several factors have been identified in the literature as being involved. This may have a negative impact on Edge AI adoption.

KEYWORDS

- **artificial intelligence**
- **edge applications**
- **edge computing**
- **healthcare**
- **IoST**
- **key performance indicators**
- **socio-technical frameworks**

REFERENCES

1. Liu, L., Yang, Y., Zhao, W., & Du, Z., (2015). Semi-automatic remote medicine monitoring system of miners. In: *Adjunct Proceedings of the 2015 ACM International Joint Conference on Pervasive and Ubiquitous Computing and Proceedings of the 2015 ACM International Symposium on Wearable Computers Ubicomp/ISWC'15 Adjunct* (pp. 93–96). ACM; New York, NY, USA.

2. Maitra, A., & Kuntagod, N., (2013). A novel mobile application to assist maternal health workers in rural India. In: *2013 5th International Workshop on Software Engineering in Health Care (SEHC)*, 75–78.

3. Yi, S., Hao, Z., Zhang, Q., Zhang, Q., Shi, W., & Li, Q., (2017). LAVEA: Latency-aware video analytics on edge computing platform. In: *Proceedings of the Second ACM/IEEE Symposium on Edge Computing; SEC '17* (pp. 15:1–15:13). ACM; New York, NY, USA.

4. Jackson, K. R., Ramakrishnan, L., Muriki, K., et al., (2010). Performance analysis of high-performance computing applications on the amazon web services cloud. In: *2010 IEEE Second International Conference on Cloud Computing Technology and Science* (pp. 159–168).

5. Bhunia, S. S., (2015). *Sensor-Cloud: Enabling Remote Health-Care Services* (pp. 3, 4). In: Proceedings of the 2015 on MobiSys PhD Forum; PhD Forum '15. ACM; New York, NY, USA.

6. Thiyagaraja, S. R., Dantu, R., Shrestha, P. L., Thompson, M. A., & Smith, C., (2017). Optimized and secured transmission and retrieval of vital signs from remote devices. In: *Proceedings of the Second IEEE/ACM International Conference on Connected Health: Applications, Systems and Engineering Technologies; CHASE '17* (pp. 25–30). IEEE Press; Piscataway, NJ, USA.

7. Althebyan, Q., Yaseen, Q., Jararweh, Y., & Al-Ayyoub, M., (2016). Cloud support for large scale e-healthcare systems. *Annals of Telecommunications, 71*(9), 503–515. doi: 10.1007/s12243-016-0496-9.

8. Chung, K., & Park, R. C., (2017). Cloud based u-healthcare network with QoS guarantee for mobile health service. *Cluster Computing*. doi: 10.1007/s10586-017-1120-0.

9. Bhunia, S. S., Dhar, S. K., & Mukherjee, N., (2014). iHealth: A fuzzy approach for provisioning intelligent health-care system in smart city. In: *2014 IEEE 10th International Conference on Wireless and Mobile Computing, Networking and Communications (WiMob)* (pp. 187–193).

10. Abbas, N., Zhang, Y., Taherkordi, A., & Skeie, T., (2018). Mobile edge computing: A survey. *IEEE Internet of Things Journal, 5*(1), 450–465. doi: 10.1109/JIOT.2017.2750180.

11. Wang, S., Zhang, X., Zhang, Y., Wang, L., Yang, J., & Wang, W., (2017). A survey on mobile edge networks: Convergence of computing, caching and communications. *IEEE Access, 5*, 6757–6779. doi: 10.1109/ACCESS.2017.2685434.

12. Yu, Y., (2016). Mobile edge computing towards 5G: Vision, recent progress, and open challenges. *China Communications, 13*(2), 89–99. doi: 10.1109/CC.2016.7833463.

13. Mao, Y., You, C., Zhang, J., Huang, K., & Letaief, K. B., (2017). A survey on mobile edge computing: The communication perspective. *IEEE Communications Surveys Tutorials, 19*(4), 2322–2358. doi: 10.1109/COMST.2017.2745201.

14. Taleb, T., Samdanis, K., Mada, B., Flinck, H., Dutta, S., & Sabella, D., (2017). On multi-access edge computing: A survey of the emerging 5G network edge cloud architecture

and orchestration. *IEEE Communications Surveys Tutorials, 19*(3), 1657–1681. doi: 10.1109/COMST.2017.2705720.

15. Yu, W., Liang, F., He, X., et al., (2018). A survey on the edge computing for the internet of things. *IEEE Access, 6,* 6900–6919. doi: 10.1109/ACCESS.2017.2778504.

16. Shi, W., Cao, J., Zhang, Q., Li, Y., & Xu, L., (2016). Edge computing: Vision and challenges. *IEEE Internet of Things Journal, 3*(5), 637–646. doi: 10.1109/ JIOT.2016.2579198.

17. Rauf, A., Shaikh, R. A., & Shah, A., (2018). Security and privacy for IoT and fog computing paradigm. In: *2018 15th Learning and Technology Conference (L T)* (pp. 96–101).

18. Salman, O., Elhajj, I., Kayssi, A., & Chehab, A., (2015). Edge computing enabling the internet of things. In: *2015 IEEE 2nd World Forum on Internet of Things (WF-IoT)* (pp. 603–608).

19. Mouradian, C., Naboulsi, D., Yangui, S., Glitho, R. H., Morrow, M. J., & Polakos, P. A., (2018). A comprehensive survey on fog computing: State-of-the-art and research challenges. *IEEE Communications Surveys Tutorials, 20*(1), 416–464. doi: 10.1109/ COMST.2017.2771153.

20. Thakar, A. T., & Pandya, S., (2017). Survey of IoT enables healthcare devices. In: *2017 International Conference on Computing Methodologies and Communication (ICCMC)* (pp. 1087–1090).

21. Kumar, N., (2017). IoT architecture and system design for healthcare systems. In: *2017 International Conference on Smart Technologies for Smart Nation (SmartTechCon)* (pp. 1118–1123).

22. AbdElnapi, N. M. M., Omran, N. F., Ali, A. A., & Omara, F. A., (2018). A survey of internet of things technologies and projects for healthcare services. In: *2018 International Conference on Innovative Trends in Computer Engineering (ITCE)* (pp. 48–55).

23. Baker, S. B., Xiang, W., & Atkinson, I., (2017). Internet of things for smart healthcare: Technologies, challenges, and opportunities. *IEEE Access, 5,* 26521–26544. doi: 10.1109/ACCESS.2017.2775180.

24. De Mattos, W. D., & Gondim, P. R. L., (2016). M-health solutions using 5G networks and M2M communications. *IT Professional, 18*(3), 24–29. doi: 10.1109/MITP.2016.52.

25. Mahmoud, M. M. E., Rodrigues, J. J. P. C., Ahmed, S. H., et al., (2018). Enabling technologies on cloud of things for smart healthcare. *IEEE Access, 6,* 31950–31967. doi: 10.1109/ACCESS.2018.2845399.

26. Gaura, E. I., Brusey, J., Allen, M., Wilkins, R., Goldsmith, D., & Rednic, R., (2013). Edge mining the internet of things. *IEEE Sensors Journal, 13*(10), 3816–3825. doi: 10.1109/JSEN.2013.2266895.

27. Wang, H., Gong, J., Zhuang, Y., Shen, H., & Lach, J., (2017). Healthedge: Task scheduling for edge computing with health emergency and human behavior consideration in smart homes. In: *2017 International Conference on Networking, Architecture, and Storage (NAS)* (pp. 1, 2).

28. Al-Khawaja, M., Webster, L., Baker, T., & Waraich, A., (2018). Towards fog driven IoT healthcare: Challenges and framework of fog computing in healthcare. In: *Proceedings of the 2nd International Conference on Future Networks and Distributed Systems; ICFNDS '18* (pp. 9:1–9:7). ACM; New York, NY, USA.

29. Gaura, E. I., Brusey, J., Allen, M., Wilkins, R., Goldsmith, D., & Rednic, R., (2013). Edge mining the internet of things. *IEEE Sensors Journal, 13*(10), 3816–3825. doi: 10.1109/JSEN.2013.2266895.

30. Meyer, J., Kazakova, A., Büsing, M., & Boll, S., (2016). Visualization of complex health data on mobile devices. In: *Proceedings of the 2016 ACM Workshop on Multimedia for Personal Health and Health Care MMHealth '16* (pp. 31–34). ACM; New York, NY, USA.

31. Rolim, C. O., Koch, F. L., Westphall, C. B., Werner, J., Fracalossi, A., & Salvador, G. S., (2010). A cloud computing solution for patient's data collection in health care institutions. In: *2010 Second International Conference on eHealth, Telemedicine, and Social Medicine* (pp. 95–99).

32. Al-Khawaja, M., Webster, L., Baker, T., & Waraich, A., (2018). Towards fog driven IoT healthcare: Challenges and framework of fog computing in healthcare. In: *Proceedings of the 2nd International Conference on Future Networks and Distributed Systems; CFNDS '18* (pp. 9:1–9:7). ACM; New York, NY, USA.

33. Baktir, A. C., Tunca, C., Ozgovde, A., Salur, G., & Ersoy, C., (2018). SDN-based multi-tier computing and communication architecture for pervasive healthcare. *IEEE Access, 6*, 56765–56781. doi: 10.1109/ACCESS.2018.2873907.

34. Lv, Z., Xia, F., Wu, G., Yao, L., & Chen, Z., (2010). iCare: A mobile health monitoring system for the elderly. In: *2010 IEEE/ACM Int'l Conference on Green Computing and Communications Int'l Conference on Cyber, Physical and Social Computing* (pp. 699–705).

35. Wu, W., Cao, J., Zheng, Y., & Zheng, Y., (2008). WAITER: A wearable personal healthcare and emergency aid system. In: *2008 Sixth Annual IEEE International Conference on Pervasive Computing and Communications (PerCom)* (pp. 680–685).

36. Rolim, C. O., Koch, F. L., Westphall, C. B., Werner, J., Fracalossi, A., & Salvador, G. S., (2010). A cloud computing solution for patient's data collection in health care institutions. In: *2010 Second International Conference on eHealth, Telemedicine, and Social Medicine* (pp. 95–99).

37. HHS.gov (2017). *HIPAA for Individuals.* https://www.hhs.gov/hipaa/for-individuals/index.html.

38. Casola, V., Castiglione, A., Choo, K. R., & Esposito, C., (2016). Healthcare-related data in the cloud: Challenges and opportunities. *IEEE Cloud Computing, 3*(6), 10–14. doi: 10.1109/MCC.2016.139.

39. Cavoukian, A., Fisher, A., Killen, S., & Hoffman, D. A., (2010). Remote home health care technologies: How to ensure privacy? Build it in: Privacy by design. *Identity in the Information Society, 3*(2), 363–378. doi: 10.1007/s12394-010-0054-y.

40. Rahman, M. A., Hossain, M. S., Loukas, G., et al., (2018). Blockchain-based mobile edge computing framework for secure therapy applications. *IEEE Access, 6*, 72469–72478. doi: 10.1109/ACCESS.2018.2881246.

41. Muhammad, G., Hossain, M. S., & Kumar, N., (2021). EEG-based pathology detection for home health monitoring. *IEEE Journal on Selected Areas in Communications, 39*(2), 603–610.

42. Yassine, A., Singh, S., Hossain, M. S., & Muhammad, G., (2019). IoT big data analytics for smart homes with fog and cloud computing. *Future Generation Computer Systems, 91*, 563–573.

43. Hossain, M. S., & Muhammad, G., (2018). Emotion-aware connected healthcare big data towards 5G. *IEEE Internet of Things Journal, 5*(4), 2399–2406.

44. Pazienza, A., Mallardi, G., Fasciano, C., & Vitulano, F., (2019). Artificial intelligence on edge computing: A healthcare the scenario in ambient assisted living. In: *Proceedings of the Artificial Intelligence for Ambient Assisted Living (AI*AAL.it 2019)*. Rende, Italy.

45. Vinayakumar, R., Alazab, M., Srinivasan, S., Pham, Q. V., Padannayil, S. K., & Simran, K., (2020). A visualized botnet detection system based deep learning for the internet of things networks of smart cities. IEEE Transactions on Industry Applications, 56(4), 4436–4456.

CHAPTER 13

Optimal Mixed Kernel Extreme Learning Machine-Based Intrusion Detection System for Secure Intelligent Edge Computing

R. PANDI SELVAM,[1] T. JAYASANKAR,[2] R. KIRUBA BURI,[3] and
P. MAHESWARAVENKATESH[2]

[1]PG Department of Computer Science, Ananda College, Devakottai,
Tamil Nadu, India

[2]University College of Engineering, BIT Campus Anna University,
Tiruchirappalli, Tamil Nadu, India

[3]Department of Computer Science and Engineering, University College
of Engineering, Anna University, Rajamadam, Pattukottai, Tamil Nadu,
India

ABSTRACT

Edge computing (EC) technologies act as an important role in resolving the issues of remote EC, such as high delay, mobility, and location awareness. Every EC service can take place in a mutual way and be accessed by users through the Internet. A few of the attacks are used to root, remote login, denial of service (DoS), snooping, port scanning, etc., can occur in EC platforms because of Internet-enabled remote services. An intrusion detection system (IDS) is an effective way of protecting the network through the detection of attacks. In this view, this study introduces an optimal mixed kernel extreme learning machine-based intrusion detection system (OMKELM-IDS) for intelligent EC. The goal of the OMKELM-IDS

Reconnoitering the Landscape of Edge Intelligence in Healthcare.
Suneeta Satpathy, Sachi Nandan Mohanty, and Sirisha Potluri (Eds.)

technique focuses on the detection and classification of intrusions in the EC environment. The OMKELM-IDS technique encompasses pre-processing, intrusion detection, and parameter tuning. Besides, the MKELM model can be designed to identify the occurrence of intrusions and classify it. Moreover, the quasi-oppositional cuckoo search algorithm (QOCSA) is applied for the optimal parameter tuning process of the MKELM model and thereby boosts the detection efficiency. The experimental result analysis of the OMKELM-IDS technique takes place using benchmark IDS dataset and the outcomes are studied under different aspects. The experimental outcome highlighted the enhanced performance of the OMKELM-IDS approach on the recent state of art approaches. The comparative outcomes portrayed the betterment of the OMKELM-IDS system with respect to distinct measures.

13.1 INTRODUCTION

With the tremendous growth of mobile networks, multi-media data on network edge devices are quickly growing. The storage space and network transmission load of conventional cloud computing (CC) smart scheme are affected. With the development of real-time requirements of the networks, edge computing (EC) rises at the historic moment [1]. Related studies show that as of October 30, 2020, 50% of multi-media information has been stored, forwarded, pre-processed, and further processed over the Internet edge [2]. The CC model of central processing would fall as to the demands of privacy and real-time security which could not complete the conventional processing of each program, and EC is becoming an innovative direction of developments [3]. EC plays an essential role in CC and services by resolving some problems at the network edge. The overall structure of EC is depicted in Figure 13.1. As a new conception, still there are several problems pertaining to privacy and security around computation, data storage, intelligent decision making, network activity, usage, and location. It is necessary to study how the features such as heterogeneity, geo-distribution, and wireless connection could be managed and how current privacy and security measures for CC could be employed to EC. Furthermore, edge server should co-operate for completing the task, under distinct operators. This could make worse the problems of privacy and security. Emerging our understanding of how to protect data and user privacy in this circumstance is important to the further development of EC [4].

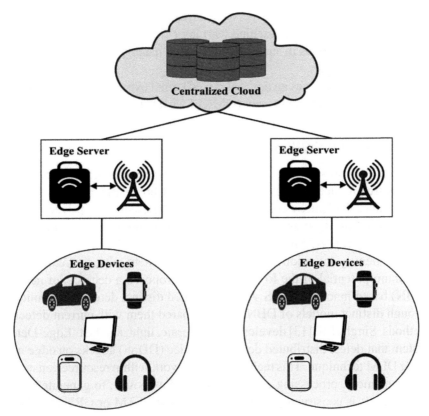

FIGURE 13.1 Overview of edge computing.

In edge-enabled IoT, the risk factor primarily includes data in system devices edge nodes, cloud servers, and edge networks. This threat comes from a different kind of sources, involving hacking, malware, unauthorized access, exploited system vulnerabilities, etc. [5]. When the intrusion is not timely detected, it will create great loss to the devices and application from the internet of things (IoT), particularly threats to security of individuals [6]. The study on edge network security was still in the developmental phase, as well a recent intrusion detection (ID) solution is suggested to be placed in the central networks [7]. But this doesn't meet the actual security requirements, and because of the turnover of the network framework, the efficiency of the ID technique has high requirements. The intrusion detection system (IDS) is a robust active defense system, and there are several ID approaches [8]. Based on the data source, IDS could be separated into two classes: host- and network-based IDS [9]. The network-based IDS is one of the solutions for the earlier recognition of network threats. Because of the outstanding classification accuracy of machine learning (ML), authors have extensively employed ML methods in anomaly-based IDS, namely Bayesian, SVM, GA, and ML models [10].

This study introduces an optimal mixed kernel extreme learning machine-based intrusion detection system (OMKELM-IDS) for intelligent EC.

13.2 RELATED WORKS

Han et al. [11] presented a face verification technique-based EC and extract the feature of face images through convolution neural network (CNN), authenticates the face by cosine similarity, and presents user privacy protection system based on secured secret sharing homomorphism and nearest neighbor algorithms. Almogren [12] introduced a method to accurately and quickly identify intrusion activities in the EoT networks, for realizing the maximum potential of the IoT. Particularly proposed a deep belief network (DBN) based innovative IDS. Also, examined distinct detection techniques, through distinct models of DBN, and compared them with current detection methods. Singh et al. [13] developed an accurate, light, and fast 'Edge-Detect' system that detect distributed denial of service (DDoS) attacks on edge node using DLM technique. This technique could work within resource constraints that is memory, processing capabilities, and low power, to generate precise outcomes. It is constructed by making layers of LSTM or GRU based cells that are renowned for the outstanding depiction of consecutive data.

Yuan et al. [14] developed an IDS to be installed on edge node. They transform network traffics into images that are employed for training a CNN to categorize the network traffics. Moreover, auxiliary classifier generative adversarial network (AC-GAN) is adapted for generating synthesized sample for extending the ID data set. Man et al. [15] developed a smart IDS, FedACNN that completes the ID tasks by supporting the DL-CNN model by using the FL method. For alleviating the transmission delay limits of FL, we incorporate the FedACNN, and the attention mechanism could attain optimal accuracy. Liu et al. [16] proposed a novel ID and defense hybrid technique for CPSS LR-DDoS in edge environments that makes use of DCNN and locality sensitive feature extraction for automatically learning the ideal feature of the original data distribution and uses DRL Q-network as an effective decision maker for protecting attack.

Lee et al. [17] presented a lightweight ML-based IDS method, i.e., IMPACT (IMPersonation Attack deteCTion utilizing deep AE and feature abstraction). It can be depending on deep feature learning with gradient-based linear SVM for deploying and running on resource-limited devices by decreasing the amount of features by using feature selection and extraction through a C4.8 wrapper, SAE, and mutual information (MI). Eskandari et al. [18] introduced Passban, a smart IDS capable of protecting the IoT device, i.e., connected directly to it. The distinctiveness of the presented solutions is that it straightforwardly positioned on cheaper IoT gateways, thus fully utilizing the EC model for detecting cyberattacks to the respective data source. Singh et al. [19] introduced an edge-based hybrid intrusion detection framework (EHIDF) which primarily considers the ML method to detect intrusive traffic in the MEC environments. The presented method comprises three ID models with three distinct classes. The hybrid detection module (HDM) uses the Meta-AdaboostM1 algorithms, signature detection module (SDM) uses C4.5 classifiers, and anomaly detection module (ADM) use Naive-based classifiers.

13.3   THE PROPOSED MODEL

In this study, an effective OMKELM-IDS technique has been presented for the detection and classification of intrusions in the EC environment. The OMKELM-IDS technique encompasses pre-processing MKELM based intrusion detection and QOCSO based parameter tuning. The usage of QOCSO algorithm assists in appropriately selecting the parameters involved in the MKELM model.

13.3.1   PROCESS INVOLVED IN MKELM-BASED CLASSIFICATION

Once the input data is pre-processed, the succeeding stage is the MKELM based classification which enables detection and classifies the occurrence of intrusions in the EC environment. Huang et al. [20] presented a particular SLFN is named ELM. An ELM only requires presenting the amount of hidden state nodes, an input weight, and hidden state bias are arbitrarily allocated without tuning. The structure of ELM is demonstrated in Figure 13.2. Besides, the resultant weight of ELM is defined with easy generalization inverse function of the hidden state resultant matrices. So, the learning speed of ELM is very quick. The ELM is obtaining the minimum norm of weights; therefore, it gains optimum generalized efficiency than gradient descent-based techniques. But, the ELM is over benefits, the generalized efficiency of ELM is uneven because of the arbitrary location of the amount of hidden state nodes.

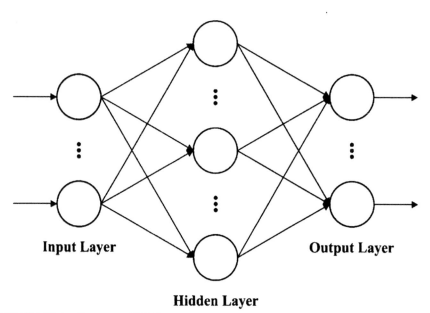

Hidden Layer

FIGURE 13.2   Structure of ELM.

Stimulated by the SVM, Huang [21] established kernel learning as to ELM and presented the KELM. Related to ELM, KELM is capable of reaching the least square optimized solutions; so, the KELM is superior and increased stability generalized efficiency than ELM. The minimum trained error and resultant weights are attained by kernel concurrently, but the learning speed of NN is increased as demonstrated in Eqn. (1):

$$\text{Min} : \left\| H\beta - T \right\|, \left\| \beta \right\| \tag{1}$$

where; H refers the hidden state resultant matrix of NN; T implies the resultant matrix; and β signifies the weight vector linking the hidden as well as resultant nodes. Eqn. (1) is resolved by least square solutions in Eqn. (2), as:

$$\beta = H^T [\frac{1}{C} + HH^T]^{-1} T \tag{2}$$

where; C refers the penalty coefficient. The resultant function of ELM is determined as:

$$f(x) = h(x)\beta = h(x)H^T [\frac{1}{C} + HH^T]^{-1} T \tag{3}$$

where; $h(x)$ indicates the feature mapping that doesn't require that recognition to user. Mercer's states were utilized for describing the kernel matrix of ELM as demonstrated as follows in Eqn. (4):

$$M = HH^T : m_{ij} = H(x_j) = k(x_j, x_j)$$
(4)

Therefore, the ELM resultant function Eqn. (3) is declared as follows in Eqn. (5):

$$f(x) = [k(x, x_1) \ldots k(x, x_N)][\frac{1}{C} + M]^{-1} T$$
(5)

The conventional KELM is a single kernel-based method. As distinct kernel function gives various similarity measures for the sample point, the efficiency of distinct kernel functions might differ significantly on the similar data set. The ECG signals have uneven distribution of samples, features of a huge dimension resulting from an imbalanced class, and higher-dimension feature space. Utilizing a single kernel for processing ECG signals could not resolve the problem. The kernel function is classified as a global or local kernel function based on either it has rotation or translation invariance [22]. In multiple kernel learning, the optimum kernel was assumed that a linear integration of a subset of base kernel, and the classifier parameters and linear combination coefficient are learned together by maximalizing the margin. The polynomial and RBF kernels are global and local kernel functions with better performances, correspondingly. For balancing the classification performance and generalization ability, an MKELM is formed by integrating the polynomial kernel and RBF kernel.

$$K_{mix} = \lambda k_{rbf}(x, x_i) + (1 - \lambda) k_{poly}(x, x_j))$$
(6)

whereas; $\lambda(0 < \lambda < 1)$ represents the weight coefficients of linear combination.

$$k_{rbf}(x, x_j) = \exp\left(\frac{-\| x - x_i \|^2}{2\sigma^2}\right)$$
(7)

$$k_{poly}(x, x_i) = (x \cdot x_i + 1)^d$$
(8)

whereas; d is fixed to 2 since the dimensions of the polynomial space represent n^d; once the index is equivalent to three and the sample size is equivalent to 1000, the dimension has attained 1 billion, and the estimation of inner product would create a dimension disaster.

Eventually, the outcome of MKELM is determined by Eqn. (9):

$$f(x) = \left[K_{mix}(x, x_1) \ldots K_{mix}(x, x_N) \right] (\frac{1}{C} + M)^{-1} T \tag{9}$$

13.3.2 PROCESS INVOLVED IN QOCSA-BASED PARAMETER TUNING

At this stage, the parameters involved in the MKELM model can be effectually adjusted by the use of QOCSA technique. The CSA method is assumed as a metaheuristic method that was initially coined by Yang and Deb. Indeed, this method stimulates the breeding behavior of cuckoo birds that are considered a type of parasitism. The cuckoo bird places their egg in another bird nests and deceives them for hosting the egg. But sometimes another bird succeeded in finding non-native eggs and hence eliminate them. The cuckoo birds try to increase the hatching possibility of its own egg by making them similar to the host egg in terms of color, shape, and size or throw other native egg out of nest with aggressive performance. Once a cuckoo chick hatches, it might remove another egg in the nests for increasing their individual feeding share [23].

During the CSA method, cuckoo eggs from various nests epitomize a generation of candidate solutions to an optimized issue. Indeed, the search starts with specific amount of nests since there is one solution for each nest. This population of solutions is evolved iteratively according to the concepts of cuckoo egg recognition (p) viz. mimics by eliminating a proportion of solution in nest and replacing them with novel one. In CS method, a random walk has been utilized according to Lévy flight distribution for yielding novel candidate solutions (cuckoos) in the present ones.

$$cuckoo_i^{(t+1)} = cuckoo_i^{(t)} + a \oplus Levy(\lambda) \tag{10}$$

whereas; $cuckoo_i^{(t+1)}$ signifies the ith Cuckoo values at iteration t. The a and λ parameters signify step size (generally fixed to 1) and Lévy distribution coefficients ($1 < \lambda < 3$), correspondingly.

Many novel solutions are produced from the existing ones by Lévy walks, as this makes CSA capable of performing a local search with ability of self-improvement. As well, any novel solution is produced away from the existing one, this reduces the chance that stuck from local minimalism and guarantee the exploration ability. Also, the application of CSA guarantees elitism as the optimal nest would be kept at the time of iteration.

Oppositional based learning (OBL) is presented to minimize the computation complexity and improve the convergence capability of evolution algorithms (EAs). With the consideration of the present and opposite population depending upon the OBL, the candidate solutions can be enhanced. It is simpler and easy to design that makes it appropriate for improving the outcomes of the CSA. Therefore, the comparative analysis of the arbitrary population-based CSA and the opposite population can result in global optima with quick convergence. With the consideration of the present and opposite population using the OBL concept, the outcome of the CSA can be improved. Therefore, the quasi-opposite number is utilized which is generally nearer to the optimum solution compared to the opposite number. Generally, the population initialization of the CSA takes place using the QOBL concept [24]. The opposite number, opposite point, quasi-opposite number, and quasi-opposite point can be defined below. In case of any arbitrary number $\chi \in [a, b]$, the opposite number χ_0 can be represented as follows.

$$x_0 = a + b - x \tag{11}$$

Here, the opposite point for multi-dimension searching area (dimension) can be represented in Eqn. (12).

$$x_0^i = a^j + b^i - x^i, i = 1, 2, \ldots, d \tag{12}$$

And the quasi-opposite number x_{qo} of any arbitrary number, $\chi \in [a, b]$ can be defined as follows:

$$x_{qo} = rand\left(\frac{a+b}{2}, x_0\right) \tag{13}$$

Likewise, the quasi-opposite point for multi-dimension searching area (d dimension) can be equated as:

$$x_{qo}^i = rand\left(\frac{a^i + b^i}{2}, x_0^i\right) \tag{14}$$

13.4   EXPERIMENTAL VALIDATION

The experimental result analysis of the OMKELM-IDS technique takes place using KDDCup99 and UNSW-NB15 [25] datasets with existing techniques [19, 26]. The accuracy analysis of the OMKELM-IDS technique with recent methods that take place on the test KDD CUP99 dataset is offered in Table 13.1 and Figure 13.3. The experimental values indicated that the OMKELM-IDS technique has resulted in improved accuracy values over the other methods. For instance, with 1000 samples, the OMKELM-IDS technique has gained maximum accuracy of 96.27% whereas the BP, SVM, and

AIoT-IDS techniques have attained minimum accuracy of 87.16%, 95.34%, and 92.74% respectively. Concurrently, with 10000 samples, the OMKELM-IDS technique has gained maximum accuracy of 95.34% whereas the BP, SVM, and AIoT-IDS techniques have attained minimum accuracy of 90.88%, 82.42%, and 93.94% respectively.

TABLE 13.1   Comparative Accuracy Analysis of OMKELM-IDS Technique on KDDCup99 Dataset

Number of Samples	BP	SVM	AIoT-IDS	OMKELM-IDS
1,000	87.16	95.34	92.74	96.27
2,000	88.18	88.37	95.25	95.99
3,000	84.37	91.44	93.20	94.50
4,000	90.04	90.60	92.09	93.94
5,000	85.58	89.30	93.85	95.71
6,000	82.51	89.20	92.09	96.27
7,000	83.82	95.25	95.90	97.01
8,000	85.49	82.79	93.94	95.34
9,000	91.16	87.63	93.11	94.69
10,000	90.88	82.42	93.94	95.34

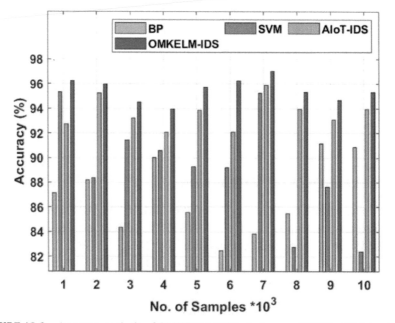

FIGURE 13.3   Accuracy analysis of OMKELM-IDS technique on KDDCup99 dataset.

The training time (TT) analysis of the OMKELM-IDS technique with recent methods that take place on the test KDD CUP99 dataset is given in Table 13.2 and Figure 13.4. The results reported that the OMKELM-IDS technique has offered reduced TT over the other methods. For instance, with 1000 samples, the OMKELM-IDS technique has accomplished lower TT of 0.011 min whereas the BP, SVM, and AIoT-IDS techniques have reached to higher TT of 0.013 min, 0.087 min, and 0.036 min, respectively. Meanwhile, with 4000 samples, the OMKELM-IDS technique has accomplished lower TT of 0.011 min whereas the BP, SVM, and AIoT-IDS techniques have reached to higher TT of 0.013 min, 0.087 min, and 0.036 min, respectively. Eventually, with 8000 samples, the OMKELM-IDS technique has accomplished lower TT of 0.073 min whereas the BP, SVM, and AIoT-IDS techniques have reached to higher TT of 0.267 min, 0.263 min, and 0.093 min, respectively. Moreover, with 10000 samples, the OMKELM-IDS technique has accomplished lower TT of 0.139 min whereas the BP, SVM, and AIoT-IDS techniques have reached to higher TT of 0.323 min, 0.158 min, and 0.139 min, respectively.

TABLE 13.2 Comparative TT Analysis of OMKELM-IDS Technique on KDDCup99 Dataset

Number of Samples	BP	SVM	AIoT-IDS	OMKELM-IDS
1,000	0.013	0.087	0.036	0.011
2,000	0.043	0.112	0.041	0.029
3,000	0.048	0.125	0.044	0.031
4,000	0.152	0.128	0.055	0.037
5,000	0.175	0.132	0.088	0.065
6,000	0.232	0.144	0.089	0.073
7,000	0.262	0.238	0.088	0.071
8,000	0.267	0.263	0.093	0.073
9,000	0.327	0.289	0.144	0.117
10,000	0.342	0.323	0.158	0.139

Table 13.3 provides a comparative result analysis of the OMKELM-IDS technique with the existing hybrid MEC technique on the UNSW-NB 15 dataset. Figure 13.5 illustrates the precision analysis of the OMKELM-IDS technique on the UNSW-NB 15 dataset. The figure portrayed that the OMKELM-IDS technique has resulted in increasing values of precision under all classes. For instance, under normal class, the OMKELM-IDS technique has attained higher precision of 80.33% whereas the Hybrid MEC technique has obtained lower precision of 97.93%. Similarly, under

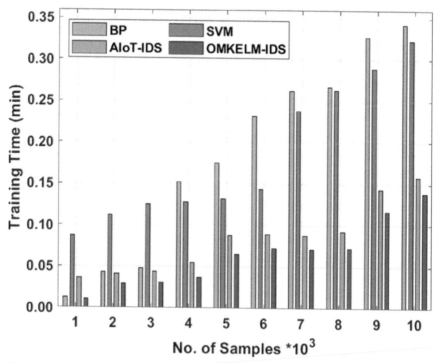

FIGURE 13.4 TT analysis of OMKELM-IDS technique on KDDCup99 dataset.

DoS class, the OMKELM-IDS technique has resulted in better precision of 84.36% whereas the Hybrid MEC technique has obtained lower precision of 84.62%.

TABLE 13.3 Comparative Result Analysis of OMKELM-IDS Technique on UNSW-NB 15 Dataset

Classes	Hybrid MEC		OMKELM-IDS	
	Precision	Recall	Precision	Recall
Normal	80.33	97.93	81.64	98.21
Analysis	82.02	17.33	83.39	27.57
Backdoor	81.65	88.79	82.05	89.18
DoS	84.36	97.69	84.62	97.99
Exploits	88.77	98.61	89.17	99.05
Fuzzers	75.84	84.49	76.21	84.87

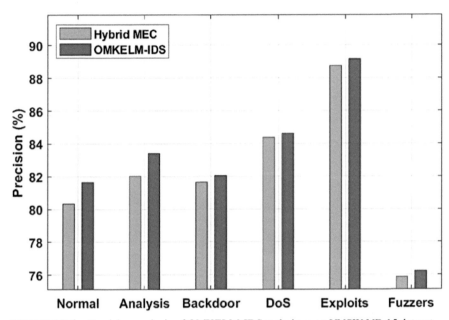

FIGURE 13.5   Precision analysis of OMKELM-IDS technique on UNSW-NB 15 dataset.

Figure 13.6 exhibits the recall analysis of the OMKELM-IDS technique on the UNSW-NB 15 dataset. Figure 13.6 represented that the OMKELM-IDS technique has led to higher values of recall under all classes. For instance, under normal class, the OMKELM-IDS technique has accomplished maximum recall of 97.93% whereas the Hybrid MEC technique has obtained lower recall of 98.21%. Along with that, under DoS class, the OMKELM-IDS technique has provided increased recall of 79.69% whereas the Hybrid MEC technique has accomplished reduced recall of 97.99%.

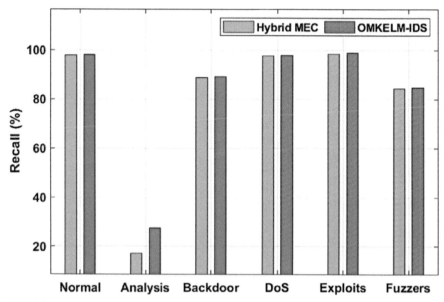

FIGURE 13.6   Precision analysis of OMKELM-IDS technique on UNSW-NB 15 dataset.

Comparative result analysis of the OMKELM-IDS technique with other methods on the test UNSW-NB 15 dataset is shown in Table 13.4 and Figure 13.7. The results show that the C4.5 technique has offered lower accuracy and F-score of 86.04% and 71.25% respectively. Followed by the Naïve Bayes model has obtained slightly improved accuracy and F-score of 86.94% and 72.49% correspondingly. Though the EHIDF technique has resulted in reasonable accuracy and F-score of 90.25% and 74.35%, the OMKELM-IDS technique has outperformed the other methods with the higher accuracy and F-score of 93.53% and 78.61% respectively.

TABLE 13.4   Accuracy and F-Score Analysis of OMKELM-IDS Technique on UNSW-NB15 Dataset

Methods	Accuracy	F-Score
C4.5	86.04	71.25
Naive Bayes	86.94	72.49
EHIDF	90.25	74.35
OMKELM-IDS	93.53	78.61

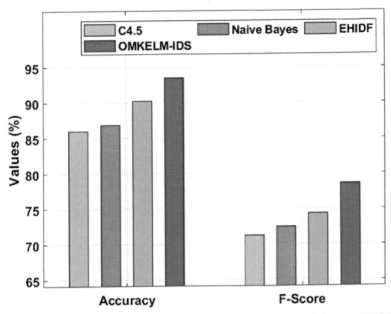

FIGURE 13.7   Accuracy and F-score analysis of OMKELM-IDS technique on UNSW-NB 15 dataset.

The result analysis of the OMKELM-IDS technique with and without MEC is shown in Table 13.5 and Figure 13.8. The results show that the overall performance of the OMKELM-IDS technique is found to be better with the MEC compared to without MEC. For instance, with respect to CPU utilization, the OMKELM-IDS technique has obtained 68.29% and 88.67% under MEC and without MEC, respectively. Similarly, with respect to RAM usage, the OMKELM-IDS technique has attained 41.56% and 61.58% under MEC and without MEC, respectively. Likewise, with respect to disk usage, the OMKELM-IDS technique has accomplished 20.39% and 24.77% under MEC and without MEC, respectively.

The experimental results analysis demonstrated the improved outcomes of the OMKELM-IDS technique over the other techniques.

TABLE 13.5   Result Analysis of OMKELM-IDS Technique with and without MEC

Parameters	With MEC	Without MEC
CPU utilization	68.29	88.67
RAM usage	41.56	61.58
Disk usage	20.39	24.77

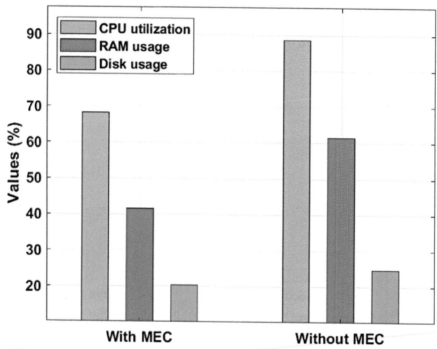

FIGURE 13.8   Results analysis of OMKELM-IDS technique with and without MEC.

13.5   CONCLUSION

The experimental result analysis of the OMKELM-IDS technique takes place using benchmark IDS dataset and the results are examined under different aspects. The experimental outcome highlighted the enhanced performance of the OMKELM-IDS approach over the recent state of art approaches. Therefore, the OMKELM-IDS technique can be utilized as a proficient tool for IDS and can be realized in practical applications. In future, advanced deep learning (DL) models with feature selection strategy is involved for improving the detection efficiency.

KEYWORDS

- **deep learning**
- **edge computing**
- **F-score analysis**
- **intelligent models**
- **intrusion detection system**
- **machine learning**
- **OMKELM-IDS**
- **parameter tuning**

REFERENCES

1. Abbas, N., Zhang, Y., Taherkordi, A., & Skeie, T., (2017). Mobile edge computing: A survey. *IEEE Internet Things J., 5*(1), 450–465.
2. Sun, Y., Zhou, S., & Xu, J., (2017). EMM: Energy-aware mobility management for mobile edge computing in ultra dense networks. *IEEE J. Sel. Areas Commun., 35*(11), 2637–2646.
3. Dong, B., Shi, Q., Yang, Y., Wen, F., Zhang, Z., & Lee, C., (2020). Technology evolution from self-powered sensors to AIoT enabled smart homes. *Nano Energy, 79,* 105414.
4. Yang, C. T., Chen, H. W., Chang, E. J., Kristiani, E., Nguyen, K. L. P., & Chang, J. S., (2021). Current advances and future challenges of AIoT applications in particulate matters (PM) monitoring and control. *J. Hazard Mater., 419,* 126442.
5. Sharafaldin, I., Lashkari, A. H., & Ghorbani, A. A., (2018). Toward generating a new intrusion detection dataset and intrusion traffic characterization. In: *ICISSP* (Vol. 1, pp. 108–116).
6. Asif-Ur-Rahman, M., Afsana, F., Mahmud, M., Kaiser, M. S., Ahmed, M. R., Kaiwartya, O., & James-Taylor, A., (2018). Toward a heterogeneous mist, fog, and cloud-based framework for the internet of healthcare things. *IEEE Internet Things J., 6*(3), 4049–4062.
7. Hajimirzaei, B., & Jafari, N. N., (2019). Intrusion detection for cloud computing using neural networks and artificial bee colony optimization algorithm. *ICT Express, 5*(1), 56–59.
8. Akashdeep, Manzoor, I., & Kumar, N., (2017). A feature reduced intrusion detection system using ANN classifier. *Expert Syst. Appl., 8,* 249–257.
9. Dovom, M. E., Azmoodeh, A., Dehghantanha, A., Newton, D. E., Parizi, R. M., & Karimipour, H., (2019). Fuzzy pattern tree for edge malware detection and categorization in IoT. *J. Syst. Archit., 97,* 1–7.

10. Keegan, N., Ji, S. Y., Chaudhary, A., Concolato, C., Yu, B., & Jeong, D. H., (2016). A survey of cloud-based network intrusion detection analysis. *Hum. Centric Comput. Inform. Sci., 6*(1), 1–16.

11. Han, Y., Zhang, W., & Zhang, Z., (2021). Security analysis of intelligent system based on edge computing. *Security and Communication Networks, 2021.*

12. Almogren, A. S., (2020). Intrusion detection in edge-of-things computing. *Journal of Parallel and Distributed Computing, 137*, 259–265.

13. Singh, P., Pankaj, A., & Mitra, R., (2021). Edge-detect: Edge-centric network intrusion detection using deep neural network. In: *2021 IEEE 18th Annual Consumer Communications & Networking Conference (CCNC)* (pp. 1–6). IEEE.

14. Yuan, D., Ota, K., Dong, M., Zhu, X., Wu, T., Zhang, L., & Ma, J., (2020). Intrusion detection for smart home security based on data augmentation with edge computing. In: *ICC 2020–2020 IEEE International Conference on Communications (ICC)* (pp. 1–6). IEEE.

15. Man, D., Zeng, F., Yang, W., Yu, M., Lv, J., & Wang, Y., (2021). Intelligent intrusion detection based on federated learning for edge-assisted internet of things. *Security and Communication Networks, 2021.*

16. Liu, Z., Yin, X., & Hu, Y., (2020). CPSS LR-DDoS detection and defense in edge computing utilizing DCNN Q-learning. *IEEE Access, 8*, 42120–42130.

17. Lee, S. J., Yoo, P. D., Asyhari, A. T., Jhi, Y., Chermak, L., Yeun, C. Y., & Taha, K., (2020). IMPACT: Impersonation attack detection via edge computing using deep autoencoder and feature abstraction. *IEEE Access, 8*, 65520–65529.

18. Eskandari, M., Janjua, Z. H., Vecchio, M., & Antonelli, F., (2020). Passban IDS: An intelligent anomaly-based intrusion detection system for IoT edge devices. *IEEE Internet of Things Journal, 7*(8), 6882–6897.

19. Singh, A., Chatterjee, K., & Satapathy, S. C., (2021). An edge-based hybrid intrusion detection framework for mobile edge computing. *Complex & Intelligent Systems*, 1–28.

20. Huang, B., Zhu, Q. Y., & Siew, C. K., (2004). Extreme learning machine: A new learning scheme of feedforward neural networks. *Neural Netw., 2*, 985–990.

21. Huang, B., (2014). An insight into extreme learning machines: Random neurons, random features and kernels. *Cogn Comput., 6*, 376–390.

22. Yang, P., Wang, D., Zhao, W. B., Fu, L. H., Du, J. L., & Su, H., (2021). Ensemble of kernel extreme learning machine based random forest classifiers for automatic heartbeat classification. *Biomedical Signal Processing and Control, 63*, 102138.

23. Bejarbaneh, E. Y., Bagheri, A., Bejarbaneh, B. Y., Buyamin, S., & Chegini, S. N., (2019). A new adjusting technique for PID type fuzzy logic controller using PSOSCALF optimization algorithm. *Applied Soft Computing, 85*, 105822.

24. Saha, S., & Mukherjee, V., (2018). A novel quasi-oppositional chaotic antlion optimizer for global optimization. *Applied Intelligence, 48*(9), 2628–2660.

25. https://www.kaggle.com/mrwellsdavid/unsw-nb15 (accessed on 10 July 2023).

26. Sui, Q., & Liu, X. (2021). Edge computing and AIoT based network intrusion detection mechanism. *Internet Technology Letters*, e324. https://doi.org/10.1002/itl2.324.

CHAPTER 14

Stochastic Approach to Govern the Efficient Framework for Big Data Analytics Using Machine Learning and Edge Computing

VAISHALI B. BHAGAT,[1,2] V. M. THAKARE,[3] and A. B. GADICHA[4]

[1]Computer Science and Engineering, Sant Gadge Baba Amravati University, Amravati, Maharashtra, India

[2]P. R. Pote College of Engineering and Management, Amravati, Maharashtra, India

[3]PG Department of Computer Science and Engineering, Sant Gadge Baba Amravati University, Amravati, Maharashtra, India

[4]CSE Department, P. R. Pote College of Engineering and Management, Amravati, Maharashtra, India

ABSTRACT

Nowadays, there is an immense demand for big data analytics framework in each area. Various types of applications have been proposed. For big data analytics different tools are available like sky tree, R Programming, Apache spark, mongo DB, rapid mine, Hadoop jasper soft, dryad storm Apache drill, and many more. Comparative table of various tools for determination of functionality of each tool which can provide more accurate analysis on big data is worked on. Every framework has its own strength & weakness which can work based on any datasets. There are a number of parameters which have to be considered in a big data analytics framework. There is hence a

Reconnoitering the Landscape of Edge Intelligence in Healthcare.
Suneeta Satpathy, Sachi Nandan Mohanty, and Sirisha Potluri (Eds.)
© 2024 Apple Academic Press, Inc. Co-published with CRC Press (Taylor & Francis)

requirement for an adequate framework for big data analytics. Thus, the aim of the work turns out to be proposing a general solution using an evaluation-based approach by utilizing tools of Big Data analytics for the benefits of the organization. In this chapter, a new framework for big data analytics for the various domains using machine learning (ML) and edge computing (EC) has been given. For data, there are a number of challenges involved when the system is working on big data. On the other hand, it has become more crucial when it is concerned with the processing. The time of processing the data is one of the important parameters which has great significance while working on the real data or applications. Another important parameter is the system requirements while applying such a system and the system must understand, interpret, and process all the features of the domain.

14.1   INTRODUCTION

Due to the wide increase in the complexity and criticality in the different modern applications, systems may provide a great variety of computational properties and facilities too. The complete optimization of applications is always difficult and critical to achieve. Nearly all aspects of recent life are in some way being transformed by big data machine learning (ML). Google and Netflix both know what kinds of movies consumers want to see & hunger to know based on their search pasts. Indeed, google has begun to replace much of its existing no machine. There is enormous hope that ML algorithms and learning technology can deliver similar benefits and improvement across many sectors through ML and big data may seem secretive at first they are closely similar to well-known classical statistical models used by most firms. We anticipate that by highlighting these relationships, these methods will become less mysterious and a set of realistic expectations for the function of ML and big data will emerge. To create a generic model which can be utilized as a foundation for evaluating big data analytics techniques in an organization is carried out.

Hadoop, HPCC, Storm, GridGain, IBM Cognos, and MongoDB tools used in big data analytics have various features, which include their volume, conversion, simplicity, and computing capacity. The main drawback of each tool is that they do not sustain transactions, but it supports some atomic operations which are at single level document. There are various challenges on data model and system level which need to be improved for the performance of big data analysis [4]. Edge computing (EC) is a distributed computing platform that puts business applications closer to data sources like local edge servers or IoT sensors. This closeness to the data's origin can have significant business advantages: greater bandwidth availability, quicker insights, and enhanced response times.

The Internet of Mobile Things includes stream data being produced by sensors, network transportations that the ability to efficiently use actionable information for transportation planning, management, and commercial advantage requires the ability to pull and deliver these data streams as well as to execute processing and analytics. With the advent of EC, communication, compute, control, and storage resources are decentralized and moved from the cloud to the network's edge.

14.2 BACKGROUND

Many research studies on different model designs and their implementations have also been done to design effective utility to produce some efficient system. Various applications and tools have adopted big data technology in which the role of each tool is specifically designed for the particular usage of various data sets for agriculture, education, medical, financial, and business to test its efficiency. Some used JDBC connection for RDBMS which is based on data storage and processing of data but there are some drawbacks that can be overcome in future research [5].

Bilal Jana et al. proposed that, the main objective is that big that requires the latest sophisticated ML and deep learning (DL) algorithm which can process real-time data with more accuracy and efficiency. They have compared various DL techniques to perform large-scale analysis Using various counts of neurons and hidden layers. They also mention that DL technology has several limitations in data processing and techniques used in data analysis. Finally, they examine that DL optimization can increase the speed with high accuracy and in the future, the comparatively study may increase the test case of DL [16].

Hung Cao et al. proposed an edge descriptive analytics is used to find significant patterns in real-time transit data streams using an EC architecture where mobile edge nodes are placed as physical devices aboard a transit vehicle. The suggested platform to facilitate descriptive analytics at a mobile edge node and produce useful information for transit managers is assessed for its benefits and drawbacks using an application experiment [21].

Chitrakant Banchhor et al. proposed the research techniques and tools used in big data computing. They have explored some computation work with some outliers over the various fields in big data. This chapter primarily focuses on cluster computing and further enhance Hadoop tools used in data analysis. The tools used in research include Hadoop, Dryad & Dryad LINQ, and CLG-MapReduce. They also mention that these services can be available through the cloud and based on features of tools the services are provided according to pay as per use. In this chapter, they compared various tools with each other based on their features which include programming-model, data handling, failure handling, and language support. Finally, they conclude that this chapter can enhance the tools and development in application over big data, but this application is in the initial stage and can increase the development growth in the future [13].

Lidong Wang in this chapter, they have used data mining, DL, and ML techniques for the analysis of big data. They have presented different challenges of application in DL and data mining techniques. They have used various algorithms which include K-mean, K-nearest neighbor, Support Vector Machine, Decision tree, Logistic regression, and neural network for processing and analysis of big data. They also compared different common methods with Ensemble methods and related features with each other. Finally, they conclude that the K-means method is efficient and more accurate but it can possibility terminates local optimization, Support vector machine work perfectly on the sparse problem but cannot handle mixed data, Native Bayes is simple to implement but it is only suitable for small scale data, and Decision tree perform more accurate on large scale data but it can cause the problem of overfitting. They also mention that in the future challenges of each algorithm can be overcome [14].

Shweta Mitta et al. In this chapter, they have studied the traditional challenges of MLT for big data analysis to find possible different solutions. They have used the Reduction technique, MapReduce, Parallel Processing, GPU, and DL which provides the best and most accurate solution for the challenges faced during the analysis of big data. During the research, they find out that if ML algorithms are optimized then we can achieve Hashing, Dimensionality reduction technique, Data cleaning, and sampling with a minimum time of execution. They also predicted that in the future we can overcome some technical challenges with the help of a hybrid machine algorithm [15].

Junfei Qiu et al. In this chapter, they have studied the latest ML techniques for processing big data. They primarily review ML techniques and methods for the representation of DL, parallel and distributed learning, transfer learning, and kernel-based learning. They also reviewed the challenges and drawbacks to overcome by providing feasible solutions to a problem. Finally, they conclude that ML can work more accurately as compared to different techniques used in big data, and in the future, there may be the latest trending research on large data machine learning [17].

Sree Divya et al. in this chapter, they have used ML techniques and Apache foundation tools for the high efficiency and computation power of big data. They have deeply explained ML algorithms and tools to know the exact challenges faced during analysis. They have mentioned that based on the challenges the algorithm can decide to overcome the problems. They have also studied and reviewed spatial resolution and performance of ML. Finally, they predicted that in the future there might be different techniques of machines for different problems [18].

Sara Landset et al. In this, they have researched various techniques which include Hadoop, Mahout, Spark, MLlib, ML, SAMOA, and H_2O. This chapter gives an overview of each tool and determines to choose the best tools for data analysis. They also mentioned each tool's features in a brief description and compared it with each other. Finally, they conclude that every tool has its advantages as well as drawbacks, so the user needs to choose the tools as per the work similarity. They also predict that in the future due to popularity these tools increase with more accuracy [19].

Gaganjot Kaur Kang et al. have discussed Air Quality prediction with the help of big data analysis tools. The main purpose of this chapter is to predict the accurate result by the tool used in air quality prediction and look into various ML techniques for forecasting the air quality. They have used DL techniques which can perform high and accurate accuracy of the result. Finally, they conclude that the reason behind choosing this topic was to make smart and pollution-free cities and based on the prediction of the government the strict action on this topic. They also mentioned that present challenges can be overcome in future research with more accuracy [20].

According to [22], size plays a crucial role in big data, and it should be considered one of the defining characteristics. Usually, the users of computers are habituated to think of data in terms of megabytes and gigabytes, but the requirement of big data is much larger units [3]. It was predicted in Ref. [3] that Bigdata will emerge as a crucial component of rivalry and expansion for particular businesses, and that if the current situation is taken into consideration the prediction stood out to be 100% true. The role of big data analytics in science research is ever increasing. Due to the cheap rate and small size of sensors, carrying out scientific experiments depends majorly on collecting so much data in order to get analyzed only by big data techniques [22].

Big data is the data production is exponential. It has various requirements and qualities, including organized, semi-structured, and unstructured data forms. According to [2], their business contains various valuable information from the numerous different types of stakeholders depending upon their needs and it is not possible to process and meet them by the use of traditional tools and methods. Here Big data technology comes into picture and plays a vital role to handle, process, store the huge amount of data. By providing analytics and techniques which are predictive, big data analytics assists entrepreneurs and companies to make more subtle and informed decisions related to business. According to [2], Apache spark can process different types of data, and not only process the high-volume data but it also concentrates on accelerating the workloads of batch processing. The prime advantage of using Apache spark is its ability to get deployed as a separate cluster or it can be combined with an already present Hadoop cluster [23].

As most of the older systems are their own strength & weakness, every tool has its own strength which can work accurately based on the user's big dataset discover some of the useful symptoms within the specified time and also fail in real time. Some of the systems developed thereafter are very useful in predicting the given systems and are very useful in properly analyzing the features of the data and they are also useful in the significance for the same. These systems can capture and analyze the large data set then take the data and can analyze it to reveal the different patterns and related trends which lead to improvement of the service and quality of the product designed [7] (Table 14.1).

14.3 PREVIOUS WORK DONE

Figure 14.1 shows analysis of different tools rapid Miner, Sky Tree, R Programming, Apache Spark, Mongo Db, Hadoop Dryad, Strom determination of best tools which can provide more accurate analysis on big data. The features comparison with respect to volume, velocity, variety, visualization, connectivity, and simplicity was taken into consideration during predicting value of each tool.

TABLE 14.1 Comparative Analysis Table of Various Existing Techniques

Sl. No.	Author Name	Tools and Technique	Drawback	Conclusion	Future Scope
1.	Karthiga, Senthil Kumar Janahan, Anbazhagu	Rapid miner, sky tree, R programming, Apache spark, and MongoDB	High computation power required, more cost, data storage.	Every tool has its own strength which can work accurately based on the user big dataset.	Due to requirement, there may a high incremental growth in tools with more accurate analysis.
2.	Ritu Ratra, Preeti Gulia	Hadoop tools, spark tools, and MongoDB	Data analysis results are sometimes misleading and speedy updates can mismatch the real figure.	This chapter was about handling the techniques and tools used during the collection of relevant data.	Future there may be a drastic change in tool up-gradation and newly invented tools which can work with minimum time span.
3.	Acharjya & Kauser Ahmed [3]	Jaspersoft, Dryad, Apache Spark, Strom Apache Drill, and Apache Mahout	Data storage, high computation, scalability is not compatible.	Every tool has its own special functionality and performs the task with a minimum time span. They have mentioned that analysis can violate principle privacy which makes customer manipulation records.	In future it can increase the efficiency and accuracy.
4.	Yogeswara Rao & Adinarayana Salina [4]	Hadoop, HPCC, Storm, GridGain, IBM Cognos, and MongoDB	Each tool is that they do not support transaction, but it supports some atomic operations which are at single-level document.	Briefly described various features of tools which include their volume, conversion, simplicity, and computing capacity.	Various challenges on data, model, and system-level which need to be improved for the performance of big data analysis.
5.	Simranjot Kaur & Er. Sikander Singh Cheema [5]	JDBC	It is less preferment, and it is inefficient.	They have used various datasets such as agriculture, education, medical, financial, and business for testing the efficiency of every tool. They said that these tools play a very important role in the storage and processing of data.	Presented challenges can be the future researchers.

TABLE 14.1 (Continued)

Sl. No.	Author Name	Tools and Technique	Drawback	Conclusion	Future Scope
6.	Bo Li [6]	Classic big data technology, cloud computing big data, and benchmark. Hadoop and MapReduce	Tool has a limited scale and cannot work on large-scale evaluation.	Big data tools can be explored and updated as per the customer requirement and can lead to incremental growth in the market.	Brief future scope in tools and techniques which can work as per the user's needs with more accuracy.
7.	Komal [7]	Semantria, Opinion Crawl, OpenText	Storage, searching, sharing, and security.	The rate of new data is more as compared to tool performance.	May increase the tools rate and performance accuracy in further research.
8.	Althaf Rahaman, Sai Rajesh & Girija Rani [8]	Storm, Apache Hadoop, Apache Mahout, MapReduce, Dryad, Apache Drill, Apache Spark	Computational complexity, data storage and analysis, scalability, knowledge discovery and information security, data visualization.	Describes each tool's potential and major impact on big data.	Research will be popular with drastic changes in these techniques and newly invented tools for solving big data analysis problems with more accuracy.
9.	Vijayalakshmi & Ramraj [09]	Lumify, Apache Strome, Apache Hadoop, Apache Samoa, Elastic search, HPCC Systems Big Data, MongoDB	Apache spark cannot limit its data processing.	They have mentioned various tools and their features which are mainly used in big data analysis. Hadoop MapReduce is one of the best tools for batch processing.	There might be drastic changes in Hadoop technologies tools that can overcome the present challenges faced during data analysis.
10.	Min Chen, Shiwen Mao, & Yunhao Liu [10]	Hadoop, computing power, and Internet of thing	Technical challenges which consist of data security, data storage, and data analysis.	They have to examine several data analysis applications including medical applications, social networks, the internet of things, and enterprise management.	Challenges faced in big data can be the further new research.
11.	Pramod Sunagar, Hanumantharaju, Siddesh, Anita Kanavalli, & Srinivasa [11]	Machine learning, deep learning	Computation speed is low.	Have analyzed various data for predicting the plan, and based upon that industries can provide a recommendation that leads to company profit.	May be a model that can predict the country and place in which the user is more additive to visit that place.

TABLE 14.1 *(Continued)*

Sl. No.	Author Name	Tools and Technique	Drawback	Conclusion	Future Scope
12.	Pramod Sunagar, Hanumantharaju, Siddesh, Anita Kanavalli, & Srinivasa [12]	Machine learning, deep learning	Computation speed is low.	Have analyzed various data for predicting the plan, and based upon that industries can provide a recommendation that leads to company profit.	May be a model that can predict the country and place in which the user is more additive to visit that place.
13.	Chitrakant Banchhor & Srinivasu [24]	Hadoop, Dryad and Dryad LINQ, and CLG-MapReduce	More cost, sharing, and security.	This chapter enhanced the tools and development in application over big data.	This application is in the initial stage and can increase the development growth in the future [24].
14.	Lidong Wang [25]	K-mean, K-nearest neighbor, support vector machine, decision tree, logistic regression, and neural network.	They have presented different challenges of application in deep learning and data mining technique.	The K-means method is efficient and more accurate, but it can possibility terminates local optimization, Support vector machine work perfectly on the sparse problem but cannot handle mixed data, Native Bayes is simple to implement but it is only suitable for small scale data, and Decision tree perform more accurate on large scale data, but it can cause the problem of overfitting.	The future challenges of each algorithm can be overcome.
15.	Shweta Mitta & Om Prakash Sangwan	Reduction technique, MapReduce, parallel processing, GPU, and deep learning	Cannot be more accurate.	They find out that if machine learning algorithms are optimized then we can achieve hashing, dimensionality reduction technique, Data cleaning, and sampling with a minimum time of execution.	The future we can overcome some technical challenges with the help of a hybrid machine algorithm.

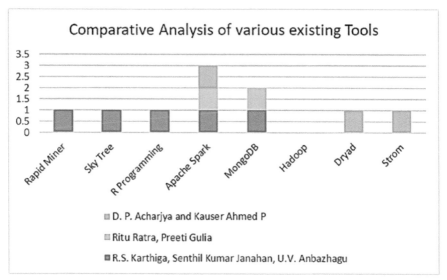

FIGURE 14.1 Comparative analysis of various tools.

14.4 PROPOSED METHODOLOGY

1. Data uploading into the proposed framework.

2. Store that data into the server.

3. Access the data from the server using user authentication.

4. The user needs to identify the methodology to be applied to the accessed data, i.e., regression for predictions, classification for categorization.

5. Once identified the methodology, the user needs to identify the technique need to be employed on the data from the in-built techniques of the proposed framework environment.

6. In this phase, feature engineering techniques will be employed on the data from the in-built techniques of the proposed framework environment.

7. Dimensionality reduction techniques will be employed on the obtained feature data from the in-built techniques of the proposed framework environment.

8   Split the dimensions of reduced data with the aid of the in-built techniques of the proposed framework environment.

9.   Identify the evaluation method for processing the split data.

10. Train the evaluation method with the aid of training data.

11. Data visualization techniques employed on the data for visualization purposes.

12. Obtained data visualization to be stored in the server (Figure 14.2).

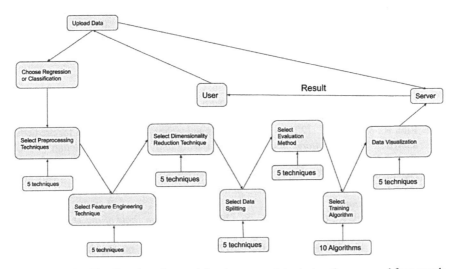

FIGURE 14.2   The flowchart that explains the approach to design the proposed framework.

14.5   CONCLUSION

The proposed framework intended to generate the graphical user interface (GUI) by integrating big data concepts along with ML methodologies and EC concepts. These ML methodologies help in identifying the hidden information and trends that exist in the massive data collected and stored in the big data management framework. Big data management framework majorly includes the gathering, storing, managing, and analysis of data. Pipelining structure considered building a complete GUI framework to avoid repeated training of the ML methodologies whenever the new data has been added. So, that the predictions will be obtained based on the combined with previously collected data.

KEYWORDS

- **Apache spark**
- **big data**
- **edge computing**
- **machine learning**
- **mongo DB Hadoop**

REFERENCES

1. Karthiga, R. S., Senthil, K. J., & Anbazhagu, U. V., (2019). Research on various tools in big data. In: *International Journal of Innovative Technology and Exploring Engineering (IJITEE)* (Vol. 8, No. 6S4). ISSN: 2278-3075.

2. Ritu, R., & Preeti, G., (2019). Big data tools and techniques: A roadmap for predictive analytics. In: *International Journal of Engineering and Advanced Technology (IJEAT)* (Vol. 9, No. 2). ISSN: 2249-8958 (Online).

3. Acharjya, D. P., & Kauser, A. P., (2016). A survey on big data analytics: Challenges, open research issues and tools. *International Journal of Advanced Computer Science and Applications.*

4. Yogeswara, R. K., & Adinarayana, S., (2016). *A Study on Tools of Big Data Analytics.* ResearchGate.

5. Simranjot, K., & Sikander, S. C., (2017). Review paper on big data: Applications and different tools. *International Journal of Advanced Research in Computer and Communication Engineering.*

6. Li, B., & Jain, R. (2013). Survey of recent research progress and issues in big data. *December10.* www.cse.wustl.edu/~jain/cse570-13/ftp/bigdata2/index.htm.

7. Ms. Komal, (2018). A review paper on big data analytics tools. published in *International Journal of Technical Innovation in Modern Engineering & Science (IJTIMES) Impact Factor: 3.45 (SJIF-2015)* (Vol. 4, No. 5). e-ISSN: 2455-2585.

8. Althaf, R. S., Sai, R. K., & Girija, R. K., (2018). Challenging tools on research issues in big data analytics. In: *International Journal of Engineering Development and Research (IJEDR)* (Vol. 6, No. 1). ISSN: 2321-9939.

9. Vijayalakshmi, J., & Ramaraj, E., (2018). Comparative study of big data analytics tools. In: *International Journal of Pure and Applied Mathematics* (Vol. 119, No. 7, pp. 825–833).

10. Min, C., Shiwen, M., & Yunhao, L., (2014). *Big Data: A Survey.* Published in Springer Science+Business Media New York.

11. Pramod, S., Hanumantharaju, R., Siddesh, G. M., Anita, K., & Srinivasa, K. G., (2020). Influence of big data in smart tourism. *Hybrid Computational Intelligence.*

12. Ms. Vibhavari, C., & Rajesh, N. P., (2014). Survey paper on big data. *International Journal of Computer Science and Information Technologies.*

13. Chitrakant, B., & Srinivasu, N., (2020). Survey of technologies, tools, concepts and issues in big data. In" *International Journal of Scientific & Technology Research* (Vol. 9, No. 4).

14. Lidong, W., (2017). Data mining, machine learning and big data analytics. *International Transaction of Electrical and Computer Engineers System.*

15. Shweta, M., & Om Prakash, S., (2019). Big data analytics using machine learning techniques. *International Conference on Cloud Computing, Data Science & Engineering.*

16. Bilal, J., Haleem, F., Murad, K., Muhammad, I., Ihtesham Ul, I., Awais, A., Shaukat, A., & Gwanggil, J., (2017). *Deep Learning in Big Data Analytics: A Comparative Study.* Direct.

17. Junfei, Q., Qihui, W., Guoru, D., Yuhua, X., & Shuo, F., (2016). A survey of machine learning for big data processing. *EURASIP Journal on Advances in Signal Processing.*

18. Sree, D. K., Bhargavi, P., & Jyothi, S., (2018). Machine learning algorithms in big data analytics. *International Journal of Computer Sciences and Engineering.*

19. Sara, L., Taghi, M. K., Aaron, N. R., & Tawfiq, H., (2015). *A Survey of Open-Source Tools for Machine Learning with Big Data in the Hadoop Ecosystem.* Springer Open Journal.

20. Gaganjot, K. K., Jerry, Z. G., Sen, C., Shengqiang, L., & Gang, X., (2018). Air quality prediction: Big data and machine learning approaches. *International Journal of Environmental Science and Development* (Vol. 9, No. 1).

21. Hung, C., Monica, W., & Sangwhan, C., (2018). Developing an edge computing platform for real-time descriptive analytics. *IEEE International Conference of Bigdata.*

22. Harry, E. P. (2014). What is big data and why is it important? *Journal of Educational Technology Systems*, *43*(2), 159–171. doi:10.2190/ET.43.2.d. ResearchGate.

23. Rawat, R., & Yadav, R., (2021). Big data: 2014-big data analysis, issues and challenges and technologies. *IOP Conf. Ser.: Mater. Sci. Eng., 1022*, 012014. ResearchGate.

24. Chitrakant, B., & Srinivasu, N., (2020). Survey of technologies, tools, concepts and issues in big data. In: *International Journal of Scientific & Technology Research* (Vol. 9, No. 4).

25. Lidong, W., (2017). Data mining, machine learning and big data analytics. *International Transaction of Electrical and Computer Engineers System, 2017.*

26. Shweta, M., & Om Prakash, S., (2019). Big data analytics using machine learning techniques. *International Conference on Cloud Computing, Data Science & Engineering.*

Index